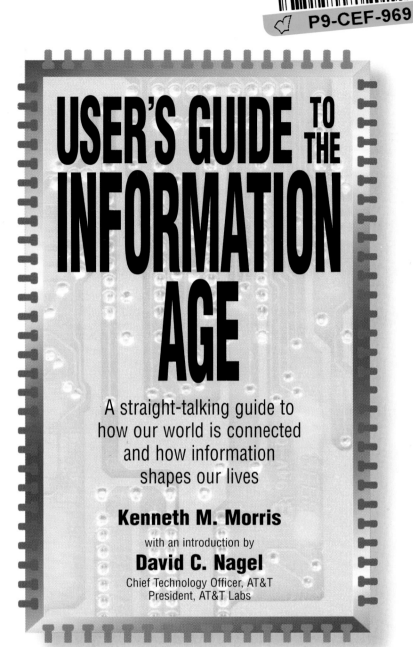

USER'S GUIDE TO THE INFORMATION AGE

A straight-talking guide to
how our world is connected
and how information
shapes our lives

Kenneth M. Morris

with an introduction by
David C. Nagel
Chief Technology Officer, AT&T
President, AT&T Labs

LIGHTBULB

PRESS

LIGHTBULB PRESS
Project Team

Chief Operating Officer Dean Scharf
Editorial Director Virginia Morris
Design Director Dave Wilder
Editor Ann Fisher
Copy Editor Sarah Norris
Designer Kara W. Hatch
Design Staff Jeff Badger, Andrea McIntosh
Sales and Marketing Carol E. Davis, Karen Meldrom
Production Holly Duthie, Marvin Douglas Emerson III, Christopher Engel, Edie Evans, Meghan Gerety, Cadence Giersbach, Sally Minker, Dennis Thomas, Thomas F. Trojan, Edie Winograde
Digital Output Quad Right, Inc.

AT&T
Special Thanks to Dick Martin, Burt Wolder and Jane Biba; and to Sam Bleecker, Greg Blonder, Ron Brachman, Ed Chen, Steve Crandall, Steve Cross, Stu Gannes, Mike Granieri, Sheldon Hochheiser, Tom Holub, David Isenberg, Dave Johnson, Nils Klarlund, Andrew Koenig, David Maher, Bill Mill, Amy Muller, Diane Nakamura, Bill Oliver, Larry Rabiner, Paul Resnick, Rich Roca, Dan Sheinbein, Barbara Sweeney, Michelle Tringali, John Tunney, Roy Weber, Bill Weiss, Mary Whelan, Jay Wilpon and Ken Wu

Picture Credits
Tom Carlson (page 55), Casio (pages 11, 146), CheckFree Corporation (page 87), Comstock/Michael Stuckey (page 63), Digital View (page 57), Echostar (page 21), Frasca International Inc. (page 148), Garmin International (page 21), Intel Corporation (page 55), John Deere-Naamc (page 17), Killer List of Video Games (page 149), Motorola Corporation (page 14), Namco Ltd. (page 149), SGI (page 56)

Acknowledgments
The following images are copyrighted and have been reproduced by Lightbulb Press with the kind permission of their owners: Amazon.com screen display ©1996–1999 Amazon.com, Inc.; Apple, the Apple logo and Macintosh are registered trademarks of Apple Computer, Inc.; Citibank screen display ©1999 Citicorp; Deja.com screen display ©Deja.com, Inc.; eBay screen display ©eBay Inc. All Rights Reserved; Echo Communications screen display ©Echo Communications Group Inc.; Excite screen display ©1994–1999 Excite, Inc. Excite is a trademark of Excite, Inc. and may be registered in various jurisdictions; Guide Dog Foundation for the Blind screen display ©Guide Dog Foundation for the Blind, Inc.; Investing for Kids screen display by Team 3096 for the ThinkQuest® Internet Challenge; Ivy Dental Consortium screen display ©Ivy Dental Consortium; Levi's screen display ©1999 Levi Strauss & Co.; L.L.Bean screen display ©1999 L.L.Bean, Inc. L.L.Bean is a registered trademark of L.L.Bean, Inc.; MetroCard is a trademark of MTA; Microsoft, Microsoft Internet Explorer and Windows are registered trademarks of Microsoft Corporation in the United States and/or other countries; MYST ©Cyan Inc.; The Netscape Communicator interface ©1999 Netscape Communications Corp. All Rights Reserved. Netscape, Netscape Navigator and the Netscape N logo are registered trademarks and Netscape Communicator is a trademark of Netscape in the United States and other countries; Oscar Mayer is a registered trademark of Kraft Foods, Inc.; Parentsoup screen display ©1999 iVillage, Inc. Parentsoup is a registered trademark of iVillage; Real Player toolbar® 1997 RealNetworks, Inc. All Rights Reserved; Seniornet screen display ©1999 Seniornet; SimCity3000 is a trademark of Electronic-Arts, 1999; Switchboard® and Maps On Us℠ data provided by Etak, Inc. 1984–1999; The Trip screen display ©1999 The Trip.com Inc.; TRUSTe logo ©1997–99 TRUSTe. All Rights Reserved; Map on page 87 reprinted with permission from The Weather Channel ©1999 The Weather Channel Enterprises Inc.; Westminster Kennel Club screen display ©The Westminster Kennel Club; William Shakespeare screen display ©Jeremy Hylton

LIGHTBULB PRESS

CONTENTS

USER'S GUIDE ^{TO}_{THE} INFORMATION AGE

Living with Technology

Ever since the first phone call, smart people have worked hard to make communicating easy.

Fifteen years ago hardly anyone had a wireless phone, hardly anybody sent e-mail, and the Internet was a phenomenon waiting to happen. Today, people have easy and instant access to networks that span the globe.

Few people understand how to derive the full benefit of the communications and information resources at their disposal. Fewer still can imagine what today's innovations will lead to in the future. That's why we at AT&T Labs were delighted to support the development of this book.

That fact is that a handful of major trends is reshaping the world. The digitization of the world's information has created new ways to practice science and engineering, reach out to people, send messages, entertain and learn.

The rise of the Internet has reshaped the way products are defined, sold and serviced. Widely available wireless communications has changed the way we work and play. And the growth of the integrated circuit and a veritable explosion of innovation have generated a tidal wave of smarter, cheaper networked devices for accessing information in all its forms.

Fitting Technology

Technology that helps people communicate has to be easy to use and fit the way people live. For example, few people wonder why a telephone is shaped the way it is, or why a telephone key pad has four rows of numbers. Most of the basic features of communicating began with groundbreaking human factors research at AT&T.

Using the first telephones involved little more than speaking into a tube and holding it up to your ear to listen. The first telephone systems had no dial tone. You picked up the telephone and told the operator the name of the exchange or switchboard you wanted, and the number of the telephone: "Get me Main 123." The operator pressed a key or pushed a plug to connect you to the person you wanted to call. Researchers began planning for the introduction of dial telephones in 1917. They needed a numbering system that was accurate and easy for people to use. After scores of tests, researchers found people remembered seven-digit numbers better than a series of five or six numbers. It seems our brains like to chunk numbers into clumps of three and four digits. Decades later, we still use the same numbering scheme.

Dial telephones brought the need for a tone to tell callers they had a working circuit. Years later, the dial tone has become friendly, familiar and taken for granted. Today, computer chips generate a dial tone that mimics the sound originally created by mechanical technology.

The design of a typical telephone receiver was directly shaped by human factors. The "candlestick" phones you see in old movies required two hands—one for the mouthpiece and another for the earpiece. By the 1920s, consumer demand for a combined handset was growing. To ensure the new handsets would be comfortable for the widest range of people, engineers measured the faces of hundreds of people to find the statistical mean distance from ear to mouth.

Pioneering work with human factors ensured that telephone numbers were easy to remember, telephone handsets were easy to hold, and people knew when it was OK to dial a phone number.

Your Intelligent Partner

Communications is a central human activity. The complexity of our communications is what makes humans different from other animals. As we imagine the communications networks of the 21st century, we need to think about how to help people stay in touch with other people, with information and with learning.

Futurists imagine a day when the dial tone is replaced by a voice tone. The network will identify you by your voice and speak to you. When you pick up the telephone, the first thing you might hear is the status of your most recent request: "Hi, Dave. I can't find your son at school yet, but I'm still paging him."

Of course, you might not like such a chatty style, or even the concept of the intelligent agent. Thanks to technology, you won't have to put up with a cookie-cutter approach to working with the network.

The new services we envision will meet your unique personal needs and preferences, and not some scientist's or engineer's view of how a network should behave. Technology should be developed to serve us rather than the other way around.

Hi, It's Me

Technologies such as speech recognition and voice synthesis are being applied in an effort to recapture the ease of communicating.

Soon you'll be able to pick up any telephone and ask for the connection you want, just as you might have done in the early 1900s. Computers will analyze your request, paying special attention to words and phrases such as "find," "I want to talk to," "get me," or "collect call." Your connection will be made easily and reliably.

If the network is uncertain about your request, it will ask you a question. Speech synthesis makes it possible for the network to speak to you in a voice that will be difficult to distinguish from that of another human being.

Interacting Naturally

Making interactions with machines easy and simple will be the hallmark of communications in the 21st century. Organizations like AT&T Labs are developing prototype applications and devices that will simplify travel, learning, play and communication.

Although we like to think it all began with Alexander Graham Bell's telephone, first demonstrated in 1876, no one invention made all this possible. The Information Age is fueled by a legion of innovators, inventors and dreamers, brilliant people working long hours in the passionate pursuit of discovery.

Until now, no single, friendly resource has been available to help understand the myriad inventions and technologies that have contributed to the Information Age. We hope this book brings you the answers to some of the questions you've asked, explains the principles behind technologies you've wondered about, and offers ideas that stimulate your personal connection to an ever-expanding world of opportunities.

David C. Nagel
Chief Technology Officer, AT&T
President, AT&T Labs

THE BACKBONE OF

Birth of a New Era

The Information Age is about extending the reach of individuals in ways never before dreamed possible.

Like the Industrial Revolution of the 1700s, the Information Age is dramatically transforming the world we know. Instead of steam, however, the driving force behind this new era is electronic technology, and the merging of computing power with the extending reach of communications networks.

But unlike the Industrial Age, which was characterized by massive machinery, standardization and the synchronization of human effort, the Information Age is about smaller and smarter machines that give us the freedom to create, share and personalize communications, and send them virtually anywhere in the world.

While the Information Age is certainly about the sheer volume of data that's being produced and transmitted, it's also about the innovative ways we obtain and use this information, the devices that give us access to it, and the latticework of systems that let us communicate information instantaneously to others.

THE NOBEL TRANSISTOR
One measure of the transistor's significance is that its inventors— William Shockley, John Bardeen and Walter Brattain—won the Nobel Prize for physics in 1956.

THE NETWORKS THAT

COMPUTERS

INTELLIGENT AND UBIQUITOUS
Information is built into the fabric of everything we do. It lets our cars cruise at a fixed speed, tells our VCRs when to record a program, and lets us withdraw money from an ATM. Programmed information also helps an airplane find the runway in the densest fog, initiates a spacecraft landing, or aims a remote camera taking pictures of the universe.

Information has also become a touchstone of power and wealth. Detailed and timely knowledge about a company's prospects helps us make smarter investment decisions than someone relying on hunches. And a company with reliable information about its customers, markets and competition can operate more profitably than one managing by the seat of its pants.

THE TRANSISTOR: USHERING

The story behind the computing power, sophisticated networks and multimedia content of the Information Age starts with a tiny electronic device called the **transistor**. Invented at AT&T's Bell Labs in 1947, the transistor

revolutionized the way electric signals travel in machines. It worked as part of a circuit. And while it could be used as an on/off logic switch, it was also an electronic amplifier— replacing vacuum tubes—that were subject to

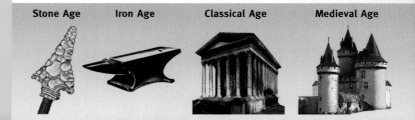

Different periods in history are identified by the innovative technologies or powerful ideas that changed the way people lived, worked and thought.

| Stone Age | Iron Age | Classical Age | Medieval Age |

CONNECT THEM

ALL TOGETHER, ALL AT ONCE

From a scientific perspective, the Information Age represents the coming together, or **convergence**, of traditionally separate technologies and industries that has enabled us to create truly interactive communications.

While two-way interactive communication is hardly new—we've been using telephones for over a century—the convergence of computers, the electronic networks that connect them, and the digitized content we can transmit over these networks has given us new ways to interact and communicate.

Computing has dramatically extended our capabilities to create and process information both as text and images. Networks have become increasingly sophisticated in directing our information as well as providing a variety of pipelines to get the information delivered more quickly.

And as content, whether simple text or full-motion video, becomes digital, it also becomes highly malleable. So we can change it, save it and act on it in highly innovative ways, giving rise to a new era of interactive, imaginative and often-entertaining communications that we experience, for example, every time we log on to the Internet.

Connectivity, computer and content—these are the building blocks that underlie the innovation and excitement of the Information Age.

STAYING IN THE LOOP

The Information Age also means we're always in touch. We can call almost anyone, anywhere in the world in a matter of seconds, get the latest-breaking news, weather and financial developments on radio, TV or the Internet. And we can do all of these things at our convenience, at any time of day or night.

In fact, the ways we receive and share information are changing so rapidly that keeping abreast of the latest devices, let alone the burgeoning amounts of information, has become an over-whelming task. As a result, providing **information about information** has emerged as a valued service, opening the way for a raft of Information Age entrepreneurs and businesses.

THE CONTENT THAT'S DELIVERED

IN THE INFORMATION AGE

wear and tear. The transistor, which had no moving parts to wear out, and no filaments to produce heat, took up less space, operated on less power, and could amplify signals much more efficiently.

This breakthrough, combined with the shrinking size and cost of transistors, set the stage for the emergence of smaller, yet far more powerful, computers in the 1970s that became the wellspring of the Information Age.

| Renaissance | Age of Exploration | Age of Enlightenment | Industrial Age | Information Age |

7

THE BACKBONE OF

Information Age Concepts

Old words, new meanings.

One way to come to grips with the accelerating pace of change in the Information Age is to become familiar with a handful of recurring concepts and themes. Knowing what they are and what they mean can help you enjoy the many benefits, and avoid some of the pitfalls, of this often-perplexing era.

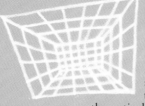

Cyber-

is derived from the term **cyberspace**, which is the virtual space created by computer systems and the networks that link them. **Cybernetics**, the theoretical study of control process, comes from the Greek *kybernetes*, meaning "one who governs."

Recently, **cyber** has been applied to things on, or relating to, the Internet. For example, a cyberlibrarian, sometimes called a cybrarian, runs a library located on the Net. There are also cybermalls, cyberlinks, and cyberbanking, to name a few. Just add the prefix *cyber* and people will know it's out there.

Multimedia

literally refers to the simultaneous presentation of two or more different media, much as the first "talkie" movies combined film and sound. Today, multimedia often involves the combination of text, pictures, video, sound and animation into a single integrated communication. Simulations of flying a plane or designing a house that appear on CD ROMs or the Internet are rich multimedia experiences.

Miniaturization

refers to the increasingly small size, yet growing functionality, of electronic and digital equipment as well as to the physical components of their underlying technology. Cellular phones, computer chips and hand-held computers are all examples of miniaturization.

Convergence

describes the coming together of several distinct technologies— computing, telecommunications networks, consumer electronics and entertainment—to create new, multipurpose devices.

Convergence has made true interactivity possible, involving not just sound but text and graphics as well. The term is also applied to electronic products with multiple functions—televisions that provide Internet access, phones with picture screens and digital message displays, and fax machines that also print and duplicate documents.

Collaboration

refers to the ability of people, usually in different locations using different equipment and programs, to share and manipulate information, often simultaneously, in order to create superior products and solutions.

Online

means using a computer or other information device, connected through a voice and data network, to access information and services. Online banking, for example, enables you to transact your business directly through a computer or phone connection.

Access

generally refers to the ability to connect or log on to a system, find and retrieve information, and use it in a meaningful way. The term frequently connotes *online* access—as in connecting to the Internet or other computer-based systems.

Network

describes a system—like the phone system—that links together a community of users through a complex but seamless integration of electronic equipment and connecting devices. A single network, which can carry voice (or sound), data (digital bits of information) or both, can also be connected to other networks. The Internet, for example, is a network of networks, and the phone system connects multiple networks. Closed networks, like company Intranets, may restrict access to certain users. But other networks, like the World Wide Web, keep expanding.

Content

means text, graphics, video and sound, and the ways they are packaged for new or interactive media, such as a website or electronic book. Content refers to the substance of a communication rather than the mechanism or code for transmitting it.

Connectivity

refers to the linking together of a wide array of complex and different networks, such as those used for telephones, computers and televisions, in a compatible way. The upshot of connectivity is that one device will be increasingly able to access many different networks and types of information.

Compression

is an algorithm, or logical set of instructions, used to shrink or filter electronic data such as text, sound or video frames to save storage space and transmission time. For example, video files would take endless hours to transmit over the Internet unless the sound and images were first compressed, then sent to their destination, and then decompressed to restore the full richness of the video presentation.

Personalization

has to do with the tailoring of information to an individual consumer or user based on the person's stated preferences, or derived from a computerized profile that reflects the person's purchases, usage patterns or other criteria. Computers can store, analyze and use this data to customize products, services and information. Many websites, for example, let visitors personalize their home page to show just the things they want to see.

Interactivity

is about two-way communication, and the ability of a person receiving information—whether as text or graphics, video or sound—to shape and respond to it and get a reply in response. Ordering a book from an e-commerce website or answering an e-mail involves interactivity, but watching TV does not. The telephone, invented in 1876, remains one of the most popular and effective means of interactive communication.

Analog and Digital Information

We live in an analog world but measure and communicate digitally.

All of the devices we use for information or entertainment—from wristwatches and telephones to computers and radios—are either **analog** or **digital**. Increasingly, they're a combination of the two.

ANALOG CONTINUITY

Analog refers to natural phenomena that move continuously, like mercury in a thermometer, a compass or a gas gauge. The sound waves that your voice generates are also analog. So is the flow of electric current.

Each analog signal varies continuously. **Analog devices**, such as a weather vane, display or transmit this continuous movement in a way that mirrors how the movement was created. When you speak on the phone, for example, the telephone translates the sounds your voice produces into continuous electrical waves that rise and fall in ways that are analogous, or similar, to the sound waves you create.

As the sound waves grow bigger and smaller, the electrical signals grow bigger and smaller proportionately. That's why the sound waves that travel in the air, and the electromagnetic waves that travel over the wires, are said to be analogous to each other—they are analog waves.

Analog signals have their limitations, however. Their fidelity—how true or faithful they are to the original light or sound wave—deteriorates as the signals move further from the source. And while you can boost, or amplify, these analog signals along the way, you also boost any noise or distortion at the same time.

DIGITAL SAMPLING

One way to preserve the fidelity of analog signals is to turn them into digital signals. This conversion is done by sampling an analog sound wave at very close intervals, say 8,000 times a second. The value of the signal at each interval is then recorded as a digital number.

Rather than mirroring nature, then, **digital devices** describe—in binary code (0s and 1s)—a representative sampling of analog phenomena. We then perceive this description as distinct sounds, or images, or very precise numbers, depending on the type of analog that's being sampled.

Analog information is continuous, in a form that reflects natural phenomena, like a waveform.

Digital information is conveyed in segments using a numerical code.

For example, a digital watch displays the time as 11:03:12, 11:03:13, 11:03:14, as if time were divided into discrete chunks of one second in duration.

The digital speedometer in your car may show your speed going from 55 to 56 to 57, as if the car moved in fixed units of miles (or kilometers) per hour.

When the reading on a digital thermometer rises from 99.6 to 99.7 to 99.8, it suggests that temperature jumps in increments of a tenth of a degree.

THAT OLD FAMILIAR SOUND

We're so comfortable and familiar with analog movement that it's become ingrained in our vocabulary. We talk about a "stream of information," the "flow of conversation," and "sweep of time" as well as "waves of change."

IN DIGITAL FORM

To understand how digital information is created, consider speech, which travels as analog sound waves. To create digital sound, the analog waveform is sampled, or measured, thousands of times a second. The value of each measurement is coded into combinations of bits (0s and 1s) by tiny switches that can operate at millions or billions of times a second.

The accuracy of digital measurements depends on the number of the samplings: the more frequent they are, the more accurate the description will be. In some ways, the digital version that results can be viewed as a synthetic replication or recreation of the analog wave. The advantage, though, is that the digitized waveform can be reconstituted and modified over and over, with no loss of quality.

The continuous and varying sound waves created by a trumpet—the high and low notes as well as the loud and the soft—can be measured at close intervals. Each value is then digitized, or converted to binary code (0s and 1s) that can be replicated on a synthesizer. To the human ear, the sound of the actual trumpet and that of the synthesizer may be hard, if not impossible, to tell apart.

DIGITAL (MIS)PERCEPTIONS

Because digital numbers appear to be so precise, we tend to think of them as being more accurate or faster than analog measures. While that's not the case—analog information is every bit as accurate as digital information—the analog version is not always as workable or convenient.

For example, when it comes to determining the winner in an Olympic speed event, a digital watch measures the time in thousandths of a second and displays it instantly in numeric form. Even a giant stopwatch couldn't do the job as well.

In many cases, digital sounds and images can be virtually indistinguishable from the originals. CDs may sound as good as, or even better than, records or some live recordings. And digital television can deliver picture quality that is much sharper than what we see on conventional TV screens.

That's because once information is **digitized**—converted and stored in digital bits (0s and 1s)—it can be manipulated to eliminate noise and other forms of interference, producing what we perceive to be a clearer sound or sharper image. What's more, digitized information is also ideal for reproducing different analogs. For example, when we play a synthesizer, we can select different instruments—a clarinet, coronet or violin—or some combination of these.

While digital signals, like analog signals, deteriorate as they travel away from their source, a digital signal can be boosted without amplifying any distortion at the same time.

That's because digital signals can perfectly replicate their source at the receiving end—in effect, it is recreated anew from its component bits each time it's sent. As a result, each new signal is "true" to the original, making it ideal for transmitting over networks where noise or disruptions can reduce the signal's quality. In addition, since digital signals can be sent at extremely rapid speeds—as fast as the latest laser equipment can transmit and receive them—they are increasingly used on networks where quick access and delivery of information is in demand.

ANALOG TO DIGITAL AND BACK

Increasingly, digital and analog equipment work together as parts of communications networks. For example, when you create e-mail, it's transmitted as a digital signal from your computer to a **modem**. The modem translates the message to analog signals, which are then carried as electric current over the phone lines.

When the analog signal reaches its destination, another modem converts it back into digital signals, which appear on your recipient's computer screen as words and numbers. If the network were entirely digital, as it is in the case of a **LAN**, or **local area network**, then converting the information wouldn't be necessary.

Binary Code

Computers handle
information in little bits
and bigger bytes.

Computers operate on a two-digit system
called a **binary code**. That means every
computer function is based on two
digits—0 and 1. The underlying principle
is that a series of endless combinations of
0s and 1s can express not only all numbers
but all information.

You get a sense of how a binary or digital
system works if you think of the word pairs
on and *off*, *yes* and *no*, or *true* and *false*.
They're clear and easy to understand, and
they don't leave room for ambiguity. Think
of the game 20 Questions: each question is
framed so that the answer is an unequivocal
yes or *no*.

Consider, for example, the difference
in controlling your lights with a switch as
opposed to a dimmer. With the switch, you
can tell instantly if the power is on or off.
But with the dimmer on very low, you can't
always be sure.

BITS AND BYTES

While looking at long strings of 0s and 1s
doesn't tell you much, they're the mother
tongue of computers. Each 0 and 1, the
smallest unit of data, is called a **bit** of
information, a contraction of **bi**nary+digi**t**
coined by John Tukey at AT&T's Bell Labs
in 1949.

The 0s and 1s are codified in a language
called **ASCII (American Standard Code for
Information Interchange)**, which assigns a string
of eight bits, or a combination of
0s and 1s, to every upper- and lower-
case letter of the alphabet, to each numeral,
to various punctuation marks, and to control
keys. For example, when you press the R on
your keyboard, it translates into 01010010
in ASCII. When you hit the number 3, it's
00110011 in ASCII. And the lowly comma
is 00100111. Each string of eight bits is
known as a **byte** and can be arranged in
128 possible patterns, or permutations.

**ONE
GIGABYTE**   1,073,741,624
bytes

A BINARY HISTORY

The system of binary logic was
invented by Gottfried Leibnitz,
a German mathematician who
simplified the communication of
numbers in the 17th century.
Leibnitz's breakthrough was to
replace the 10-digit decimal system
(0, 1, 2, 3, 4, 5, 6, 7, 8, 9) with a
two-digit system that expressed all
numbers by using a series of
combinations of 0s and 1s.

In the early 19th century,
George Boole extended
Leibnitz's binary system
into a form of math. He
used only three basic
operations—**AND, OR**
and **NOT**—and the use
of "true/false" switches
to show that every
written declaration
could be conveyed through binary
math. With Boolean algebra,
statements could be encoded, or
expressed in symbolic language.

One more breakthrough—the
work of Claude Shannon, in 1937—
bridged the gap between algebraic
theory and practical applications.
Shannon substituted electrical on/off
switches for Boole's mechanical
true/false switches. Also in 1937,
George Stibitz developed a binary
circuit based on Boolean algebra.

Eventually, this work contributed
to the creation of the **transistor**—
a tiny on/off switch that could open
and close extremely rapidly to direct
electric current, making it possible
to render large amounts of information in binary code, the language
that computers could understand.

IT'S ALL YIN AND YANG

Legend has it that the inspiration for
Gottfried Leibnitz's development of
the binary code was his introduction
to the Chinese classic *I Ching*. It
portrays the universe and all its
complexities as a series of
dualities—either/or propositions—
including dark and light, male
and female, open and shut.

COMPRESSION

How does a computer handle all the data you want to store, or programs you want it to run, without quickly running out of storage space? That's where **compression** comes in. Compression means squeezing or shrinking data to save storage space and transmission time.

For example, if there are a lot of the same letters or numbers in a string of bytes, it's possible to insert a code that tells the computer "When you see this character, it actually means the word *elephant*, and, by the way, there are 17 elephants in what follows."

QUICK BYTES

Information travels electronically in bits per second. How fast is that? Using a standard 56K (kilobyte) modem, you can send approximately 6 pages of text containing 56 kilobytes in a second.

In fact, electronic transmissions are so fast that speed is measured in tiny fractions of a second. A **millisecond** is a thousandth of a second. A **microsecond** is a millionth of a second. And a **nanosecond** is a billionth of a second—virtually no time at all.

ONE TERABYTE = 1 trillion bytes

A NIBBLE IS 4 BITS

ONE MEGABYTE 1,048,576 bytes

ONE KILOBYTE 1,024 bytes

ONE BYTE 8 bits 1 bit

Compression also works by using a kind of abbreviation or shorthand, similar to using *St.* for *Street*. For example, you can use fewer bits for common letters, or a number of other coding shortcuts. Whatever the method, your computer can reconstruct the information in its original form when it's needed.

1,000 characters

18 characters

10 repeated 100 times

16, 32, 64...YIPE!

Bits are also the key to measuring a computer's capacity to process information. A 16-bit machine, for example, can handle numbers that are 16 bits long. As a rule, the greater the number of bits, the faster the computer can work, and the more complex tasks it can handle. Most PCs are 32-bit computers, so they handle numbers 2^{16} longer.

The Magic Chip

Chips are miniature circuits that give new meaning to the idea that good things come in small packages.

Embedded in an increasing number of devices that help run businesses and households—from computers and cellular phones to microwave ovens and cars, not to mention the most sophisticated medical and military equipment—are a host of tiny chips, or **microprocessors**.

These chips, consisting of highly intricate, miniature circuits, are the brains of an electronic device: they govern the way modern electronic machines operate as well as the complexity and speed of the tasks they perform.

Initially, circuits consisted of discrete, or separate, transistors. With the introduction of the microprocessor, however, the transistors were combined into a single integrated circuit, greatly increasing the speed and efficiency of the current flowing through it. As a result, chips have been able to handle far more complex tasks than individual transistors could.

SWITCHED ON, AND OFF

Each microprocessor, which is the size of a thumbnail, contains thousands, or millions, of even tinier transistors. Each transistor is a logical switch that creates the **binary code** (on = 1, 0 = off) that a computer can interpret to perform certain operations.

By interpreting the electronic pulses that flow through its circuitry, the microchip determines what commands to follow and what logical decisions to make—for example, which file to open, which names to select from a database, or which words to flag as misspelled.

SMALLER AND FASTER...

When you touch the keyboard of a computer, punch the buttons on a microwave, or apply the brakes on a car, you expect instant results. And that response time is directly related to the speed of the chips that control the machine's functions.

THE CHIP is composed of many thousands of **transistors**.

THE TRANSISTORS and other solid-state components sit on a **silicon wafer** less than 0.4 inch (1 cm) thick.

ELECTRICAL SIGNALS are conducted to the motherboard through rows of **pins**.

CHIP

SILICON VALLEY

Since the semiconductor companies that manufacture chips have been predominantly located in northern California, this area has earned the sobriquet Silicon Valley. The term is also used generally to refer to an area that abounds in companies developing innovative computer and computer-related products. Silicon Alley in New York City is the home of many hot web development and Internet technology companies.

Chip speed is determined by size—the smaller and more cleverly designed the circuits, the quicker the electric pulses can travel to complete the requested tasks. It also means that many more instructions can be processed in fractions of a second, so that even small computers can perform very complex tasks.

For example, some chips now have thousands of times the power of **ENIAC** (**Electronic Numerical Integrator and Calculator**)—the first electronic computer. What's more, these chips operate at an infinitesimal fraction of the cost, using a few watts of electricity (which costs about 0.1¢) compared to the ENIAC's need for 130–140 kilowatts (which is $18.20 at 13¢ a kilowatt).

...AND EVEN SMALLER AND FASTER

In fact, reducing size and increasing speed have been a major priority of the **semiconductor** industry, which develops and manufactures the chips. Semiconductors are materials that conduct electricity at high temperatures but act as insulators at low temperatures. Common semiconductors are silicon, germanium and gallium arsenide.

Because of the premium placed on speed, the announcement of a new chip, such as the Intel 486 in 1990 or the first Pentium microprocessor in 1993, caused a big stir: it meant that the machines containing these chips—in this case, primarily computers—could perform more complex tasks, such as transferring large files, far more quickly.

As chip development has evolved, each new chip to hit the market has had smaller and more complex connections, so that as of 1998, nearly 32 million transistors could exist on a single chip.

A new generation of chips, however, called **multilevel memory chips**, can store double the amount of data—2 bits instead of 1—in each transistor, expanding the capacity of a single chip to 64 million bits. (Remember, a typical letter of the alphabet is only about 8 bits.) This increase means added speed and the ability of a single chip to handle more and more complex tasks simultaneously.

...AND EVER CHEAPER

A transistor that sold for around $70 in the 1960s now costs a tiny fraction of a cent. And a microchip with over 16 million transistors costs just a few dollars. The result: far more computing power for far less money.

CYBER ETCHING

Another breakthrough is reconfigurable chips, or chips that can be upgraded or reprogrammed over the Internet once customers have them. That means product glitches and upgrades can be handled online, without the need to replace existing chips.

LITE CHIPS

If light travels faster than sound, why not use light—or photons—to transmit signals? That's exactly what a new generation of chips is designed to do, pushing data hundreds of times faster than the silicon version. Because of this speed, photonic chips are specially suited to fiber-optic switches in telecommunications networks.

MOORE'S LAW

In 1965, semiconductor pioneer Gordon Moore articulated the law that computer chip capacity would double every 18 months. Not only did this principle help people plan buying replacement machines, but it reliably predicted that prices would decline as faster chips were made available.

A CHIP OFF THE OLD BLOCK

A chip begins life as a block of silicon, a principal element in the manufacture of glass. Silicon is a natural semiconductor, which means it's not a good insulator or a good conductor of electricity. But these same features make it perfect for controlling a measured flow of electrons. When ultrapure silicon is combined with tiny amounts of chemicals called **dopants,** it can be used to detect, convert, alter and amplify electric currents, making it ideal for the tiny switches, or transistors, in a chip's circuitry.

Typically, silicon blocks are sliced into **wafers** 1/30 of an inch thick and imprinted with scores of integrated circuits. These wafers are then cut into single chips no larger than a fingernail.

Changing a wafer from a disk of silicon into a group of identical chips is a complex process called **photolithography**. It resembles an artist's etching process, but with one major difference: the work is done in microscopic detail, using many photographic overlays.

Because the minutest imperfection can ruin the chip, the manufacturing process is carried on in a **clean room** free of dust, lint and other impurities. And the people who work in these plants wear special gear, resembling spacesuits, to prevent impurities from affecting the chips.

Here a Chip, There a Chip

Inside every smart machine is a microcomputer, or dozens of them.

When we step on the gas of our cars, or apply the brakes, or set the cruise control, we are transmitting instructions that are carried out by microchips, or microcomputers, embedded in the car's operating system. Some chips, called **embedded controllers**, are by far the most common and are found in appliances like coffeemakers and toasters. They are hard-wired to perform a single function—like turning the appliance on or off at a predetermined time or temperature. For example, the automatic headlight control in a car senses when there is not adequate daylight for safe driving and turns on the headlights.

A special kind of microprocessor, called **digital signal processing** (**DSP**) chips, show a lot more "intelligence." These chips are, in effect, sensors that respond to sounds or voice impulses and then translate these incoming signals almost instantaneously into digital bits that trigger an appropriate reaction in the machine. For example, a digital phone knows when the phone is off and will record your messages, or even indicate an incoming call while you're on the phone. You also find DSP chips in CD players, answering machines, modems and digital VCRs.

GETTING SMARTER ALL THE TIME

Even the "single-minded" controller chips are getting smarter—or at least more versatile. New microprocessors use software to replicate old functions while adding new ones to the same chip—a process much simpler and less costly than rewriting a program and creating a new set of transistors every time a new feature is added.

COMPUTERS

Computers have several different kinds of chips, all with special functions: **memory chips**, which provide capacity for storing and processing data; **ASICs**, or **application-specific integrated circuits**, which are custom-produced for specific programs; and **microprocessors**, which combine both logic and arithmetic and control functions. These chips are used in the computer's CPU, or central processing unit.

AUTOMOBILES

Step on the gas. Set the cruise control. Open the sun roof. Turn on the heat. Lower your side-view mirror. Hit the brakes. All these mechanical functions, and dozens of others "under the hood," are controlled by microprocessors in the car. Some luxury cars have upwards of 40 different chips, monitoring a range of operating and safety features, including air bags, that are all transparent to drivers.

By responding instantly to the slightest changes in the vehicle's movement, speed or stability, and signaling corrective actions, microprocessors make cars a lot safer, more fuel-efficient—and in the case of dashboard control systems—a lot more fun to drive.

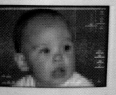

SYSTEM-ON-A-CHIP

System-on-a-chip devices combine digital signal processing, memory and controller functions on a single chip using very little power consumption. And they're very economical to produce.

Furby, the popular furry toy created by Tyger Electronics, contains two such chips—and has the processing power of an Apple II. This is the same processor used in the Atari 2600—the popular home video game system from the late 1970s.

Furby is programmed to interact with the environment through sight, touch, hearing and physical orientation. And it can "speak" in response to conditions detected by built-in sensors and an infrared device.

Sharper Image's Weebots and Mattel's Rugrats are other toys designed to mimic learning by slowly releasing preprogrammed behavior over days and even months.

BABY IDS

The little ID bracelets traditionally placed around a newborn's ankle may now contain a data chip that has been programmed with an identity number. And the new baby's mother and father wear matching bands. To insure that infants are matched up with the right set of parents, hospital staff scan the chips each time they move a baby to and from its mother's room as well as when the baby and parents check out of the hospital.

Chips are used for the LCD, or display, on a boom box as well as on such functions as timing, tracking and skipping.

DSP chips are essential ingredients in cellular phones, handling voice compression and decompression, and filtering out noise.

HITTING THE MICROCHIP JACKPOT

Microprocessors have even found their way into slot machines. There they not only generate random numbers that determine the odds of winning on a single machine but they also communicate with other machines linked via a network. The result: a much larger running jackpot that taps the winning pools of the connected machines.

Bandwidth

In its travels, information can run into traffic jams.

Whether your image of a traffic jam is three lanes of cars crowding into a two-lane exit, thousands of people jockeying to go through a stadium gate, or some equally frustrating bottleneck, you've got a sense of why **bandwidth** gets so much attention in the Information Age.

Quite simply, bandwidth is how much stuff—voice, text, video—you can send through a connection, or pipeline, in a given amount of time. The basic premise is that the higher the bandwidth of a particular transmission medium, such as copper wire, coaxial or fiber-optic cable, or the airwaves, the more information that medium can carry.

The catch, though, is that the actual rate at which information arrives, called **throughput**, is determined by the slowest part of the route, generally the wiring to your home, which is often described as "the last mile."

HERTZ AND BITS

More technically, bandwidth measures how much information, in the form of pulses of electricity (electrons) or pulses of light (photons), can move through a transmission medium. In analog networks, the measurement is in **hertz**, or frequency of wave repetitions per second. In digital networks, bandwidth is measured in **bits per second** (**bps**)—the number of 0s and 1s that flow through the switches or transistors.

So, for example, an analog voice telephone call traveling over copper wire has a bandwidth of 3 kilohertz (KHz), which in digital terms would be 64,000 bits per second. Compare that to broadcast video, which requires moving 10 million bits, or 10 megabits, per second through the pipeline. Bandwidths that are this high or higher are generally referred to as **broadband** service.

MEASURING THE PIPE

The wires and cables of network transmission systems are often referred to informally as **pipes**. Though the analogy isn't perfect, you can compare the bandwidth of voice and data moving through pipes to water moving through different-sized hoses.

The larger diameter of a fire hose, for example, can push through a much larger quantity of water than an ordinary garden hose can. Even if you increase the water pressure in your house, the garden hose can still let only so much water through.

BROADBAND

To understand broadband, picture a suburban street in mid-afternoon, where an occasional auto occupied only by the driver ambles along. That's the equivalent of a low-bandwidth telephone call on analog copper wire. At rush hour, the same street may be bumper-to-bumper with single-passenger cars. So there's more traffic but still low bandwidth.

Now think of a four-lane interstate, crammed with trucks, buses and car pools as well as single-passenger cars. And throw in a light-rail system running down the highway median. Not only do you have vehicles carrying more people but you also have more lanes, or channels, of traffic integrated into a single transmission path. That's broadband.

Analog phone call on copper wire
64,000 bits per second

Broadcast video
10,000,000 bits per second

The higher the bandwidth, the more information the transmission medium can carry.

STRIKE UP THE BAND

Volumes of information travel quickly and reliably through the existing telecom network, as telephone conversations have always done. Fax transmissions, e-mail messages and most text-based data arrive intact within seconds of being sent or downloaded from the Internet.

But that's not the case with graphics, music or multimedia content. Unless there is enough bandwidth, such transmissions arrive painfully slowly, in fits and starts or out of synch. Similarly, true interactive transactions, like videoconferences or collaborative long-distance learning, need delivery systems with enough bandwidth, or broadband service, to be effective.

SQUEEZING THE CONTENT

One approach to meeting higher bandwidth requirements is to shrink the content so it moves through the pipeline more efficiently.

Compression involves squeezing the content, or reducing what has to be transmitted, so that it takes up less space in the pipeline. The content is converted to digital form, and special computers compress the signal. When the signal is received at the other end, the digital message is reformed into words and images.

Multiplexing is a way of combining or timing transmissions so that more information can travel through the same communications medium at the same time. There are several ways to do this.

With **space division** multiplexing, for example, transmissions are arranged so that several different "packages" of data can travel through the same communications medium at the same time. This technique uses bandwidth more efficiently by filling in the pauses in transmissions with the smaller packages, which are then reassembled at the receiving end.

With **time division** multiplexing, the release of the signals is carefully controlled and timed to maximize transmission during a specific time period. There is also **dense wave division** multiplexing, which increases the capacity of fiber-optic cable by putting up to 16 different wave paths or more on a single strand of fiber.

THE SEARCH FOR GREATER BANDWIDTH

Delivering broadband service to people's homes is a national goal. To make it a reality, bandwidth is being increased in a number of ways, including:

- **Developing two-way cable connections.** The average cable TV connection provides plenty of bandwidth, but up until recently it's been one-way. You could receive the transmission but couldn't send anything back. But companies like AT&T, working with local cable companies, are using a technology for making cable a two-way transmission medium. The result is dramatically higher bandwidth to your home, creating a hybrid system using fiber-optic and coaxial cable. This mix of technology brings two-way broadband communication to people's homes.

- **Replacing existing wires.** The wires to homes and public buildings, like schools and libraries, are being replaced with coaxial or fiber-optic cable.

- **Enhancing the existing wired connections.** Bandwidth can be increased with **ISDN**, or **Integrated Services Digital Network**. ISDN is an all-digital network that connects to your home or office using a special interface that combines voice, data and video on a single phone line.

  ADSL, or **Asymmetric Digital Subscriber Lines**, use the same copper wires that carry regular voice telephone service, but the circuit is much faster than a normal phone connection. ADSL also have digital signal processors that suppress the noise created when you cram high-speed data down a standard copper-wire phone line.

- **Using satellite transmissions and fixed wireless receivers.** These technologies avoid the bottlenecks that can be created, particularly on copper-wire lines, when content requiring higher bandwidth is being transmitted.

Communications Spectrum

Silent, invisible waves carry wireless communications around the globe.

One of the hallmarks of the Information Age is the increasing use of the airwaves to get information from one point to another.

All wireless communications travel through air and space on designated **frequencies**, or wave patterns, in a section of the electromagnetic spectrum known as the **radio spectrum**.

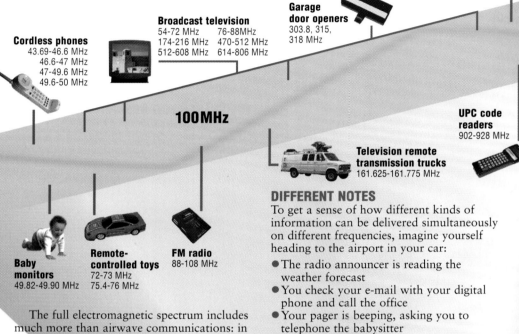

Cellular phones
824-849 MHz
869-894 MHz

Garage door openers
303.8, 315, 318 MHz

Broadcast television
54-72 MHz   76-88MHz
174-216 MHz 470-512 MHz
512-608 MHz 614-806 MHz

Cordless phones
43.69-46.6 MHz
46.6-47 MHz
47-49.6 MHz
49.6-50 MHz

100MHz

UPC code readers
902-928 MHz

Television remote transmission trucks
161.625-161.775 MHz

Baby monitors
49.82-49.90 MHz

Remote-controlled toys
72-73 MHz
75.4-76 MHz

FM radio
88-108 MHz

DIFFERENT NOTES

To get a sense of how different kinds of information can be delivered simultaneously on different frequencies, imagine yourself heading to the airport in your car:

- The radio announcer is reading the weather forecast
- You check your e-mail with your digital phone and call the office
- Your pager is beeping, asking you to telephone the babysitter
- Flashing lights on your tracking map alert you to a backup at the next exit
- Your radar detector squeals, warning you to slow down

The full electromagnetic spectrum includes much more than airwave communications: in fact, it encompasses everything that travels in waves—from radio signals carrying voice to extremely high-frequency cosmic rays.

In the US, the **Federal Communications Commission (FCC)** allocates the radio spectrum by assigning a range of frequencies to each type of communication. Cellular telephones, for example, broadcast in one range of frequencies, broadcast television and fixed satellites in still another. The FCC licenses individual frequencies within each range.

RIDING THE WAVE

The radio spectrum is a critical natural resource with a limited supply. Unlike oil and coal, however, airwaves don't get depleted. But they can get crowded. And the spectrum is getting fuller as demand for all types of wireless service increases.

There are some potential solutions to over-crowding, though, such as technologies that can transmit more layers of information at the

THE ELECTROMAGNETIC SPECTRUM

The full electromagnetic spectrum includes much more than wireless communication: it encompasses everything that travels in waves, from very low frequencies to cosmic rays.

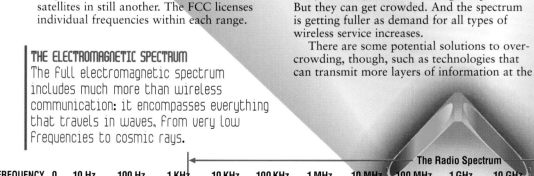

The Radio Spectrum

FREQUENCY	0	10 Hz	100 Hz	1 KHz	10 KHz	100 KHz	1 MHz	10 MHz	100 MHz	1 GHz	10 GHz	100 G
BAND DESIGNATION		VLF (Very Low Frequency)				LF (Low Frequency)	MF (Medium Frequency)	HF (High Frequency)	VHF (Very High Frequency)	UHF (Ultra-High Frequency)	SHF (Super-High Frequency)	EHF (Extremely High Frequency)
ACTIVITY		Audible Sound Range					AM Broadcast		FM Broadcast			

Personal communications services
1850-1990 MHz
1910-1930 MHz

Microwave ovens
2540 MHz

Global Positioning Satellite system
1610-1626.5 MHz
2483.5-2500 MHz

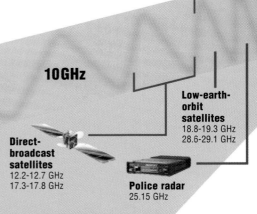

Fixed satellites
17.7-18.8 GHz   19.7-20.2 GHz
28.35-28.6 GHz 29.5-30 GHz

10GHz

Low-earth-orbit satellites
18.8-19.3 GHz
28.6-29.1 GHz

1000MHz/1GHz

Direct-broadcast satellites
12.2-12.7 GHz
17.3-17.8 GHz

Police radar
25.15 GHz

Automatic teller machines
928-929 MHz   932-932.5 MHz
941-941.5 MHz 952-960 MHz

same frequency at the same time, compressing data for more efficient transmission, or finding ways to use parts of the spectrum that haven't been used before.

UNDERSTANDING FREQUENCY

Frequencies are measured by the number of wave repetitions, or completed cycles, per second. The radio spectrum contains more than 300 million frequencies, but fewer than half are currently used for wireless communication.

Guitar strings can help clarify how frequencies differ. The thickest string vibrates more slowly than the thinnest string. Since the thick string produces fewer completed cycles in the same period of time, it has a lower frequency than the thin one. (We hear the thicker strings as "lower" notes, and the thinner strings as "higher" notes.) Because the frequencies are different, you can hear the different sounds created by the two strings even though they're struck at the same time.

IT'S HERTZ TO MEASURE FREQUENCY

The frequency, or the number of cycles an airwave completes in a specific period of time, is measured in **hertz**, or units equal to one cycle per second. The measurement gets its name from Heinrich Hertz, a 19th-century German physicist who investigated radio signals and other portions of the electromagnetic spectrum.

The more oscillations a wave completes in a second, the greater the hertz measure, or frequency. A frequency of five hertz, for example, means that a wave completes five cycles or repetitions in a second.

Because the frequencies in the radio spectrum are very high, they're actually measured in kilohertz (KHz), or thousands of hertz, megahertz (MHz), or millions of hertz, and gigahertz (GHz), or billions of hertz.

A radio station that broadcasts at 96.3 on your radio dial means that the station operates at 96.3 megahertz—that is, the waves emitted by the station go through a cycle 96.3 million times a second.

SALE OF THE CENTURY

When commercial radio and television were the primary users of the airwaves, the FCC granted licenses at little or no cost but restricted the number of licenses a broadcaster could hold. Since 1994, however, the FCC has been actively auctioning airwaves, selling off parts of the spectrum to individual owners who will be able to provide a range of services using those frequencies.

From the government's perspective, it's been a profitable venture. And there's lots of the spectrum—more than 80%—that's not for sale, at least so far, because it's reserved for the government or is just not practical to use.

1 THz	10^{13}Hz	10^{14}Hz	10^{15}Hz	10^{16}Hz	10^{17}Hz	10^{18}Hz	10^{19}Hz	10^{20}Hz	10^{21}Hz	10^{22}Hz	10^{23}Hz
	INFRARED LIGHT	VISIBLE LIGHT		ULTRAVIOLET LIGHT		X-RAYS		GAMMA-RAYS			COSMIC-RAYS

Communicating across Time and Space

Many systems have evolved for sharing information.

Communication is often easiest when you're face to face. You're sure your message has been delivered, and you can usually get an immediate response. But when you're trying to send a message—across the city, the country or the world—you're dependent on some sort of system to get it there.

With access to e-mail, a fax machine or overnight delivery, you probably don't give **telecommunications**—*tele* is the Greek word for distance—a second thought. But communications systems have a long history. Early methods of communication included drumbeats, fire, smoke signals and lantern beacons, all of which could be heard or seen over a distance.

MESSENGER SYSTEMS

The oldest communications systems used messengers to carry information. To announce their victory over the Persians in 490 B.C., the Greeks sent runners to Athens from the city of Marathon—hence our word *marathon* to describe long-distance races.

Long distances were later covered by carrier pigeons. Their first recorded use was in 12th-century Iraq by the Sultan of Baghdad, and they were still in use during World War I.

Governments have employed couriers (from the French verb *courir*, "to run") to carry important messages, especially in wartime. This system could be used by citizens, who were charged a fee, or tax, which was indicated by postage stamps.

Despite its popularity, the Pony Express lasted just 18 months as part of a publicity stunt in 1860 by Central Overland California and Pikes Peak Express Company to secure a government mail contract. The fastest delivery was of President Lincoln's Inaugural Address, taking 7 days and 17 hours between existing telegraph lines. The completion of cross-country telegraph lines in 1861 officially ended the Pony Express.

VISUAL SIGNALS

Early communications systems could relay information that the receiver was expecting—for example, an alert of an impending attack or a celebratory message. The Greek playwright Aeschylus recounts that news of the destruction of Troy was relayed by means of fires lit on mountaintops. Hannibal is said to have communicated by fire signals in Africa and Spain, and the ancient hill forts of prehistoric Britain were situated so people could relay signals across the countryside.

For these systems to work, the sender and receiver had to agree on the message ahead of time. When Paul Revere waited for the lantern signal from the Old North Church so he would know which way the British were coming, he was absolutely clear about the alternatives: one if by land, two if by sea. There was no accurate way to convey something that hadn't been anticipated or agreed on.

SIGNS AND SYMBOLS

A visual signaling system is based on an alphabet code and uses flags, lights or semaphores—with mechanical or human arms—to relay information. The messages you send with visual signals can be more complex because you can spell out words and sentences. And the person on the receiving end can use the same code to respond.

The ancient Greeks had a system that used five tables of five letters, plus signalers to indicate which table and which letter on the table was being used.

In 1793, Claude Chappe began construction of a French semaphore system that ultimately grew to 556 telegraph stations, covering roughly 4,800 kilometers (3,000 miles). The network connected 29 of France's largest cities to Paris.

And the semaphore or flag systems devised by James Elford of South Carolina in 1816 used 7 blue and white flags, allowing sailors to create up to 8,000 coded combinations.

SOUND SYSTEMS

Communications systems based on sound were initially limited by how far the sound could travel. But the messages conveyed were much richer and more detailed than a simple code. African drums, for example, were more sophisticated than early visual systems because they could use two tones—high and low—to simulate the speech patterns of languages structured on alternating tones.

It was the telegraph, though, that radically altered long-distance communications. After almost 100 years of experimentation and discovery in Europe and the US, Samuel F. B. Morse patented his version, developed with his assistant Alfred Vail, in 1844. Using a coded system of dots and dashes, operators could send messages anywhere by wires. By the 1860s, the wires stretched across the Atlantic.

Since then, new telecommunications methods and systems have mushroomed. The telephone was invented in 1876 by Alexander Graham Bell. In 1885, the company he founded—the American Telephone and Telegraph Company—began linking together telegraph exchanges to form a nationwide system.

Wireless telephone messages using radio waves were first sent in 1896, and the first wireless transmission of the human voice across the Atlantic took place in 1915. Commercial radio telephone service was established between New York and London in 1927, and the first radio programs were broadcast in 1936 by the BBC.

NETWORKS

Unlike earlier signaling systems, such as flags, fires or lanterns, communications in the Information Age travel over networks as sound waves, light waves, microwaves and radio waves that you can't see or hear. To move information over these networks, you need switches, which guide and direct the information from source to destination, and a transmission medium, such as copper wires, fiber-optic cable or the air.

Even as these communications networks grow, they continue to become more "intelligent," providing an array of services from call forwarding and caller identification to finding the quickest and most economical path for Internet traffic. As you consider the rich variety of communications networks throughout this chapter, you may be reminded of the first telegraph message sent over the experimental line between Washington, DC, and Baltimore, Maryland: "What hath God wrought!"

How Networks Network

With information, as with trains, switching and routing gets the freight to the right destination.

Networks are the veins and arteries—some would even say the heart and soul—of the Information Age. That's because networks are designed to move information, a commodity that grows in value the more it's shared and the more accessible it becomes. The network's job is to speed up the rate for exchanging information, ensure the accuracy of the transmission, and do it all for as little cost as possible.

Some networks are connected physically, like the wires that link your home to the telephone company, or cables that carry programs to your TV. Other networks use radio or microwave signals to transmit information, and still others use a combination of wired and wireless systems.

A network can be as small as the connections linking the equipment in a home office or as vast as a telecommunications system that crisscrosses the globe. And while no network is as complex as our own nervous system—a network that has evolved over millions of years—the elements in a global telecommunications system rival the number of brain cells and synapses in our bodies.

Networks are everywhere. When you make a phone call, log on to the Internet, use an ATM to withdraw cash, or switch on your radio, you are relying on networks to get the job done. And while the closest we get to a network is through the access devices we use every day—phones, computers, faxes, beepers and televisions—behind the scenes these devices are seamlessly connected by a mass of electronic equipment, software and millions of miles of wires and cables, all synchronized and working together.

In 1998, AT&T's long-distance networks consisted of **51,000** of miles of fiber-optic cable. Together, that's enough wiring to cross the country 14 times.

SWITCHES INSIDE BUSINESSES

Most medium- and large-sized businesses use a **private branch exchange**, or **PBX**, which provides internal switching on site and connects directly to the company's local and long-distance carriers. Used to manage the phone traffic within a building or campus, PBXs help simplify a phone system and lower the costs.

MAKING THE RIGHT SWITCH

Like transportation networks—highway, airline and rapid transit systems, for example—land-based telephone networks operate around central hubs. There sophisticated computers switch incoming signals, routing them to their ultimate destination.

When you make a call, the network creates a circuit or pathway between you and the person you're calling by pulling together hundreds of network components—and billions of possible connections—in a unique combination. When you hang up or finish sending the message, the components are released, probably never to reassemble again in quite that order.

As you speak, your telephone converts sound waves from your voice into electrical waves, which are then

transmitted across long distances as pulses of electricity or light. Along the way, the signals are routed or directed through a series of processing points controlled by **switches**, the equivalent of a colossal, globally coordinated force of electronic traffic cops.

These switches can shift from on to off and back again many millions of times a second. They respond to software commands to act on the numbers you dial and also provide the "intelligence" to activate specific services, such as 800 numbers, call waiting and caller ID. That's why networks like the telephone system that were originally designed to carry voice are called **switched circuits**.

THE SWITCH TO DATA NETWORKS

Originally, people needed a network that let them talk to each other. So the **voice network**, which sent signals over analog sound waves, provided POTS, or plain old telephone service. But increasingly, networks designed to carry voice are also being used to transmit electronic data in the form of text, graphics, sound and video—but often far too slowly for people doing business or surfing the Internet.

Digital information can be transmitted far more efficiently over **data networks**, which are designed to carry digital bits of information (strings of 0s and 1s) in special packets or bundles. The intricacies of these **packet-switched** circuits, which are ideal for moving large files, especially those with pictures and sound, are described in greater detail in "Voice and Data" in the following pages.

INTERNET PROTOCOLS

In addition to the traditional voice networks, you can also make phone calls over the Internet. But there are some down sides: you and the party you're calling will probably have to install special software and equipment on your PCs, and you may well experience network delays and erratic sound quality.

That's changing, however, now that large telecommunications companies have begun using **IP—Internet Protocol**—as the standard for their global networks. IP is a set of rules or procedures for moving all forms of digital information—voice, video, data and images—in packets across many kinds of networks. With so much of the world's brainpower focused on developing new IP applications and services, Internet Protocol is the likely choice for next-century communications.

MAKING THE

Voice and Data

Networked information travels as voice or data, and sometimes both.

While voice networks that carry telephone messages are still used extensively, the demand for transmitting **data**, such as text, graphics, video and sound, has increased dramatically. So much so that the amount of data being sent over the telephone network now exceeds the amount of voice traffic.

The result has placed greater demands on the existing networks—for faster speeds, for greater bandwidth (a larger pipeline) to carry the richer mix of multimedia information, and for still lower costs of transmission. To meet the demand, digital networks use special data packages and switches to transmit information in the most efficient way.

PACKET IT UP

Unlike the sound of your voice, which is analog and travels in continuous waves, data is transmitted in bursts. That means the information travels in bunches, or clumps, with long pauses in between, wasting a lot of network capacity.

To use the network more efficiently, a special type of transmission, called **packet switching**, is used:

1. The data is chopped into **packets**, or groupings of digital bits (0s and 1s) that contain the unique identity and address to which each packet is headed.
2. A single packet is then bundled, or **multiplexed**, with other packets being sent from the same office, building or serving area. In this way, there's almost always data traveling the network at any moment—like a highway at rush hour 24 hours a day.
3. When a bundle is full, the system seizes a physical circuit and holds it open long enough to transport the bundle to the next point along the route.
4. When the packet reaches its final destination, the circuit is released, and packets with the same identity and address are reassembled to form a complete message.

While this system works exceedingly well for data, it's not as effective for voice signals. That's because the data packets, which can travel in any order and take different routes through the network, can arrive at their destination late, out of sequence, or damaged. As a result, even though voice signals can be digitized and transmitted as data packets, the quality and reliability of the transmissions is generally poor.

IT'S NOT A FRAME-UP

A special broadband transmission service that's ideally suited to businesses is called **frame relay**. This service is based on the premise that data streams originating in companies are checked for errors when they're sent and when they're received. So they don't need error checking on the network while traveling to their destination—a process that reduces costly delays. The primary benefit of frame relay, then, is that users get broadband transmission speed when they need it but don't have to pay for private line networks that may not be fully used.

SEEKING THE SHORTEST ROUTE

The incredibly complex job of getting the right packets to the right location in the right sequence is the job of **routers**. The software in these computerlike black boxes looks up the addresses for each packet it receives, inspects each one, and selects the best path to get the packet to its destination.

This same procedure occurs in every router along the network—a tedious task that gets slower as the traffic grows. For example, the delays you may experience using the Internet are often the result of routers up and down the line groaning under the weight of checking every packet.

VOICE NETWORKS ARE NOW HANDLING DATA

- Voice messages are created as sound waves.
- Voice messages travel effectively over basic 26-gauge copper wires.
- Voice messages are sent in real time, so that you hear what is being said as it is spoken.
- Voice messages go to a specific receiver, or limited number of receivers, linked to an internal telephone system.

MERGING VOICE AND DATA

The distinctions between voice and data networks are constantly blurring. Voice networks are handling data transmissions—faxes and e-mail, for example—but not as efficiently as data packets can. And networks created for transporting data, like the Internet, are moving toward carrying voice, though they lack the quality that voice networks provide.

But voice networks are being adapted to carry data, especially text, by innovative switching and transmission techniques and higher-capacity wires and cables. In addition, wireless digital phones and other devices are being designed to receive voice and data equally well.

NETWORKS NEAR AND FAR

Many organizations use a **local area network**, or **LAN**, to enable their employees to share software, information and applications over a common network. Typically, LANs consist of various PCs or desktop terminals connected to a central and powerful computer, or server. Because LANs are entirely digital networks and operate at broadband speeds on a single, broad pipe rather than several smaller ones, they speed the flow of information to individual desktops within a workgroup or across the enterprise.

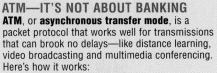

ATM—IT'S NOT ABOUT BANKING

ATM, or **asynchronous transfer mode**, is a packet protocol that works well for transmissions that can brook no delays—like distance learning, video broadcasting and multimedia conferencing. Here's how it works:

ATM breaks information flows into separate cells of 53 bytes each, with 48 bytes carrying data and five bytes carrying address and routing information. These cells then flow along virtual paths on a virtual channel, taking advantage of whatever capacity and route is available to reach their destination. At higher transmission rates, an ATM data stream can seize cells at the rate it needs to support its flow at any point in time, so no bandwidth is wasted.

LAN PROTOCOLS

LANs work because they use a set of common procedures, or protocols, to regulate the flow of data. One popular protocol, called **Ethernet**, first checks to make sure other data isn't being transmitted before it sends information—like looking both ways before crossing the street. With multiple access, however, two computers may transmit data at the same time, resulting in a collision. A detection system identifies collisions and then resends the messages. The busier the network gets, however, the more collisions are likely to occur, weighing down the network with resent messages.

Another protocol, called **token ring**, takes its name from an order-keeping procedure the ancient Romans used in their Senate: a member could speak only if he held the token. In the modern version, a special packet of data, known as a token, is passed around the network. A computer must wait until it receives the token to transmit a message. Token ring is more orderly than Ethernet but also more expensive.

LAN AND WANS

Many LANs hook into a **wide area network**, or **WAN**, which allows widely separated LANs to communicate. For example, if an office in Madrid using a LAN sends data to a home office in Milwaukee, which has its own LAN, the transmission probably went via a WAN.

The Internet is basically one gigantic WAN, linking government, business, educational and private computer networks around the world.

DATA NETWORKS ARE MOVING TOWARD CARRYING VOICE

- Data is created as binary digits and chopped into packets.
- Complex data transmissions have too much information to travel efficiently on basic copper lines.
- Data is transmitted in bursts, at a different rate than it is created or can be absorbed.
- Multiple receivers around the globe can get the same data simultaneously.

A Phone Is a Phone Is a...

Simple, versatile and constantly evolving instrument of communications.

Though over 100 years old, the telephone remains one of our most modern appliances. One of the earliest examples of true two-way communication, the telephone has continued to evolve, taking on new shapes and sizes (mostly smaller), adding a bevy of special features—from speakers to answering machines—jettisoning its attached wires, and even becoming digital.

While the basic principle of **telephony**—transmitting sounds between distant locations—hasn't changed since its inception, the convenience and usefulness of the phone has shot ahead thanks to continuous infusions of technology. Yet all you need to control this versatile machine is a simple rotary dial or key pad—a human interface so elegant and easy to use that even small children can make a telephone call.

LOUDER AND CLEARER, PLEASE

Though you might not explain it exactly this way, a telephone is a device for converting acoustic waves produced by your voice box into electrical waves that can be transmitted over a telecommunications network.

At the receiving end, the procedure is reversed: electrical waves are converted to acoustic waves that vibrate the eardrum, producing intelligible sound.

The earliest telephones converted sound into electrical waves using a diaphragm that vibrated a piece of wire suspended in a mag-

netic field. This electromagnetic mechanism was capable of converting only one-thousandth of the available electrical power that the listener could hear to acoustic power—and only

Key pad enters numbers in the form of tones and accesses special calling services

Microphone and mouthpiece captures analog waves

Automatic redial

a millionth when used as a transmitter. That was powerful enough to summon Mr. Watson from the next room in 1876, but not practical for long-distance communications.

THE EVOLUTI

Alexander Graham Bell, age 22, 1876

1876

1877

1878

1882

1897

1921

1928

1937

Old wall telephones had a wooden box with a crank, which was used to spin a magnet that powered up the phone's circuitry to alert an operator to get on the line. Improved central office battery equipment got rid of the crank. The operator, by the way, was the first truly "intelligent agent," who understood what you said and made the necessary connections.

The candlestick phone was an upright arrangement that took both hands to operate: one held the transmitter to the mouth, the other held the separate receiver to the ear. The two parts had to be separated because the transmitter and receiver interfered with each other, causing howling and other noise.

In 1886, Thomas Edison patented a transmitter with a microphone that converted sound to electrical energy by varying the resistance between two contacts.

Speaker and earpiece

The material he selected was carbon black, and with further improvements, carbon elements served in millions of telephone sets for decades.

Then, in the 1970s, Jim West of AT&T's Bell Labs developed the use of the foil-electret microphone. In the electret, sound creates an electric charge, which in turn generates the electric signal that carries voice on phone lines. This technology is still standard in 90% of the world's phones.

CORDLESS PHONES

If you like wandering around the house when you're on the phone, then a cordless phone is probably a good buy. Cordless phones transmit voice signals between the handset and phone base by radio waves that use different parts of the radio spectrum.

In recent years, the use of less crowded parts of the radio spectrum has dramatically improved the range and clarity of cordless phones, while the introduction of **spread spectrum** technology has made eavesdropping almost impossible. To provide this security, the sound waves are first converted to digital form. The digital signals are then transmitted over a broad range of frequencies and even jump from one frequency to another. As a result, only the person receiving the call can get the full message.

WIRELESS PHONES

Unlike cordless phones, wireless phones have no phone base but transmit signals directly, so you can take the phones anywhere there are receptors to pick up the signals. (See "Look, Mom, No Wires" in this chapter.) Some wireless phones are analog, and send and receive sound waves, while others, including **personal communications systems**, or **PCS**, transmit digital data.

In fact, some of these phones also double as walkie-talkies or mobile speaker phones, enabling several people to hold a conference call over the airwaves—without a single wire.

THE INTERNET PHONE

For people who want to get on the Internet but don't have PCs, an Internet phone— complete with viewing screen—is available. AT&T's PocketNet Phone, for example, as well as Cidco's iPhone, lets you make calls but also gives you direct, wireless access to the Internet. When the phone is turned on, it automatically connects to the network. While not best suited for surfing the Net, these phones let you send and receive e-mail, check your daily planner, and get a range of information, from financial reports to sports scores.

O N A R Y   P H O N E

1949 1959 1956 1964 1976 1968 1987 1999

The one-piece handset has prevailed since it was introduced in 1926. The new key pad introduced in 1964 included the ★ and # keys for enabling interactions with data services and equipment.

Advances in microelectronics technology created tiny amplifiers and solid-state memories that resulted in **speaker phones** for hands-free conversations, **repeat dialers** that store dozens of numbers to be dialed simply by touching a button, and **fax terminals** and **modems**, which enable machines to talk to each other over telephone networks.

MAKING THE

Getting in Touch

A telephone call is all about connections and interconnections.

When you make a phone call, you're using a network that can move your voice anytime, anywhere, without delays. The network is organized around hundreds of interconnected switches, junction points and transmission lines—or links.

SETTING STANDARDS

For this connectivity to work, all the elements in a telecom network, from the most basic telephone to the most complicated switch, need to meet physical, electrical, performance and safety standards.

Manufacturers and designers, through a number of different standards groups, use complementary specifications so that everything works together. That's the reason you can plug a phone into any working jack, dial the appropriate numbers, and reach the person you're trying to call.

Making the

YOU	lift the receiver,	dial the number you're calling, and

| THE NETWORK | When you pick up your telephone, you signal the switch in your local phone office that you're ready to make a call. The dial tone you hear means the system is ready for you. | As you push numbers on your key pad, the office switch decides how to route your call. It's programmed to react in specific ways if you choose **0** (assistance), **1** (long distance), **411** (directory assistance), **611** (repair), **911** (emergency) or **011** (international). If you start with any other digits, it knows you're making a | local call. If you press 1, a switch checks your account to identify your long-distance carrier. It then sends the number you dial along a trunk line to your carrier's point of presence (POP), where the local and long-distance networks meet to hand off calls. |

READY!

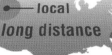

— local
long distance

| PHONE TALK MAKES WAVES | 1. When you speak into the phone, your voice enters the phone's mouthpiece as sound waves, which are transformed into electrical waves, or signals, by a device called an **electret.** | 2. The electrical waves travel along one strand of a pair of copper wires to your phone company's local office... | 3. ...where they are converted to binary digits, or bits, and combined with groups of bits from many other calls. |

MANUAL OPERATION

In the days of the manual switchboard, there was a pair of copper wires running from every house to a central office in the middle of town. A switchboard operator sat in front of a board with one jack for every pair of wires entering the office. Above each jack was a small light or

metal flag. When someone picked up the handset on his or her telephone, the hook switch would complete the circuit, allowing current to flow through wires between the house and the office. This would light the light bulb or activate the flag above that person's jack on

ALTERNATE ROUTES

In the AT&T long-distance network, there are 141 giant switches that create possible routes for getting a call across the country. Each switch in the system communicates with every other switch at five- to ten-second intervals to check their status. If there's congestion on one route, another is opened up.

Because the routing is done in real time, the quickest path is almost always chosen, so your call goes through instantaneously.

Although it is primarily fiber-optic, the long-distance network may use a combination of coaxial cables, fiber-optic lines, and microwaves to transport the signals along the route. To travel on the fiber-optic pathways, the electrical signals are changed to light signals and then back to electrical signals for the final leg on local copper wire.

SINGLE DIGITS, BIG VIBES

If you're calling from a rotary phone, the digits you dial produce short pulses that interrupt the dial tone. Dialing 1 produces one set of pulses, dialing 2 produces two sets of pulses, and so on.

If your phone is a touch-tone, each button you press generates a pair of tones that electronic receivers in the central office recognize and associate with a particular number. The number 7, for example, is represented by tones at 1,209 and 852 **hertz**, which is a measurement of how fast something is vibrating per second to produce sound.

The double tone is used to avoid producing harmonics—frequencies that cross over from the input to the output channel—that can trick the network into signaling that the call should be dropped.

Connections

the person you're calling picks up

There, a switch sends the number along a high-speed data network called a common channel signaling network (CCSN). The network checks the routes to the call's destination, finds the most direct path, and contacts the local office that handles the number you're calling.

A switch at the local office of the number you're calling checks the number, rings it if it's free, or sends you a busy signal if it's not. If someone (or a machine) answers, the voice path, or circuit through the networks—all the switches, contacts, trunks and lines—opens at once and stays open until one of you hangs up.

When you finish talking, the circuit is released, and equipment in your local office goes back to a ready state, continuously scanning your line until you pick up again to make another call.

BUSY · NOT BUSY

READY!

4. They are then sent to the nearest POP and onto the long-distance network. Along the way, the signals are amplified, or boosted, to make them stronger.

5. When the signal reaches its destination, the bits are reconverted into electrical waves…

6. …which move by copper wire into the phone's receiver. There they strike a plate that transforms them back into sound waves so the person you're calling can hear your voice. When she replies, her voice travels the same way in reverse.

the switchboard. The operator would plug the handset into that jack and ask who the person wanted to talk to. She would then ring the receiving party. Once the receiving party picked up, the operator would connect them with the caller.

CONNECTING UP
Better than 99% of all calls reach their destination and about 65% are actually completed. The others don't go through because the line is busy or there's no answer.

What the Numbers Mean

By picking the right numbers, you can call almost any country in the world.

The numbers you dial or touch on your phone will send your call to a specific destination almost instantaneously.

Seven digits let you call someone next door or across town. By dialing eleven numbers, you can get in touch with anyone in North America. Just a few more digits let you reach almost anyone on earth who has a telephone. In fact, from the United States you can dial directly to 250 nations and territories of the world.

Direct dialing works because a uniform numbering plan, combined with sophisticated switching technology, can interpret and hand off calls from one network to another. This technology allows all local, long-distance, and international telecommunications companies to understand the signals you're sending, thereby taking all the hassle and much of the expense out of long-distance calling.

The innovation that made direct long-distance dialing possible—one of the biggest leaps forward in modern telecommunications—was the North American Numbering Plan, developed by AT&T in 1948. It meant that every telephone with its own line had a unique, 10-digit number.

011·44·171

INTERNATIONAL CODE **COUNTRY CODE** **CITY CODE/ AREA CODE**

CALLING ABROAD

When you direct dial an international call, you start with 011 to alert switching equipment that the call is going overseas. Then you add a country code, a city code for major metropolitan areas, and finally, the individual number.

If you're calling London from the US, for example, you dial:

011 (this is an international call)

44 (it's going to the United Kingdom)

171 (it's going to central London) followed by a seven-digit local number

Not all of the numbers you can dial directly resemble the 10-digit US model, especially if they're in rural areas or developing countries. For example, 7 is the country code for Russia, but you have to dial 389 to reach Macedonia.

Area or regional codes are also different in every country. You have to dial a four-digit area code to talk to a friend in Xiamen, China, but it only takes one digit to call Helsinki. India's area codes can be anywhere from two to four numbers, while small countries like Fiji, Malta and the Solomon Islands have no area codes at all.

1. In the US, the country was divided into 152 area codes, called Numbering Plan Areas (NPAs).

Each area code was a unique three-digit number, known in telephone jargon as a N0/1X. N was any digit 2 through 9 followed by 0 or 1, and X was any digit from 0 through 9, producing codes like 203 and 914. The sequence couldn't start with 0 or 1 because local callers used those numbers to contact operators.

By 1962, it was clear that the original set of 152 area codes couldn't meet the growing demand, so an NXX format was added, increasing the number of possible codes to 792, and phone numbers to more than 6 billion. The system still avoids a 0 or 1 to start but allows any number in the middle position, as in 423 or 947.

Instead of the long waits that were once typical of overseas calls, direct-dialed calls reach their destinations almost as quickly as calls in the US. That's because the switching offices that handle the calls in each country enable different networks to speak to each other without confusion or delay.

THIS NUMBER'S FOR YOU

Busy people are kept even busier by having to deal with separate numbers for home phone, office phone, home fax, office fax, pager, car phone and portable phone. Ironically, having more numbers actually increases your chances of missing an important call.

Personal phone numbers, provided by AT&T and other telecommunications companies, simplify the problem by giving you a single, personal, 700- or 500-prefix number that you can take with you anywhere. These services rely on sophisticated voice response systems, databases and routing systems similar to those used for toll-free (800) business services. They let you:

- Have calls forwarded to any phone that you're near (including pagers, wireless phones and faxes)
- Have your calls forwarded to preselected callers who can reach your personal number (and allow you to pay for the calls)
- Ring multiple phones (home, office and car) to cover all bases
- Ring specific phones at selected times

-225-5288

TELEPHONE NUMBER

2. The next three digits of a number identify the central office code, or the local company's exchange office in the city or state covered by the area code. Each area code can have up to 720 exchanges.

3. The final four digits are the individual phone's identification number. Each exchange can have up to 10,000 unique combinations, which means the system could accommodate more than 1 billion numbers.

You must remember this...

It's hard to fault direct dialing, but it did mean the end of distinctive alpha-numeric phone number prefixes, like BUtterfield 8, PEnnsylvania 6 and WAlnut 9, which had been around since 1930.

Alphabetic exchange names predate alphanumeric prefixes by 50 years, but we still remember the glamour of the exchanges that added a historical, poetic or even whimsical dimension to making a phone call. They lent their names and their allure to fiction, movies, musical compositions and even restaurants. But there were just too many NIghtingale, HYacinth and CRestview exchanges, and only 640 potential combinations—far from enough to give everybody his or her own 10-digit phone number.

BUtterfield 8

John O'Hara

THE FIRST CUT

When area codes were assigned, New York got 212 on the grounds that people calling the most populous city in the nation needed the quickest and simplest dialing sequence. Washington, DC, got 202, which was considered the next easiest, and other major cities in the country got similar preference.

CODATHON

In 1998, the state with the most area codes was California, with 15. There are 11 states with one area code, plus Washington, DC. They are Delaware, Hawaii, Idaho, Maine, New Hampshire, New Mexico, North Dakota, Rhode Island, Vermont, West Virginia and Wyoming. There are 282 assigned area codes, of which 216 are currently active.
There are just over 400 area codes remaining for assignment.

Toll-free Calls

The way to get a customer on the line and calling back for more.

The success of many businesses, particularly those in the service industry, is increasingly linked to the intelligent services provided by modern telecommunications networks. In most cases, businesses don't even need extra equipment—just a subscription to the services they want. The network takes care of the rest.

Undoubtedly, one of the most successful and widely used of these services is toll-free calling available through 800 and 888 numbers.

Before 1967, these calls were handled as collect calls through phone company operators, a process which, as companies grew, turned out to be very costly. It didn't take businesses long to discover that with 800 numbers, they could create new 24-hour nationwide and even worldwide customer services from a single telephone number. The result: better service at a lower cost. In fact, the 800 number became so popular that a second toll-free number, 888, was introduced in 1996 and a third number, 877, in 1998 to absorb the increased demand.

HOW AN 800 CALL WORKS

The network knows from the minute someone dials 1-800 to treat the call differently from other long-distance calls. The first step is to get instructions about where to send the call by factoring in:

- Where the call originates
- The day and time of the call
- How much call traffic there is at the possible destinations

For example, if a customer used an 800 number to reach a mutual fund company with offices in Baltimore, a switch could be programmed to route the call to Tampa if that office were less busy, or to Phoenix if it were after normal business hours on the East Coast.

The company could also choose to block calls from some states or area codes, either because they're too close or too far away to justify the expense.

Even if you run a very small business, you can have your 800 calls forwarded to a number where you can be reached so you never risk losing an important call.

NOT MANY SECRETS

The person who answers an 800 call can often greet the caller by name thanks to **automatic number identification (ANI)**, which displays the calling number and sometimes the name linked to it on a display screen. Then, using account information stored in the company's database, the sales agent or company representative can speed up an order, resolve a problem, or set up an automated service without having to ask questions that were answered the last time the customer called.

WHAT'S YOUR INFO WORTH?

In contrast to 800 services, which are free to the caller, 900 services charge the caller. That's because they connect to information providers who believe the information they're dispensing is worth paying for.

Premium billing arrangements enable the provider to set a per-call or per-minute charge for dispensing advice, helping with financial services, arranging charitable contributions, or connecting to chat lines. The telephone company puts the charge on the caller's bill and forwards it to the information provider, keeping part of the charge as a billing fee.

To see if a business has a toll-free number, you can call

1-800-555-1212

TOLL FREE*

NO CHARGE

WATS LINES

In contrast to inbound services like 800 calls, outbound services have evolved steadily since 1961, when **wide area telephone service** (**WATS**) was introduced as a way of giving businesses a bulk discount on calls to specific regions—for example, a New York company with a lot of traffic to Chicago and Milwaukee. WATS calls aren't free but can save money for some businesses.

WHAT'S IN A NAME?

Many 800 numbers have used names or mnemonic (that is, memory) devices to make their toll-free numbers easy to remember. Some of the more popular are 1-800-FLOWERS and 1-800-CALL ATT. Of course, if you're accustomed to pressing numbers on your key pad, picking out the letters can be time-consuming and even frustrating.

By the way, you won't find 800 numbers with Q or Z. That's because they don't appear on all phone key pads.

1-800-GET SMART

The average American makes purchases over an 800 or 888 number 16 times a year, and retail businesses handle more than $100 billion in sales over these toll-free numbers annually. Millions of other callers check their financial records, make travel reservations, or contact customer service representatives. In fact, about 40% of a typical day's calls go to toll-free numbers.

* ON WHOSE NICKEL?
Describing the calls as toll-free may be a bit misleading. There is no charge for the person making the call, but the receiver, or subscriber, pays the freight, as businesses taking phone orders have customarily done.

A lot of numbers use mnemonic memory devices

1-800-DONT-4GET

Central Intelligence

Downloading network software can make even dumb appliances smart.

The devices we use to connect to networks—phones, computers, televisions, fax machines—are all endowed with certain features or capabilities. Some are dumb and serve simply as passive devices for sending or getting messages. Others, including computers and most of the phones built since 1980, are smart: they contain microprocessors that can be programmed to remember and act on instructions.

While the machines we use to access networks are getting smarter, so are the networks to which the machines are attached. For many in the telecommunications and computing businesses, the question of where intelligence should reside—in the equipment or the network—is being slowly answered in the marketplace, as people buy what they want.

A simple case involves the telephone answering machine. While this device still exists as a separate unit, it is becoming a standard feature on new phones. But you can also get an answering service supplied by your telephone company where the network, not the machine, handles the messages. In choosing one type of message system over another, you have several factors to weigh, including convenience, cost, reliability and future capabilities.

INTELLIGENT NETWORKS

EASY TO UPDATE?

MORE ECONOMICAL?

NEVER OBSOLETE?

INTELLIGENT APPLIANCES

The increasing intelligence being built into networks is already accessible in the devices we use daily. Custom calling services, such as call waiting, call forwarding and caller ID have transformed the plain old phone into what is becoming known as an **information appliance**—a terminal or device that gets its smarts from a centralized source, whenever it needs to.

Many operating systems can be downloaded over the Internet. And users of the World Wide Web already download plug-ins to receive sound, video or other advanced software, greatly enhancing the capability of their PCs. In the future, access devices known as **network computers** may supplant more powerful PCs for people who want to be connected to the Internet but don't use a computer for other tasks.

ALL NET

Appliances that are, in effect, extensions of a network rather than stand-alone devices offer several advantages:

- Since the intelligence is built into the network, the cost of producing appliances without complex circuitry and microchips drops dramatically.

- The devices themselves are far less likely to become obsolete since they can be upgraded when the network software is enhanced.

- The growing number and complexity of various features and functions would make it impractical to house the intelligence in individual appliances.

- The information could be rendered to suit a particular appliance and the user. For example, information could be tailored to a wireless phone or computer, sent as voice rather than text, appear in large letters for easier reading, or even be translated into a certain dialect or language.

UP CLOSE AND PERSONAL

Advocates of increasingly smarter devices point out that usage patterns built up over many years will not quickly disappear, and that people will want the intelligence in their machines, not out in cyberspace somewhere. They also argue that an individual's PC will become, in effect, a personal agent whose uppermost concern is filling individual needs— a type of dedication that won't exist out on a network.

While there is little doubt that electronic devices will keep getting smarter, whether they will eventually outsmart the networks remains to be seen.

COLD LOGIC

Frigidaire's prototype of an Internet refrigerator called the Screenfridge is in the works. It's equipped with a bar-code scanner and a touch screen (which has an Internet link, including e-mail). The scanner can be used to swipe items, entering them directly into a Web shopping list.

And AT&T Lab's Cyber Fridge makes it as easy to leave a message on the family Web page as it is to tape a note on the door of the family refrigerator.

vs. SMART MACHINES

INTELLIGENT FEATURES?

MORE POWERFUL?

PROGRAMMABLE?

MACHINES AIN'T DUMMIES, EITHER

In fact, the intelligence being built into digital devices, especially computers, telephones and faxes, is giving the networks a run for their money.

Phone/fax machines, for example, can be programmed to greet all calls with a voice message. If the software detects a fax tone, it automatically switches into fax mode. If not, the software assumes it's a voice call and invites the caller to leave a message.

Desktop computers are becoming increasingly powerful, and some of their processing capability is being used to make them more accommodating to people. For example, computers are capable of recognizing not only speech but individual voices and even facial expressions. And they can also "learn" from previous experience to recognize individual preferences or patterns of behavior so they can personalize the experience for the computer user.

Digital wireless phones have also acquired an array of intelligent features, including the ability to keep directories, take and display voice- or e-mail messages, and signal different rings for different callers. Some can even operate as remote speaker phones.

How May I Help You?

Virtual personal assistants are not only intelligent but awfully polite.

The first telephone networks depended on people instead of switches to connect calls. When you picked up your phone, the operator responded, "Number, please?" And if your town was small enough, you could often ask for the person by name. The local operator may also have shared other information—like who tried to call while you were away, or even where someone you wanted to call could be reached.

GETTING AN ASSIST, DIGITALLY

The quaint, personal touch of the first operators may not be as old-fashioned as it seems. Today, a new breed of electronic operators, **virtual personal assistants**, with names like Wildfire, Webley and Portico, can handle many of these helpful tasks, from screening calls to taking and forwarding e-mail messages, all at the sound of your voice.

In reality, these virtual assistants are intelligent software programs that recognize and respond to your voice in what appears to be natural conversation. These programs can not only pick out key words but can put them in a context to produce the desired response or action. For example, if you say, "Get me Alice," your assistant will not only recognize the name but put the call through.

The range of services a virtual assistant can perform keeps growing, including telling you who called, sorting through your e-mail messages, forwarding your calls to a place where you can be reached, or even telling people you don't want to hear from that you're not available.

QUICK LEARNERS

Virtual assistants are programmed to learn about you and to respond to different situations. For example, some assistants provide more tips and helpful advice as you learn to work them, and then stop offering suggestions once things are running smoothly. In other words, the assistant is learning to understand and adapt to you rather than the other way around, which is typically how you would interact with a conventional computer.

ONCE MORE, WITH MEANING

Sophisticated intelligent agents have evolved far beyond speech recognition that elicits a fixed response. These agents, which are being tested at AT&T Labs, can put words into a context. They "understand" spoken language and can respond as if carrying on a conversation.

In the following screen sequence, the caller's words are indented, the agent's "understanding" of the message is shown in red, and the agent's actual response to the caller is shown in blue.

Hi! I'd like credit for a call!

```
AT&T. How may I help you?
>   hi I'd_like_credit_for_a_call
Do you need me to give you credit?
>   yes please
Okay What is the reason for the credit?
>   this seems I_dialed_a_wrong_number
What was the number that you dialed?
>   nine_oh_eight_five_one_eight_nine_two_zero_six
Was the call billed to the phone you're
calling from?
>   yes
I've given you credit for that call. Thank you
for using AT&T
```

AVATARS: A PERSONAL REP ONLINE

Even with a virtual assistant handling your communications, you may still need help in keeping up with the information you want or tracking down the best bargains available, particularly on the Internet. What you need is an **intelligent agent**, or **avatar**, that is programmed to identify your interests and preferences, and travel the networks on your behalf, seeking the things of interest to you.

Imbued with their own personalities and able to recognize your voice, avatars will be able to scan the Internet and its voluminous databases, searching for everything from stock prices to sports scores to research reports as well as providing custom news, travel updates, and even movie and book reviews.

HELLO!

TRAVERSING THE LANGUAGE BARRIER

Another goal of researchers involved in developing electronic assistance is instant language translation. While you can call anywhere in the world, the person at the other end needs to speak your language for the two of you to converse.

That may not always be the case. In experiments, AT&T Labs has already demonstrated an English-to-Mandarin translator. In the future, the language barrier, over the phone at least, may be a thing of the past.

COMING DOWN THE ROAD

Speech-recognition technology in cars will soon allow you to make calls on a wireless phone, change the radio station, play a tape or CD, or adjust the heat or air conditioning using simple spoken commands. In America these systems are programmed to understand American accents, and some auto manufacturers are using programs that will let you add commands in your own voice, which will help if you have an unusual accent.

COMMUNICATIONS, SPOT ON

Computers that speak and listen have been around for many years. For example, when you want to make a collect call, you can make your request through an interactive voice response (IVR) system that understands what you want.

The IVR system uses a technique known as **word spotting**, which identifies key words or phrases, whether you say them separately or in a sentence. It uses a pattern-recognition technique that can distinguish a command, such as "collect call," from everyday conversation. For example, the system ignores the words "I'd like to make a..." and acts on "collect call." "Collect call, please" and "I'm calling collect" work just as well.

The real challenge in speech-recognition technology lies in teaching computers to understand many different accents and speech patterns. For instance, the slurred words and disorganized sentences that some children speak make sense to their parents, but to a computer, a child's language is difficult to understand.

For PCs, speech-recognition software is already on the market. You can give simple verbal commands, such as dictating words into a microphone on your computer.

AUDIO RESPONSE UNITS

A crude ancestor of virtual assistants that has gained immense popularity with cost- and service-conscious organizations is a special answering system called an **audio response unit (ARU)**.

When you call an 800 number, for example, you are often asked to identify the kind of information you want by pressing the appropriate numbers on your key pad.

These audio response units provide a menu of options to choose from (the final one, and court of last resort, often being to wait for the next available operator).

ARUs are used by most airlines to give you flight arrival and departure times, reservation confirmations, and other travel-related information. Service providers, like banks and mutual fund companies, use these systems to provide timely financial information, though you'll need a code to access your personal account.

Wired

Physical connections—wires and cables—carry a steady stream of information.

Did you ever make a telephone call with two tin cans and a piece of string? If you did, you'll remember that the string—your transmission system—was the critical link. Of course, there's not much string in the nation's land-based communications networks. But there are millions of miles of copper wire, coaxial cable and fiber-optic cable providing the connections people and machines need to send and receive information.

COPPER WIRES

A pair of copper wires called a loop connects your home or office phone to the nearest source of a dial tone—either a telephone company's central office or your company's private branch exchange (PBX). One wire in the pair carries outgoing traffic, and the other carries incoming traffic.

Copper wires don't care if they're carrying analog or digital signals, or if the signals represent voice, data or video traffic. They only care about conducting electricity. But, like the wires that route electricity through your home, you can overload them. What's more, electrical surges, lightning and other kinds of interference affect copper wire and can disrupt data sessions more severely than they do voice calls.

Copper wires work best for carrying a two-way phone call. They're not ideal for complex data transmissions because they've traditionally had limited bandwidth, or capacity for carrying heavy loads of information.

But copper wires are getting a new lease on life: they can carry up to 1.5 million bits of data or more when they're operated digitally, as they are in T-carrier systems. T-carriers, sometimes referred to as T-1 lines, use two pairs of wires, which are shielded from each other to protect against disruptive crosstalk.

And newer digital techniques such as **Integrated Services Digital Network** (**ISDN**) and **Asymmetric Digital Subscriber Line** (**ADSL**) enable even ordinary phone lines to deliver high-speed Internet traffic or even movies into customers' homes.

Voice/**DATA**

YOU'RE

CABLED TOGETHER

Coaxial cable can carry up to 13,000 long-distance calls on each pair of cables that runs between telephone company switching offices. In many communities, cable is the standard for TV transmission because one cable can carry many channels at the same time. While cable systems need modems to deliver data, they can carry it hundreds of times faster than copper wires, and over 80 times faster than ISDN lines. (Cables are described in greater detail in the following pages, "Cable Able.")

WIRING

Twisted pair describes copper phone wires bundled in color-coded pairs that carry electrical impulses. Each wire pair is twisted at a different rate to reduce interference.

Coaxial cable is a solid piece of metal wire covered with insulation and surrounded by a metal tube. It can carry lots of voice and video signals quickly, and because it's highly immune.

Fiber-optic cable converts electrical signals into light pulses that travel along thin strands of glass or plastic that act as pipes, sealing the light

FIBER-OPTICS

The newest, highest-capacity systems use fiber-optics—hair-thin fibers of silica glass so pure that if the oceans were as transparent, you'd be able to see to the bottom of the deepest trench.

Fibers carry infrared light generated by tiny lasers, no bigger than grains of salt, that blink on and off billions of times per second, speaking a digital code in which a pulse of light represents a binary 1, and no pulse represents a 0. A single pair of fibers today carries more than 50,000 phone calls, or the equivalent in data or TV programs.

New fiber-optic systems are being built to what is known as **Synchronous Optical Network (SONET)** specifications, which take advantage of the ultra-high bandwidth of fiber-optics to transmit at much higher rates than current fiber systems. A single cable not much thicker around than your thumb can carry all the nation's long-distance calls.

Fiber-optics, which are increasingly the standard in telephone networks, may some-day come right into people's homes. But fiber-optics don't conduct electricity, which means they can't ring your phone.

ONE FIBER, MANY CALLS

A typical SONET fiber-optic cable carries 288 separate strands of fiber, with each strand capable of carrying 48,000 voice circuits. A technology called dense wave division multiplexing has increased that capacity by putting multiple wave paths on a single strand of fiber. In 1999, that number is forecast to be 80 wave paths, which means a single strand would carry nearly 4 million voice circuits.

INFORMATION MADE LIGHT

Although it may begin its journey as electrical pulses, or electrons, most information travels over long-distance networks as light pulses, or photons. The transformation occurs when pulses moving on copper wire and coaxial cable converge on an optical terminal, or black box, whose circuitry uses the pulses to drive tiny, solid-state lasers.

At the other end of the fiber-optic link, solid-state devices called photodetectors convert the light pulses back to electrical pulses that can be delivered to receiving terminals, like phones or fax machines, by wires, cables or radio systems.

or noise, and both wires in a pair can send and receive signals. But transmission speeds can be slow.

to noise, it has a low error rate. With a modem, it can also deliver high-speed data.

inside the fiber. Not only does information travel at the speed of light, but fiber-optic cable is nonconductive, which means that it can't be distorted by electrical noise.

Cable Able

There's a new twist to the common cable that provides television service to your home.

If you've ever sat listlessly in front of your computer watching a Web page download line by line over a slow modem, you'll appreciate the benefits of **home broadband** service. With broadband service and a **cable modem**, you can download even complex graphics, such as weather maps and video clips, at astoundingly high speeds. In fact, with cable access, you can even watch full-color, full-motion video over the Internet.

Home broadband also means you'll be able to receive a full range of communications services through a single pipeline. For example, in addition to high-speed Internet access, the cable connection can bring you multiple telephone lines, each with its own number and distinctive ring. You'll also receive hundreds of cable TV channels, including big-screen DVD, and dozens of radio channels with CD-quality sound.

One major advantage of cable access is that you're always "on," which means you're

> One way that cable access speeds up connecting to the Net is that the most frequently visited websites can be stored locally in the network so that they are instantly available. The process is akin to a local newsstand or market that knows from experience which publications or products sell the most and keeps larger quantities of those in stock.

constantly in touch with the network. Without having to dial a phone, or go through the ritual of connecting to the Internet, you can have immediate access to a broad range of communications—e-mail, reminders, the weather, your stock portfolio. You can also see who else is currently on the network.

← IT'S NOW A TWO-WAY STREET →

COAXING THE CABLE

Although cable television has given us access to broadband cable services for the past several years, until recently this medium has been only one-way: we could receive high bandwidth signals, such as full-motion video, but we couldn't use cable to send anything back out.

So while cable worked well for TV, it was impractical for phone calls or the Internet, which require true two-way communications. Over the last five years, the cable industry has incorporated

technology capable of delivering two-way voice and data transmissions.

More recently, AT&T has developed ways to push optical fiber, which carries an enormous amount of information at the speed of light, even closer to your home. Optical fiber increases the capacity of the network to deliver a broad array of communications services at very high speeds while decreasing the operating cost of delivering the service.

In the years ahead, high-capacity optical fiber connections will be extended directly into people's homes.

UPSTREAM   DOWNSTREAM

THE CABLE EDGE

There are many advantages to broadband service provided by cable:

- You're always "on," so Internet access is immediate, and you're always in contact with the network.
- Downloading times are incredibly fast—roughly 25 times faster than a 56K modem and even quicker than a T-1 line.
- One pipeline provides service to an array of devices—TV, radio, phone, Internet, fax.
- All of your access devices can be used simultaneously—you don't have to give up time on the phone to receive a fax or use the Internet.

WORKING OUT THE KINKS

Connecting PCs to the Internet through digital cable modems dramatically improves download times, since no time is needed to translate between analog and digital signals, as is the case with conventional modems.

But the cable modem itself is a lot quicker than your PC's network interface. It's also quicker than even the fast lines (called T-1 and T-3 lines) your cable company uses to seek and retrieve information from the Internet. That means the greater speeds that cable modems can deliver may be limited by other parts of your system. But download times are so much faster overall that this discrepancy should prove to be of little or no concern at all.

A single broadband cable is attached to a box on the side of your home. A splitter then separates the different channels in the cable to provide phone, fax, TV and radio, and Internet service.

ONE WIRE, ONE SERVICE CALL, ONE BILL

For most people, one of the appeals of cable data network services, such as @Home or Road Runner, is that you can get amazingly fast Internet access. You can also buy a bundle of various services together, pay one bill, and make one service call if something goes wrong. And there are often special plans and discounted rates available. The trick is to decide how many of the services you'll actually use, and how the cost stacks up against services from several different providers.

A New (Tele)Vision

The boob tube is about to get smart. Real smart.

As a medium for delivering information and entertainment, the TV has a major advantage over the PC—it's inherently simpler to use. You turn it on, select the channel, and adjust the volume. PCs, on the other hand, can be persnickety: you need to know how they work, how to run the software, and how to interpret the various symbols and functions.

What's more, computers and computer software require frequent upgrades, while TVs last for many years, even though the programs change each season. That's one reason, perhaps, that over 99% of households have TVs while around 50% have PCs.

LOOK SMART, BE SMART

Thanks to home broadband service and cable modems, TV's simplicity and outstanding picture quality are being combined with the interactivity and functionality of a PC browser.

No longer a one-trick pony, TV will be more like a multi-ring circus—a highly interactive **communications portal** that shares the features of a television, VCR, Internet access device, personal communications network and entertainment center, all wrapped into one. From an Information Age perspective, the TV or portal epitomizes the convergence of voice and data communications with entertainment—a unique coming-together of the phone, the PC and the television in a highly versatile appliance that is always connected to the network.

As a network appliance, TV will enable you to enjoy many of the benefits of new technologies without having to replace your TV. At the same time, as TV becomes totally digital and uses microchips that can integrate many different functions, your TV will become smarter, letting you interact more directly with the information you receive.

For example, you might see an ad for a car and immediately arrange for a test drive at a nearby dealer. You might notice a special sale on a product you want to buy and print out a coupon on the spot. Or you may want to fast-forward or rewind a movie you are watching, or instantly record it for future viewing.

SIMPLE SYSTEM UPDATES

As a communications portal, your TV will constantly be canvassing the network for system changes, such as upgrades to your browser or operating system, or new plug-ins. By clicking a button or hot link, the upgrade will be done automatically, without fuss and without delay.

SOMEONE TO LOOK OUT FOR YOU

Your TV screen will also show you the up-to-the-minute efforts of your smart agent, or online concierge, who will fill special requests, such as getting tickets to a concert, letting you know when a book you wanted is available, or telling you about the best fares available on a vacation you are planning.

THE ULTIMATE ORGANIZER

With your TV as portal, you won't have to store lists of phone numbers in different places—on your PC, wireless phone and hand-held computer. Nor will you need to keep mental lists of documents and correspondence stored on office and home computers, zip drives and floppy disks.

That's because the TV can serve as an always-accessible repository for this information: you'll be able to look up files on your TV, or on any other device that's linked to the network, from wherever you are. And you won't have to worry about misplacing these records, or having them inadvertently erased or destroyed.

Your TV organizer can also store your addresses and calendar, financial records and bills, and can even serve as an online album for your digital photographs.

MY TV

Part of TV's new vision will be to present you with your own window on the world, displaying the local weather, news and show times at local theaters as well as the latest stock prices in your portfolio.

PERSONAL NETWORK CENTRAL

On your screen, you'll be able to see whether a person you want to contact is already online somewhere—for example, on their wireless phone, on the Internet, or even watching TV. You can then send them a message instantly or speak with them directly, since they'll be connected to the network, regardless of the device they're using.

INTERCHANGING VOICE AND DATA

A very special feature of the TV as portal will be your ability to choose whether you want to activate the system by voice command, or by keying in or clicking a button. You can also decide whether to read the text or hear it spoken. Voice activation will also allow the blind to listen to e-mail, and the hearing-impaired to read captions when they view movies and television.

THE (DIS)PLAYGROUND FOR INTERNET SERVICES

The TV screen, like the computer screen, will become a primary display for all Internet services. For example, you'll be able to participate in newsgroups, check a variety of directories, send and receive e-mail, and enter chat rooms. And if a picture or video clip of the speaker is transmitted along with the message, you'll be able to view that as well.

ENTERTAINMENT GALORE

The TV will become a type of personalized home multiplex, where you can view not only programmed shows and movies but also those available on demand. Any program you download will be in digital form, so you'll be able to treat it as you would a video—you can fast-forward or reverse it, show it in slow motion, or even freeze a frame. There will also be a comprehensive guide of all the programs so you can select online those you want to record.

SCREENING YOUR PURCHASES

Your TV will also become your own center for e-commerce, where you can shop online for everything from groceries to cars, just as you can on the World Wide Web today.

Look, Mom, No Wires

Airwaves are becoming the preferred
channel for staying connected.

Because you never want to be out of touch,
but you can't trail endless lengths of wire
from cars, trains or planes, let alone
pocketbooks and briefcases, wireless
communication is quickly emerging as
the medium of choice in the Information
Age. With wireless, or mobile, communications, the vision of being in touch anytime,
anywhere is becoming a reality. The wires
that now connect your phones and other
electronic devices may soon be as obsolete
as the horse and buggy.

There are two distinct types of wireless
communications: **cellular** (both analog
and digital) and **personal communications
systems**, generally known as **PCS**. While
the technologies are different, the two are
alike in one way: they are both person-based,
rather than home-based or office-based,
systems. That means that your phone rings
where you are, provided it's turned on.

CELLS WITHOUT WALLS

In a cellular system, phones don't send electric signals over wires. Instead, they broadcast
radio signals over the airwaves to a local
transmitter/receiver, which then connects the
call to a switching center for routing to a
long-distance, local or wireless carrier.

A cellular network is divided into adjacent
cells, or geographic areas. Each cell has a low-
power transmitter/receiver that determines how
far its frequencies can travel, thereby creating
the cell's boundaries. As a result, the exact same
frequencies can be used in nearby cells without
causing any interference or having callers share
their conversations. Cells can range from one
to 20 miles in diameter, depending on the ter-
rain and the density of service being provided.

MOBILE CALLS TO GO

As you travel out of one cell and into the
next, your call is monitored by a computerized switch that hands off your call from the
radio frequency in one cell to the radio frequency in the next. The process is so seamless
and so fast, you're not aware of the switch.

If you're dialing any phone that's linked to
a land-based system, your call is routed
through conventional network connections to
its destination. But if you're calling another
mobile phone, your call is sent to the nearest
switching office of the wireless carrier used by
the person you're calling and is then broadcast as radio waves on an available frequency.
As both of you move, your call is transferred
from frequency to frequency among the cells
you move through.

CELLULAR MITOSIS

Each cell starts out with 999
radio frequencies. As the
volume of calls increases,
the cells can be subdivided,
increasing the capacity by
expanding the number of
available frequencies that
can be used simultaneously.
So, for example, an area
divided into five cells
would provide 4995
frequencies. Sub-
divided into 10,
there would
be 9990.

CELLULAR OPTIONS

Cellular phones can be analog (the sound
travels as waves or electric pulses) or digital
(the sound is converted to binary code—0s and
1s—and travels as data packets). There are
some substantial differences between them.

ANALOG VS.	DIGITAL
Blanket coverage in continental US in key areas	Better coverage in urban areas; weaker in rural areas
Voices sound natural	Voices may sound mechanical or tinny
More subject to inter-ference and distortion	Elimination of "hiss" or noise
Not practical for data transmissions	Ideally suited for data transmissions
Not secure; easy to clone	Very secure; built-in encryption prevents fraud
Few special features: directory, instant redial	Many features based on network intelligence: text messaging, multiple rings, call forwarding
Special plans available, but often more expensive	Special bargain rates for heavy users

HAVING IT BOTH WAYS

If you want the blanket coverage of wireless
but the fun features of digital, you might
consider a digital multinetwork phone that lets
you shift to analog mode when out of digital
territory and back again when the digital mode
works for calls.

WHEREVER YOU ROAM

If you make a call outside your home area, the local switching office is programmed to recognize your phone's area code and to signal a switching office there to forward your calls to the mobile office you're physically closest to. This system is called **roaming**. While phone companies initially charged separate rates for these calls, listed as roaming charges, many are offering various one-rate plans that charge the same amount for local and roaming calls.

THE WIRELESS TRAVELER

Current analog or digital wireless systems use a technique known as TDMA (time division multiple access) to carry voice conversations. Another technique, CDMA (code division multiple access), divides the radio wave more finely to provide over three times the capacity for digital transmission. That means that more information can be delivered more quickly. However, CDMA is more costly and not as widely used.

A third standard, GSM (Global System for Mobile Communications), offers many advanced features and is widely used in Europe and Asia. It also has some subscribers, mostly through Omnipoint, in the US.

Using your cellular phone overseas can be complicated, since phones in Europe, Asia and elsewhere operate on different frequencies. If you subscribe to AT&T Wireless Services, however, or to a service that uses GSM, you can rent a handset that accepts a tiny "smart card" that you insert into the rented phone to activate your account. You can then make and receive calls as you would at home, and even use special features like call forwarding.

Some companies are starting to manufacture multiband phones that work on the GSM standard but will also function on the lower frequencies used in the US.

DIGITAL PLUS

Personal communications systems, or PCS, share many of the characteristics of cellular digital phones but are even richer in the range of features they provide. In fact, some of them, like Qualcomm's handsets and AT&T's PocketNet Phone, are actual minicomputers that allow you to do things like send and receive e-mail and faxes, get stock quotes, newsbriefs and ball scores, and activate your calls by voice.

The reason PCS devices are more versatile, and can send and receive information more quickly, is that they can operate on different radio frequencies and also take up less spectrum for transmission. That leaves more spectrum available for special features. For example, while cellular phones operate in the 850-megahertz part of the radio spectrum, PCS can use this band or the 1.9-gigahertz range opened up by the Federal Communications Commission in the 1990s.

Eventually, PCS will provide a host of intelligent network services and allow you to have a single telephone number instead of multiple numbers for home, office, mobile service and even fax.

WHY CALLS FAIL

While wireless telephony has improved by leaps and bounds, technology hasn't been able to conquer the laws of physics that affect radio transmissions. Your conversation can be interrupted by tall buildings, mountains, tunnels and underpasses that don't let radio signals through. Lightning and other forms of electrical interference can wreak havoc with a call, too. And sometimes you just can't get through because too many people are trying to use too few frequencies at the same time.

TRACKING THE POLLS

Every few minutes, your wireless phone (when it's on) sends a message back to the nearest cellsite letting the switch center know where you are and how to route calls to you. This process is called **polling**.

The Outer Limits

Communications of every stripe are taking to the airways.

While often used to describe the TV and radio business, **broadcast** actually describes a number of ways to send information to two or more receivers, or to people in different locations. In Information Age terms, though, broadcast means sending voice and data using radio waves and microwaves transmitted by earth- or satellite-based antennas.

The waves travel through the atmosphere to receiving antennas that may be part of either a wireless or wired network. One clue to a broadcast transmission is the brief lags in conversation you sometimes detect in overseas calls that have been routed the 22,300 miles up to a satellite and back down.

INTO THE AIR

Over-the-air networks depend on antennas to transmit radio waves and microwaves carrying voice and data into air or space and to retrieve, or pluck them out, again. The size antennas that a network needs depends on the **frequency** at which its signals are broadcast, with higher frequencies needing smaller antennas. That's because the higher the frequency, or rate at which a wave completes a cycle, the smaller the **wavelength**. The smaller the wavelength, the smaller the antenna has to be.

For example, cellular phones are portable because they transmit and receive at frequencies above 850 megahertz (MHz), which requires an antenna less than 6 inches long.

But a TV antenna for channels 2–13 (operating at 54–74MHz) has to be five feet long.

Microwaves, with frequencies above 890MHz, use **dish**, or **parabolic**, antennas that reflect microwave energy, focusing it on the actual antenna, which is a tiny element inside a plastic covering at the center of the dish.

TWO-WAY STREETS

Unlike TV or radio broadcasts, voice and data networks are two-way systems. That means every antenna in the network can both transmit and receive, as the situation requires.

At the start of an over-the-air exchange, the information is modulated onto a radio wave and broadcast by the transmitting antenna. At the receiving end, the second antenna—whose elements are about the same size as the first—picks up the signal. It's then amplified and converted back into a form that lets you hear or see it.

In the case of a voice call, for example, the antenna in your phone switches roles, from receiver to transmitter, as you begin to reply. This two-way capacity makes it possible to carry on a conversation, ask questions or register a complaint.

Information Age commentators point out that this dynamic way to share information fosters the free exchange of ideas around the world in a way not possible with underground newspapers or censored TV or radio programs.

Unlike the antennas on global satellites that are boosted miles into space, antennas that reach wireless phones and pagers have to be just a little higher than what's around them. So in New York City, for example, lamp-posts, church steeples and building facades are being pressed into service as convenient parking places for the devices.

REALLY LONG DISTANCE

Your local radio broadcast station may have a radiating power of 50 kilowatts, and the transmitter is probably no more than 60 miles away. Spacecraft have nowhere near that amount of power available for transmitting—no more than 20 watts—yet they must bridge distances measured in millions of miles. How can they do it? To span these distances using low wattages, satellites use microwave frequencies concentrated into a narrow beam.

DATA BROADCAST

Data broadcasting uses radio waves and wireless data networks to send simultaneous, individually addressed text messages, or **data packets**. A data broadcast system is built around a central transmitter and a number of antennas. Data packets are sent from the originating source, such as a networked computer or handset, to a transmitter that beams radio signals into the air either in all directions at once or in a single direction.

With **adaptive array**, or **smart, antennas**, it's possible to launch packets in specific directions by forming instantaneous narrow beams. Since all the broadcast power is concentrated in those beams, they are able to get through any obstructions and reach their destinations at the same time. Sending a signal to a select group of receivers rather than making it available to many is sometimes described as **narrowcasting**.

SATELLITE COMMUNICATIONS

Many of the systems that are currently being developed use satellites, either in low-earth orbits (LEOs) or different types of fixed systems. The LEOs are designed for digital wireless voice and text communications, while the fixed systems are designed to provide high-speed Internet services.

For instance, Iridium has developed a global LEO network that combines 66 low-earth-orbit satellites with land-based wireless systems. The system will allow you to communicate using wireless phones and pagers virtually anywhere in the world. When you place a call or page, the signal travels several hundred miles into space to the nearest satellite and is sent to another satellite nearest the person you're calling. Your signal is then transmitted directly to your contact's phone (if it's an Iridium phone) or to a ground station, which then routes it to the proper destination.

It's expensive to establish a global data broadcast system. A satellite system like Teledesic is a $9.5 billion project, and the three licensed LEOs (Iridium, Odyssey and Globalstar) weigh in between $1.5 billion and $3.7 billion, based in part on the number of satellites placed in orbit.

WIRELESS CONNECTIONS

Companies like AT&T are exploring ways to connect people's homes to the network using wireless technology. A small box on the side of your house will provide high-speed, two-way voice and data communications.

MAKING THE

Anytime Anywhere Anyhow

"A telephone service for this nation, so far as humanly possible free from imper-fections, errors or delays, and enabling anyone anywhere at any time to pick up a telephone and talk to anyone else anywhere else in this country, clearly, quickly and at a reasonable cost."
—AT&T president Walter S. Gifford's vision, 1926

Message Center of Cy Berman

Email
☐ 05/08/99 07:43 pm   1K   April Rubin   Another announcement
☐ 05/08/99 06:20 pm   252K 📎 Fred Grant   MIME Attachments

Vmail
☐ 05/08/99 03:23 pm   1'   Sandra Smit   732-345-3371
☐ 05/07/99 06:20 pm   2'   Michael Kodder 732-345-3376

Fax
☐ 05/08/99 04:44 pm   1P   Sam J. Cross   CCITT Document 1
☐ 05/07/99 08:05 am   7P   Laura Brit   CCITT Documents 2-5

The equipment that gives us access to the world of networks—phones, computers, pagers, television and radio—were originally designed for a specific purpose: we use telephones to converse, fax machines to transmit documents, pagers to leave messages, television to view broadcasts, and computers to create and share information. It's been easy to tell these devices apart because they look and work differently. But that may no longer be the case.

THE ANYTHING DEVICE

One of the byproducts of inventing more-versatile digital devices and connecting them to ever-more-intelligent networks is that the distinctions between the different kinds of equipment begin to blur.

We already see this convergence in televisions that let you access the Internet and transmit e-mail (WebTV), computers that work like phones and can show on-demand movies, and PCS devices that work as a phone, computer, Internet access device, and mobile office communications center.

And increasingly, it won't even be necessary to enter your commands on a computer keyboard or phone key pad. Instead, you can tell machines what you want them to do—in technical terms, you can **voice activate** them—and expect them to get the job done, whether it's simply a matter of putting a call through or getting the latest information on your portfolio holdings.

In the anyhow world, you'll be able to send and receive messages in different voice and text formats interchangeably. For example, you'll convert a voicemail message into e-mail or a fax, or send a fax you've received as e-mail to someone else. How you want to receive or send a message will be your choice.

THE VOICE AND DIGITAL ONE-MAN BAND

Eventually, the distinction between voice and data communications, including broadcast video, may disappear altogether, and you'll be able to use the exact same device for voice, data and video transmissions.

Just as certain wireless phones can switch from analog to digital reception in different geographic areas, scientists anticipate that handsets will be able to distinguish between satellite, wireless and wired communications, deciding which to use at any particular moment.

Today, it's the sender who determines what kind of data you receive—text, sound or video. But in the future, experts predict that you, as the receiver of information, will be able to decide which format a particular message will take. The ability to make this choice

Today, most networks are an amalgam of parts, protocols and transmission media. The network of the future will be more layered, each layer having a distinct but complementary function.

This structure provides the flexibility to keep pace with rapid growth while ensuring an open architecture, making it easier for customers and innovators to use or create new features.

At the top will be an Internet Protocol (IP), which will handle all the actual communications services. Intelligence for custom features, such as call forwarding or caller ID, will be stored here.

At the bottom will be the transport layer, where all the hardware—wires and cables—are located.

GOING A-WIRE

As access devices and their functions continue to converge, so will transmission channels. In addition to the blending of voice and data networks, there will be increased integration of wired and wireless systems. That means you'll be able to plug into a telecommunications network virtually anyplace you are with any kind of device. The connections and intelligent switches residing in the networks will handle the entire transaction so seamlessly, you'll never notice any difference.

will be embedded in software, whether in the network that's transmitting the data or the equipment that's receiving it, or in some combination of the two.

What all this means is that the information becomes very malleable: it can move from voice to data and back almost seamlessly and can be sent and received on any number of different devices. As the sender of the message, you'll be able to choose whether to say it or key it in. As the receiver, you'll decide whether to hear it or view it. And once you have it, you can save it or share it in the form in which you receive it, or convert it to voice or data and send it on to another device.

Keeping the Lines Humming

Every network needs watchdogs and a repair crew.

Telecommunications networks are designed to prevent accidents like cable cuts as well as recover from disasters like earthquakes. So the entire system is constantly under scrutiny.

Somebody has an eye on every switch in every network all the time, and traffic is constantly monitored and tracked on large electronic boards. When warnings flash, computers and software move into action to avert a potential problem or to mobilize an effective response.

Other information networks, from online service providers to in-house data networks, also focus on keeping their systems operating at full steam. Their major challenges tend to be internal software and traffic problems rather than external disruptions.

INTERRUPTIONS ON THE LINE

You've probably noticed on occasion a certain noise, or interference, when you're talking to someone, or that a phone conversation has been interrupted by a sudden crash or crackle. You may have trouble understanding a regional dialect or an unfamiliar accent, or be thrown off by a lilt, a twang or a lisp. Or you may be distracted by someone speaking very quickly or very slowly.

But you can usually get the gist of the message because language has built-in clues, or **redundancies**, that help you understand what's being said. And you can always ask the speaker to repeat herself.

Digital signals, on the other hand, such as those used to transmit a fax or send e-mail, give no clue as to their meaning if they're disrupted by interference and distortions. As a result, some information may never arrive or may be indecipherable. That's why **error-checking** systems are built into data transmissions.

Phone calling into the area was so heavy following the October 17, 1989, earthquake in San Francisco that circuits quickly became overwhelmed.

KEEPING CABLES SAFE

Fiber-optic cables get cut regularly despite constant ground- and air-based surveillance along cable routes, and alerts to farmers, utility crews and others when they're digging near a below-the-ground installation. For added protection, Qwest, a telecommunications carrier, locates its cables inside polyethylene conduits buried three to five feet underground, while MCI Worldcom puts its cables inside unused natural gas transmission pipelines.

GETTING THE DATA RIGHT

One form of error checking is the echo method. The receiving device echoes the data it gets back to the transmitter, which checks the data—as received and echoed—to make sure that it's correct. Unfortunately, errors can occur in echoed data as well, so the method isn't always foolproof. **Parity checking** is more common in digital equipment and is also more effective. This safeguard looks for equivalence, or parity, between the number of data bits sent and the bit or bits that have been designated for testing purposes.

Although error detection and correction take up a lot of bandwidth, they help ensure that information is transmitted and received correctly. But as networks become increasingly digital and use more fiber-optics for transmission, the bit error rate (the number of bit errors per millions of bits transmitted) should decrease significantly, as will the need for error checking.

DOUBLE, NO TROUBLE

If you describe something as **redundant**, you often mean it's wasteful or unnecessary. But redundancy is music to the ears of network engineers.

For example, central offices have large banks of rechargeable batteries that automatically step in to run the systems if commercial electrical power fails or fades. That's why your phone keeps working even when your lights go out. Switching systems, the brains of telecommunications, have a duplexed or twin processor, so if the main brain of the system fails, a duplicate takes over without interruption.

DISASTER RECOVERY

The key to disaster recovery is restoring the communications system to the same level of service it provided before catastrophe struck. But it's also critical to maintain connections while things are still disrupted to keep important information flowing.

For example, when the 1989 San Francisco earthquake produced a torrent of calls to the city, the response team worked the circuits to let more calls leave San Francisco than enter it. That meant that residents could call anxious relatives in other parts of the country to tell them they were okay.

Carriers are also installing **SONET** rings, which use **Synchronous Optical Network** technology in dual, concentric ring patterns around cities and high-traffic areas. Because phone traffic is routed two ways, the network provides nearly instantaneous rerouting, often called self-healing, in the event of a cable cut.

A LITTLE HELP FROM YOUR FRIENDS

Software that can crunch mountains of data and can anticipate and head off problems greatly simplifies the jobs of the people who keep the networks running. Instead of having to read and interpret reams of raw data, a manager can get a printout that analyzes a situation and offers suggestions for resolving it in language that an experienced worker might use. The result is faster identification and resolution of problems, and more reliable service.

In addition, AT&T uses **FASTAR (Fast Automatic Rerouting)** and **FASTAR II**, which are proprietary, computerized systems that monitor the entire fiber-optic network in real time. If a cable is cut or goes out of service, both systems instantly know where to find additional capacity and immediately start routing traffic away from the broken cable.

From Bean Counter to Communicator

What the wheel did for transportation, the computer has done for information.

When we think of computers, we often think of **PCs**, or **personal computers**, the machines we use to write papers, solve math problems, access the Internet, search databases, or run programs that help us prepare our taxes, keep track of our investments, or even create music.

But there are millions of computers—many of them tiny **microprocessors**—that we don't see and would not look familiar to us. They control switches that direct our phone calls, keep track of financial records, and create digitized cartoons. Most of these "computers" are designed to handle a dedicated task rather than many different ones, like the PC. But they all use the same digital technology and process information the same way.

EVOLUTION OF THE COMPUTER

Over the centuries, computers have evolved from mechanical calculating machines into highly sophisticated electronic devices that we use both to create information and share it with others via global networks.

The first 300 years of computer history—from the mechanical adding machines of the 1640s to the electrical calculating machines of the 1930s—were not, however, about producing and communicating information but about crunching numbers more efficiently. In fact, a "computer" was a person who handled calculations with a mechanical device, like a book-keeping machine.

But the challenges of World War II, from cracking German military codes to building the atomic bomb, created a synergy between businesses, governments and academic institutions that produced major breakthroughs in computing. The creation of the **transistor** and miniature **integrated circuits**—which enabled computers to process digital information at blinding speeds—as well as the movement from punched cards to internal stored programs made it possible to create efficient machines that could handle multiple, and extremely complex, tasks.

Most recently, the processing power of the computer, and especially its ability to handle

The **abacus**, a wire-and-bead construction, was invented in Babylonia in **3000 B.C.**, though it was not commonly used until 1300. Each bead has a value based on its placement, and is "counted" when moved along the wire. Complex calculations, including those with decimals, are made by counting off and shifting the beads to specific positions.

In the **1640s** Wilhelm Schickard, Blaise Pascal and Gottfried Leibniz developed the first mechanical addition, subtraction and multiplication machines. Leibniz also developed the binary code, the basis for digital information.

ABACUS

digital information, has been linked to electronic networks, transforming the computer into a highly versatile communications device. This convergence of computing and connectivity—especially when combined with rich multimedia content—has been instrumental in shaping the Information Age.

LEFT IN THE DUST

How fast have computers improved since 1946? If cars had evolved at the same rate as supercomputers, they would travel 100 miles on a thimbleful of gas, go 3 million miles an hour, and cost less to replace than to park overnight.

In **1804** Jacquard's loom, a machine that could simultaneously follow a number of different instructions stored on punched cards, was introduced to speed up the production of intricately patterned textiles. Charles Babbage worked on the development of a mechanical computer between 1822–1833 using punched cards as memories, but he never finished it.

1889 Herman Hollerith developed the first electric-powered computer to simplify data collection in the 1890 US Census.

1939 The Electrical Digital Computer, an electromechanical machine, was developed by George Stibitz of AT&T's Bell Labs.

MICROPROCESSOR

1944 The Harvard Mark I—the first fully automatic digital computer—got its instructions from punched cards and punched tape, and handled complex mathematical simulations for the atomic bomb project.

1946 The electronic digital computer, the Electronic Numerical Integrator and Calculator, or ENIAC, weighed 30 tons, took up an area the size of an airplane hangar, and ran on 18,800 vacuum tubes. It could handle 5,000 additions a second.

HOLLERITH CARD

VACUUM TUBE

1971 The PC era began with the first commercially available microprocessor and floppy disk. Apple IIs were introduced in 1976 and IBM PCs in 1981.

1951 The UNIVAC, or UNIVersal Automatic Computer, the first commercial electronic computer, had its operating instructions coded on magnetic tape instead of punched cards—a revolutionary innovation. One of its first jobs was handling payroll calculations.

A Gallery of Computers

Size and shape don't always tell what a computer can do.

Computers come in a broad continuum of shapes and sizes, and, more recently, colors. For example, supercomputers are the size of a walk-in closet. Personal digital assistants (PDAs), at the other end of the spectrum, can fit in the palm of your hand. A computer's distinguishing features, though, are not its shape or size but what it can do and how fast it can do it. And increasingly, smaller and smaller computers can do more things faster and faster.

SUPER-COMPUTER

Supercomputers, the largest, fastest and most powerful computers in use today, perform the world's most massive and complex calculations, often involving thousands of interdependent variables.

Among the tasks that supercomputers perform are testing new drugs, predicting the weather, simulating nuclear explosions, and designing cars and airplanes.

The latest supercomputer, built by the Intel Corporation, is capable of 1.34 trillion operations per second and sells for more than $55 million.

SERVER

Servers are typically used in office environments. The central computer, often known as the **network server**, stores and distributes data and sometimes controls voice- or e-mail. With a server, many individual users can have access to the same information at the same time.

Many servers are even more powerful than mainframe computers, and because of their flexibility have replaced mainframes, even in large corporations.

MAINFRAME

Mainframe computers are data processors at the heart of many large corporations and university research centers. In the past, data from a mainframe was usually accessed by hundreds of users with what are known as **dumb terminals**, which couldn't compute on their own.

LAPTOP/ NOTEBOOK

Laptop computers are portable personal computers light enough to carry easily. They come with a built-in monitor, or liquid crystal display, keyboard, hard drive, battery and AC adapter. Many include a CD ROM reader and a modem, making them extremely versatile.

In place of a mouse, most laptops and notebooks use some type of touch ball or touch pad located in or close to the keyboard.

The first laptops were dubbed luggables because they weighed 10 pounds or more. Today's weigh as little as two and a half pounds, and they keep shedding the ounces.

WORKSTATION

A workstation is a powerful computer usually used for complex scientific, engineering and mathematical calculations. Workstations are also used in computer-aided design and computer-aided manufacturing, or what is known as CAD/CAM. However, as PCs increase in power and speed, the distinction between them and workstations seems to be blurring.

PC

Personal computers are machines designed for the desktop.

While PCs are not portable, they can be linked together in an office or classroom environment. And unlike the liquid crystal displays of laptops and notebooks, desktop monitors use the cathode ray tubes (CRTs) also used in television sets.

The more memory a PC has and the faster its processing speed, the more software programs it can run.

PERSONAL DIGITAL ASSISTANT (PDA)

PDAs—hand-held or palm computers—are the smallest ones on the market.

Most PDAs perform a list of specific tasks, including serving as calendars, schedule planners, address books and records of to-do lists. They can also send e-mail and faxes using a built-in modem. Some PDAs can link up to desktop computers to upload or download information.

ANATOMY OF A PERSONAL COMPUTER

TUNE UP YOUR SCREEN
If you want to make sure your screen is showing at its best, consider a tune-up on the Web at **www.displaymate.com**. The site provides a series of slide images to help you make the necessary adjustments.

HARD DRIVE

A hard drive is a computer's long-term internal memory and stores both software programs and data files. The more capacity your hard drive has, the more information you can store. Currently, most new machines come with at least a 4-gigabyte (4GB) hard drive, and ones with four or six gigabytes are also available.

PROCESSOR

The brains of a computer, the **CPU**, or **central processing unit**, enables the computer to understand commands and carry out specific operations. Computing power is measured in instructions per second (MIPS equals 1 million instructions per second). Megahertz measures the speed of the processor's internal clock. The clock speed sets the pace at which operations can proceed. When you compare clock speeds, you should only compare computers that use the same kind of microprocessor. That's because even different microprocessors with the same megahertz may execute instructions per second at different rates.

MONITOR

With monitors, the size of the screen and clarity of the display are the main issues. Clarity is determined by the **dot pitch**, the distance between the small dots that create the image. The lower the number, the greater the clarity.

The built-in monitor in laptops and notebooks is called a liquid crystal display, and there are two types. With an **active matrix display**, each tiny screen dot, or pixel, has its own controlling transistors, turning the pixel off and on. In a **passive matrix display**—also called dual-scan displays—columns of pixels are controlled as a unit instead of individual pixels. As a result, active matrix displays have more contrast and are easier to read than passive displays. They're also more expensive.

MOUSE

The mouse is the device that controls the cursor and helps you to select applications or documents, launch pull-down menus, and highlight text or images within a file.

Mice come in a variety of different shapes and sizes, and ergonomic mice that help you rest your hand in a more natural position are also available.

KEYBOARD

The keyboard, which is modeled on a typewriter, is the main way to enter, or input, information. Extended keyboards with 101–105 keys have a numeric keypad and special delete, command and function keys.

Ergonomic keyboards, which allow you to type with your hands and arms in a more natural position, are designed to avoid repetitive stress injuries from prolonged computer use.

PORTS

Computers connect outside devices, or **peripherals**—such as printers, external modems and external hard drives—through **parallel** or **serial ports**.

Printers connecting to the parallel port print faster than serial printers because parallel ports deal with data one byte (eight bits) at a time, while serial ports take data only one bit at a time. Serial ports are common, however, because they can handle a wide variety of peripheral devices, not all of which follow the same standards.

Other peripheral devices, such as scanners, attach to a **SCSI (Small Computer Systems Interface)**, pronounced *scuzzy*, through an interface adapter card that comes with the device. Macintosh computers have SCSI ports built into them, so all you need to do is plug the device into the port.

USB (**Universal Serial Bus**) is a new plug-and-play interface that allows up to 127 peripherals to plug sequentially into a single external port. USB is fast, processing data at 12MB per second.

WHAT'S THE SKINNY?

Pressed for space? New flat panel monitors that attach to high-end PCs may be the ticket. These streamlined LCDs (liquid crystal displays) enhance viewing but can take a bite out of your wallet—though the price does keep coming down.

How Computers Compute

Computers are soldiers, not generals. They follow orders.

A computer is a numerical transformer, or rearranger, of information that has been coded into binary digits, or combinations of 0s and 1s. For example, every time you hit a letter or number on a keyboard, that information is converted to a string of 0s and 1s and transmitted as electronic pulses through a series of microscopic, rapidly changing on/off switches, or gates.

Since all kinds of information can be coded into binary digits, it doesn't matter to a computer how information starts out—as words in a document, numbers in a complex mathematical problem, or a photograph of your little sister. And the computer doesn't care how the information will be used. It handles all **input**, or everything it receives, in the same way and with the same basic calculations: it adds, subtracts, multiplies, divides and compares electronically.

Based on the information you provide, a computer does what you want it to do because it follows a program, or set of instructions, for each task it performs. In addition to its **operating system**—a program that tells it how to do the basics—every computer uses **application programs** for particular jobs.

For example, a designer and an accountant might own the same model computer with the same operating system, but the designer would need graphics programs, while the accountant would need a program capable of generating spreadsheets.

THE WHOLE IS GREATER

Computers have several distinct systems or sections, each handling a specific part of the machine's operation. The sections are linked together electronically, and information is transmitted from one to the other with high-frequency electrical signals, or impulses.

CPU

The brain of the computer is the **central processing unit**, or **CPU**—an integrated **processor** that does the computer's work. It understands the commands, runs the programs, and coordinates everything that goes on.

You can classify a CPU by its clock speed, measured in **megahertz** (**MHz**). Major operations in a computer happen in lockstep, and this is controlled by the microprocessor's clock speed. The greater the hertz, the faster the CPU can handle its work, and the more complex tasks it can do. A 200MHz machine, for example, typically operates about 25% faster than the 166MHz version.

Inside the computer's microprocessor, or CPU, stored instructions determine the flow of data and commands, and control the tasks you're asking the computer to perform.

The actual computing is done by **arithmetic and logic units** (**ALUs**) and the **floating point unit** in response to the instructions they receive. The ALUs add, subtract, multiply or divide data, and compare it. The floating point unit deals with decimal fractions in the data, processing numbers like 1.25 or 66.6.

ON THE BIOS

The BIOS, or basic input/output system, works first and last, getting information from you, managing the machine's internal information flow, displaying text or numbers on your screen, and directing the data that's printed, faxed or shared between your computer and another one. The BIOS

PU

kind of instructions the computer uses, the amount of memory it has, and the capacity of its hard drive. Generally, whatever processor speed is fast today will be the norm tomorrow and slow before long.

Many machines today use **CISC**, or **complex instruction set computing** architecture, in which the CPU supports as many as 200 instructions. An alternative architecture is **RISC**, or **reduced instruction set computing**. By reducing the full set of instructions to the most frequently used, the computer can get more work done in a shorter amount of time.

MANY HANDS MAKE LIGHTSPEED WORK

Parallel processing involves linking microprocessors for greater speed, since different parts of a task can be handled by separate processors. By analogy, think of several people working simultaneously on a research project, looking for answers to different questions and getting the job done faster than any one could by working alone.

has been described as the link or arbiter between the software and the hardware.

HARD DRIVE

A hard drive is a computer's long-term internal memory, which stores software programs and data that you input, or that were previously installed and are activated as the machine operates. Current data is held in **RAM**, or **random-access memory**, before and after it is manipulated, or acted upon.

The more capacity your hard drive has, the more information you can store. In general, the tasks you'll be doing determine the storage capacity you'll need—for example, you'll need much greater capacity if you're moving large graphic files than if you're only generating text. The capacity of a hard drive is currently measured in gigabytes, or billions of bytes.

Speed is also an issue. The time it takes the hard drive to provide the information the CPU needs—its **access time**—is measured in microseconds. Lower numbers indicate faster response times.

SPEED

A computer's speed determines how fast it can handle the tasks you want it to perform. Speed is determined by the number of cycles per second the CPU's clock makes, the

OUT **PUT**

EXIT

IT'S EITHER YES OR NO

If you've ever played 20 Questions, you know how computers process information. *True/false* or *yes/no* provide unambiguous responses that let you sort through the information one logical step at a time. That's the foundation of digital communications, where:

- *Yes/no*, or the idea that something is or is not, is the basic unit of all information, and

- *Yes/no* can be expressed in electronic circuits as the binary numbers 0 and 1

And because computers can process lengthy strings of yes/no or 0/1 queries almost instantaneously, they can tackle extremely complex problems.

ORY

Computer Logic

Logic reigns when the answer to any question is yes or no.

If computers were human, we'd describe them as logical because they arrive at their conclusions in a methodical way, and the answers they get are always clear-cut: either true or false, yes or no.

Actually, since computers work in numbers, not words, the answers are really combinations of 0s or 1s. It's precisely that certainty of being one thing or another that allows the computer to process information so efficiently.

HOW LOGIC WORKS

Logic is about structure, not content. When you follow the principles of logic, you handle the *relationship* between ideas or numbers, not what those ideas or numbers are about. In the decimal system, five added to five is always 10, whether it's apples or puppies. The logical system that computers follow is concerned with the

**If A is true
B is false.
If B is true
A is false.**

Can I Cross the River?

A is true only if both B AND C are true.

INPUT   OUTPUT

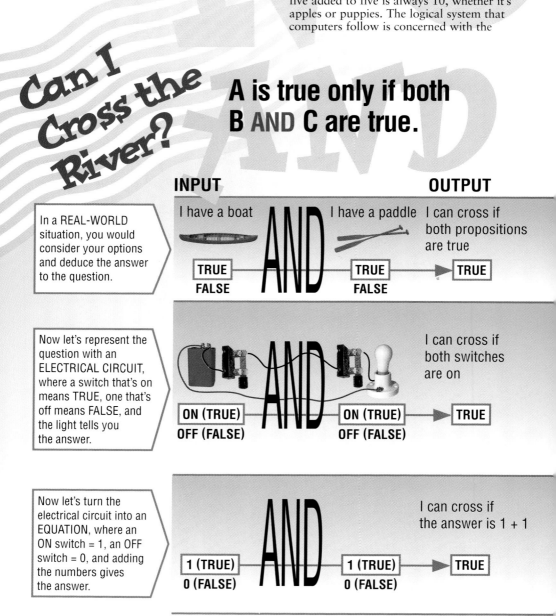

In a REAL-WORLD situation, you would consider your options and deduce the answer to the question.

I have a boat   **AND**   I have a paddle   I can cross if both propositions are true

TRUE — TRUE — TRUE
FALSE   FALSE

Now let's represent the question with an ELECTRICAL CIRCUIT, where a switch that's on means TRUE, one that's off means FALSE, and the light tells you the answer.

I can cross if both switches are on

ON (TRUE) — ON (TRUE) — TRUE
OFF (FALSE)   OFF (FALSE)

Now let's turn the electrical circuit into an EQUATION, where an ON switch = 1, an OFF switch = 0, and adding the numbers gives the answer.

I can cross if the answer is 1 + 1

1 (TRUE) — 1 (TRUE) — TRUE
0 (FALSE)   0 (FALSE)

relationship between two numerical bits of information:

- Are they both 0 or both 1?
- Is at least one a 1?
- Is it a 0 or 1?

As the illustration below demonstrates, the computer handles the first of those questions using the AND function. The answer is yes only if both bits are the same. It handles the second question with the OR function. The answer is yes if either one of the bits is a 1.

It handles the third question with the NOT function. While OR and AND compare two bits to arrive at an answer, NOT looks at one bit at a time.

BIT PARTS

When a specific set of conditions is met—for example, one bit = 1 in an OR operation, or both bits = 1 in an AND operation—a part of the system known as a **gate** produces a signal. If the conditions aren't met—neither is true, or both are false—the gate blocks a signal.

In the case of NOT, whatever comes in, the opposite goes out, so the gate is also called an inverter, converting a 1 to a 0, or a 0 to 1.

By using each yes or no answer to set up the next comparison, the computer can do very complex logical problems by following the same AND, OR and NOT patterns over and over.

A is true if either B OR C is true.

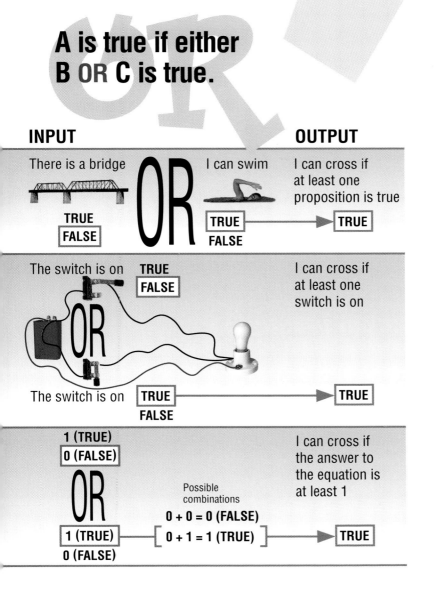

INPUT

There is a bridge
TRUE
FALSE

I can swim
TRUE
FALSE

The switch is on **TRUE**
FALSE

The switch is on **TRUE**
FALSE

1 (TRUE)
0 (FALSE)

OR

Possible combinations
0 + 0 = 0 (FALSE)
0 + 1 = 1 (TRUE)

1 (TRUE)
0 (FALSE)

OUTPUT

I can cross if at least one proposition is true
TRUE

I can cross if at least one switch is on
TRUE

I can cross if the answer to the equation is at least 1
TRUE

NOT AS EASY AS IT SOUNDS

While computers can deal with all logical problems by using AND, OR and NOT, they also use the additional functions NAND, NOR and XOR. NAND refers to "not AND," NOR refers to "not OR," and XOR to "exclusive OR."

A good example of the way XOR logic works is a light that you can control using either of two switches. If you were looking at just one of the switches, you couldn't tell if the light were on or off. But if you could see them both, you'd know which was true—even if you couldn't see the light.

Software Is the Hard Stuff

Computers are really a combination of brains and brawn.

Before the word **software** entered the language, hardware generally meant merchandise or tools made of metal. Today, strongly influenced by computer speak, many people use the word **hardware** to refer to all the equipment—circuit boards, boxes, cables and other components—that form a computer. (But you still don't buy computers in a hardware store.)

Software, on the other hand, provides the instructions that computers follow to perform basic tasks, like recognizing the keys you type on your keyboard or displaying your document on a monitor. Software also handles particular jobs such as word processing or financial calculations.

Without software, hardware may look like a computer, but it can't act like one. In fact, you actually need two types of software to run a computer: **system software**, also known as the operating system (OS), and **application software**, which lets you handle particular tasks, or applications.

ALL SYSTEMS GO

When you turn on your computer, it looks for the system software, or **operating system**, like UNIX, Windows or Mac OS, by checking the ROM or a floppy disk. If it's there, the machine loads and runs it.

The operating system, which works behind the scenes as a director and coordinator, allows your central processing unit to interact with printers and other peripherals, and tells the computer how to find and load other programs. It also manages input and output, and the tasks you ask the computer to do. For example, if you type the command for copying a file, the operating system gets it done.

You use only one operating system at a time to run a computer, although several can be stored in the machine. In fact, there aren't very many different operating systems, and it's hard to create new ones, since people won't buy them if there aren't software programs to use with them. And companies won't go to the expense of creating programs for operating systems that people don't have. That's

why new operating systems have a hard time penetrating the market, even if they have advantages over existing systems. One exception may be Linux, an operating system created by a group of software writers as an alternative to Unix and distributed as freeware.

MS-DOS, Windows NT, Windows 98, OS/2, UNIX (pronounced *U-knicks*) and Apple's Macintosh OS are the most popular operating systems. UNIX is frequently used by engineers and scientific and computer professionals, while the other operating systems are more familiar to home computer and business users.

Making It Look

FILES
are the products you create

Text

Images

DTP

Spreadsheets

"Create a file"

APPLICATION SOFTWARE
are the tools you use for specific functions

"Open an application"

"Start up the computer"

HARDWARE
is the nuts and bolts of your computer.

MAC VS. PC

For many years, an industry battle raged between two popular operating systems—one that ran Macintosh computers and another produced by Microsoft that ran PCs, including IBM, Compaq, Dell, Hewlett-Packard and numerous others.

There are still staunch devotees in each camp, with the Macs being favored for design and creative applications and the PCs being preferred for business and processing tasks.

The fact is, however, that the differences between the systems—from a user's perspective—have largely disappeared. Macs can be configured to run PC programs, and when Macs and PCs are part of a common network—as they are on the Internet—information can be seamlessly exchanged between them.

CREATING AND MANAGING FILES

When you're finished creating something on a computer—a letter, a spreadsheet, a presentation—you'll usually want to save it for future reference.

When you save the material you've created, you set up a **data file**. You save the file by naming it, ideally with a name that makes it easy to remember when you want to use it again. Individual data files can be grouped together into larger files, called directories or **file folders**. For example, if you create a series of letters, posters and flyers to announce an annual event, you could create a directory to hold all of those files, making a record of what you'd done so it would be easy to find the following year.

Files aren't permanent: you can revise what's on them, copy them, move them or delete them. Even when you delete a file, you may actually be able to retrieve or reconstruct it. What actually happens is that the file name is removed from your directory, although the file itself still occupies the same place in the computer. As long as the space where the deleted material is stored hasn't been reused, that information will still be there, even though you may need a special program to resurrect it. Smart systems store new files in the space occupied by the oldest deleted files.

PUTTING IT TOGETHER

If you're buying a computer, you generally buy the hardware first. But the software programs you want to use can help you determine which new hardware to buy. Since some programs need more computer memory and speed than others, you want to be sure your hardware has the capacity to run the software you plan to use.

While a computer is a major investment, most software is available at relatively modest cost. You can build up a library either on your hard disk, floppies or CD ROMs. And now most computers come with a variety of preinstalled software.

Easy

"Open a new file"

"Save what's been done"

"Turn off the computer"

OPERATING SYSTEMS are the master control programs that work behind the scenes to coordinate your computer's internal, functions, operations and file systems

OTHER WARES

Other types of software include **groupware** and **shareware**. Groupware allows many people to use the same data to work on the same project at the same time. Shareware is software that people want to share and make available for free, or at nominal cost, to others. Some shareware, also called **freeware**, can be downloaded from the World Wide Web. Software that's used all the time, like the instructions that operate a pocket calculator, are burned into a chip. It's then called **firmware** or said to be hard wired.

Software Everywhere

There's a universe of applications to handle almost anything you want your computer to do.

Software applications are tools that you use to do specific jobs. Just as you might choose a broom over a mop, or a hammer over a screwdriver, you select the software that's right for a task you want to handle.

Each application has its own vocabulary and its own set of instructions, but they all have one thing in common: they are designed to process information that you provide.

Some applications allow you to create information from scratch—for example, drafting a document or setting up a spreadsheet—while others specialize in organizing or arranging what you've created. Still others allow you to transform that information into something else entirely, like changing text and columns of numbers into a chart or graph.

You can use many kinds of application software on the same computer as long as each one is compatible with the operating system.

WORD PROCESSING

With a word processing application, you can create and edit documents as simple as a memo or a letter, or as complex as a report, proposal or book. Word processing applications range from basic text editors to full-featured publishers, which allow you to create footnotes, automated indexes and tables of contents. They also let you use a range of formats, typefaces and other stylistic features.

SPREADSHEETS

Dan Bricklin designed the first computer spreadsheet program, which was released in 1979. Spreadsheet applications are designed for processing numbers. They can handle a wide range of mathematical, financial and scientific functions, and turn raw numbers into graphs or charts. Individual spreadsheets can be linked, too, so that information that's updated in one place is automatically recalculated in another.

For example, if a salesperson records a sale, the billing department's spreadsheet reflects the anticipated income. Because spreadsheets are made up of rows and columns, they're also used to keep lists and create tables.

DATABASES

A variety of database applications store and retrieve information.

- A personal information manager, for example, is a database of contacts—names, addresses, phone numbers. You can use it simply as a phone book or to keep in-depth information about friends and associates.
- A checking program functions like your checkbook but actually stores your records so that you can get updates and pull personal financial reports at any time.
- Scheduling applications allow you to keep track of appointments and the time you spend on projects.

Businesses use other, larger databases to monitor everything from employee records to sales figures, and from raw material to shipping status. And the Web is full of useful databases such as online libraries and e-mail address and phone directories.

PRESENTATIONS

Presentation applications create slides that may be printed on plain or transparent paper, turned into film or used as an on-screen presentation with an LCD projector. An organizer, or sorter, lets you look at miniature images of the slides and arrange them by dragging them from one position to another. When you give a show on-screen, you can assign fade times so that each new slide comes up automatically at a fixed interval (say 10 seconds). You can also choose the transition pattern from one slide to the next—for example, a new slide may appear from the top, bottom or from either side.

A key feature of any presentation application is its ability to incorporate color and graphics. Multimedia applications go one step further, combining graphics, images, animation and sound. They're frequently used for special effects in film editing and can create high-end presentations.

FREE DOWNLOADS

Lots of software is available free of charge on the Internet. You can find e-mail readers, instant message systems, games, music and virus protection programs. Web browsers can be upgraded as well.

$0.⁰⁰

WYSIWYG

Pronounced *Whizzy-wig*, this acronym stands for "what you see is what you get," a visual standard for today's personal computers. When you look at a document on your screen, you see the format, type and image size, and layout just as they will appear when they're printed.

This is a change from earlier DOS-based applications, in which text formatting, for example, was indicated by a coded tag, and there was no way to know for sure what it would look like before it was printed.

SOFTWARE VERSIONS

Software developers are constantly improving and adding features to their products, if only to stay one step ahead of their competition. This accounts for the numerals tacked onto the end of most application names—for example, Microsoft Word 6.0 or Quicken 7.0. A full number increase, say, from 4 to 5, or 6 to 7, indicates a major new release. A partial number, like 6.2 or 6.4, indicates minor enhancements or additions.

It's important to remember that newer isn't necessarily better. If a new version is larger, it may run more slowly. Also, in the rush to get products to market, some manufacturers may not test new software adequately for operating glitches, called bugs.

UTILITIES

A comprehensive utilities program, such as Norton Utilities, maintains the integrity of your operating system.

The program scans for viruses, analyzes your hard drive for problems and repairs them, and optimizes the storage capacity on your hard drive.

CAD AND CAM

Computer-aided design (CAD) applications generate and manipulate three-dimensional objects like rooms or cars in two dimensions—that is, on your computer screen. Engineers and architects use CAD to design everything from airplanes to apartment buildings. CAD is also used by interior and lighting designers to manipulate objects in a room or on a theatrical stage. Personal CAD applications can help you create a blueprint for a home or plan your garden landscaping.

Related to—and often used in conjunction with—CAD are CAE (computer-aided engineering) applications, which diagnose an object's structure, and CAM (computer-aided manufacturing) applications, which analyze the material makeup of an object.

GRAPHICS APPLICATIONS

Graphics applications show you how to work with and manipulate images in innovative ways. Drawing applications use mathematical equations to create and fill in shapes. With painting applications, you can create images using a variety of commands that imitate older methods like brushes or sponges, or you can work with images that have been scanned.

Photography applications let you transform photographs, changing the lighting, altering the size or shape, or adding (or subtracting) elements so that the final image may be quite different from the original. The images can be incorporated with text using page-composition applications.

ARE WE HAVING FUN?

Computer applications are sometimes fun and, quite literally, games. In fact, some people credit the excitement of playing computer-based action games as a major force in inspiring many creative programmers as well as popularizing computer use.

Screen saver images—originally designed to extend the life of CRT (cathode ray tube) monitors by avoiding a single image being burned into the screen—let even sober users enjoy whirling stars, dancing bears or exploding fireworks. Today's energy-saving monitors shut off if they're not being used after a set amount of time, making screen savers an expression of personal taste.

Programming

When you program, you tell a computer what to do.

If your eyes glaze over when you hear the word **program**, it may be because you associate the term with trying to record a show on your VCR. In fact, that isn't programming at all—it's just filling in the numbers for the date, time and channel.

More accurately, you might compare programming to writing a manual that tells someone how to deal with every single element of a particular task: managing an office, running a public transportation system, or billing credit card accounts. The program itself is a long string of small steps for the computer to follow as it handles each aspect of a job.

Programming is also like creating a recipe for other people to use. You know what you want the dish to taste like, so you figure out the necessary ingredients, how much of each to use, and the order in which to combine them. Your recipe might be a little different from someone else's, but both can produce tasty results.

OUT OF HAND

Some early computers were programmed by hand. Programmers actually plugged wires into boards, much as the early telephone operator did, to handle the mathematical computations—a procedure that could take hours, days or even longer to set up. Today, when computers run complex programs and provide the solutions we expect, millions of electronic switches are turned on or off almost instantaneously.

WHAT'S RELEVANT?

The key to successful programming is being able to figure out what's relevant to a particular problem and what's not. That means a good programmer has to be able to think in the abstract and to put things in perspective, whether the problem is creating a basic chess game—something that experts say would take one good programmer perhaps a week to do—or putting together an air-traffic control system for New York City—a job that has taken thousands of programmers several years to complete.

DIVIDING UP THE PROBLEM

Regardless of the job, developing a programming solution usually involves the following steps:

- Initially, a programmer decides how to **divide**, or slice up, the problem so that its components can be tackled separately. Dividing not only takes time—at least one expert estimates it to be 50% of the total creation process—but it ultimately affects how the system performs.

- After the major components are identified, the programmer specifies the **communication links**, or connections, between the segments.

- Then each segment is broken into a series of steps, which are, in turn, **subdivided** into smaller ones until every element of the problem is isolated.

- At that point, the work of programming, or building the **code** that provides the solution, begins.

The program itself must be unambiguous because computers can understand only *yes/no, on/off, and/or*. They have no tolerance for *uhs, ahs,* and *maybe*s. Every program is also tested, both along the way and when it's completed, to be sure it handles the task it has been created to do and that no **bugs**, or glitches, exist.

WHY 2000?

In the 1960s companies started computerizing their operations using large mainframes. These machines had to be custom programmed for each individual business, and memory was expensive. So programmers cut corners by using only the last two digits for the year—73 for 1973, for example.

It was assumed that these programs would be obsolete by the year 2000. Unfortunately, many of these programs are still in service. When the year 2000 arrives, the programs will think it is the year 1900 and may shut down or perform in unpredictable ways.

Because so many companies rely on code written 30 and 40 years ago, and the dates are embedded in millions of lines of code, the Y2K bug will be difficult to fix. But most large agencies and companies have been working on the problem for some time and are taking steps to handle the situations that may arise.

COMPUTER LINGO

Just as you need to speak a language to communicate with others, programmers must speak to computers in a way computers can understand.

Computer languages have their own vocabularies, with keywords, letters, numbers and symbols that stand for particular operations, or sequences of operations, that the computer performs. And, like other languages, those used by programmers must follow certain rules to make sense.

Though there are thousands of programming languages, just a handful dominate the market.

FORTRAN (for Formula Translator),

one of the earliest languages used for scientific, technical and graphic applications, was developed by IBM in 1953. It's now used for numerical computations, like weather forecasting or airflow simulations.

BASIC (Beginners' All-Purpose Symbolic

Instruction Code), developed in the 1950s at Dartmouth, is widely used in a variety of applications. Microsoft, for example, uses a variation called V-Basic.

COBOL (Common Business Oriented

Language) is an old language, and as its name suggests, is used for commercial data processing. ANSI, the American National Standards Institute, standardized COBOL in 1968.

JAVA (believe it or not,

named after the island where coffee is a prime crop because, in the arcane life of computer programmers, coffee is a programming fluid, required for the arduous, endless, around-the-clock work) was adapted for programming on the Internet by Sun Microsystems. Examples of Java applets, or small applications, are calendars or calculators that appear on web pages.

A FLY IN THE OINTMENT

There's some debate about when *bug* was first used to describe programming glitches. One popular version dates to 1945, when Grace Murray Hopper glued a dead moth she'd found in Harvard's Mark II computer in the lab's log book and announced that she'd debugged the machine.

However, Thomas Edison is known to have used the term while working on the telegraph in the 1800s.

REDUCE BY HALF...OR MORE

One way programmers can save time and space is by using **subroutines**, which are sections of existing code that always do the same thing and that serve as a kind of shorthand. Using a subroutine for handling a particular computation, for example, means you don't have to spell out the instructions for that computation every time it occurs.

You can compare subroutines to using a term to describe a specific cooking process, such as "reduce by half." If you're talking to other cooks, you don't have to explain that you mean "simmer the liquid slowly until there's half the quantity you started with left in the pot" each time the recipe calls for this step.

C and **C++**, which were developed at AT&T, are widely used in modern systems programming. Most computer operating systems are a mix of C and C++, and most consumer applications are created in C++. For example, when you make an 800-number telephone call, the telephone switching systems that connect you use programs written in C and C++.

Thinking Machines

Computers perform great intellectual feats, but do they understand what they're doing?

When a computer runs a spreadsheet or checks the spelling in a document, we don't tend to think of the machine as thinking.

We know that the software—the lines of code used to create the program—has been fed into the machine and that the computer is simply applying the rules, and doing calculations at a very rapid rate. Sometimes these rules are more complex, as when a computer automatically corrects common misspellings as we type, flags repeated words, and anticipates how to present text based on the style we've already established.

But computers start seeming really intelligent when they respond to our voice, diagnose an illness, or beat an international master at chess, as IBM's Big Blue has done.

HOW NOW, BIG BLUE

When IBM's supercomputer beat Kasparov, the world chess master, many people said that the machine could in fact learn and was "smarter" than a human. But Big Blue merely uses brute computer force: by calculating all the possible moves at a very rapid speed, the machine could anticipate all of the possible outcomes of each move and eventually won. But that doesn't mean that the machine plays chess or thinks like a person.

ARTIFICIAL INTELLIGENCE

Whether or not computers can actually think remains an ongoing philosophical debate, centered on such questions as: Do computers really learn or simply mimic human behavior? And even if they can learn to modify or improve their performance, are they really conscious of what they are doing? Do computers really know what's going on?

Whatever **artificial intelligence** a computer may have, some theorists maintain that we will never write a program complex enough to handle the daily issues of life as well as a normal three-year-old can. These experts agree that computers cannot react to their environment as humans do. For example, computers cannot adapt to constantly changing situations, anticipate unforeseen events, make a long-term plan, or deal with things they haven't come across before.

Yet there are many things that computers can do that strongly suggest that they have, by some definitions, actual intelligence.

LEARNING ALGORITHMS

Children learn what the color blue is by abstracting the color from objects in their surroundings. Computers can learn to recognize objects through learning algorithms that enable them to extrapolate certain forms or configurations. For example, if you feed a computer enough examples of trees—scenes with trees, pictures or drawings of trees —it will eventually be able to identify a tree without having a tree described to it as such.

Provided with such **training sets,** computers can crunch through overwhelming amounts of data, such as pictures of the galaxy, and identify specific formations, such as a supernova.

Computers also learn from online algorithms in which humans interact with the machines to tell them when they're right and when they're wrong.

AN INTELLIGENT RESPONSE

The Turing test was invented by Alan M. Turing (1912-1954). In his 1950 article "Computing Machinery and Intelligence," Turing suggested that if the responses from the computer were indistinguishable from that of a human, the computer could be said to be thinking. The Turing test connects a questioner to a person and to a machine via a terminal. The interviewer must figure out which is the machine and which is the human by asking questions. If the interviewer can't distinguish between the two within a certain time (Turing proposed five minutes), the machine is generally considered intelligent.

"The whole thinking process is still rather mysterious to us, but I believe that a thinking machine will help us greatly in finding out how we think ourselves."
—Alan Turing, May 1951

AI KICKOFF

In 1956 John McCarthy, regarded as the father of AI (artificial intelligence), organized the Dartmouth summer research project on artificial intelligence to draw together the talent and expertise of psychologists, mathematicians, logicians and others interested in machine intelligence. The Dartmouth conference brought together the founders in AI and laid the groundwork for future research.

EXPERT SYSTEMS

Some machines mimic human intelligence by sorting through a number of variables, or factors, to solve a problem. These **expert systems** are created by programming into the computer the collective experience of knowledgeable people in a particular field.

The computer then analyzes the information it receives, following a set of rules, to arrive at a logical solution. For example, doctors use expert systems to identify infectious diseases based on symptoms and other patient data. Loan approval programs that qualify or disqualify an applicant—based on financial ability, income, monthly expenses and debts—are also types of expert systems.

But expert systems are only as smart as the data they have been programmed to evaluate. They can't function properly if a factor changes, which is why they are also considered **fragile systems**. Quite simply, expert systems can analyze a staggering number of variables, but they have no common sense.

INTELLIGENT AGENTS

Some computers exhibit intelligence that is more generalist than specialist. These so-called **intelligent agents** can "understand" words in a context and then respond to this information in what appears to be a human interaction.

For example, intelligent agents can function as telephone operators, essentially interpreting what people are asking and then responding in appropriate phrases or sentences. The agents appear to be more human because they exhibit adaptive behavior. Their responses suggest that they are following a conversation and providing the information sought after.

RESPONSIVE ROBOTS

A real-life but still-in-the-future humanoid robot, Cog, is being constructed by Rodney Brooks and the Cog team at MIT. Cog's brain is silicon chips and all its body parts are inorganic. It is designed to go through an embodied infancy and childhood, reacting to people it sees with its video eyes, making friends, learning about the world by playing with real things with its robot hands, and acquiring memory. You can visit MIT's site about the Cog project at **www.ai.mit.edu/projects/cog**.

AI ACTION

You can chat with some AI programs yourself. Try one of these programs at **http://ciips.ee.uwa.edu.au/~hutch/Hal.html**.

Thanks to the Memory

The more memory a computer has, the faster it can operate.

A computer can do what you tell it to because all the information it needs is stored, either permanently or temporarily, in its memory. The programs that the machine uses all the time are stored as **read-only memory**, or **ROM**. But the particular program it needs to perform a current task, plus all the data that the task produces, are stored in the machine's **random-access memory**, or **RAM**.

FLEETING MEMORY

Random-access memory is temporary. When the machine is turned off, everything that's been stored in RAM disappears. That makes the memory capacity available again when you turn the computer back on. The same chips are used over and over to store different data or programs—like a glass you can fill with different kinds of liquid, depending on what you want to drink.

What's more, information that's stored in RAM can be changed while the machine is running. That's because the CPU can either **read** a program or **write over** it. When information is read, it is left as is, in the same location. But when new information is written, it destroys whatever had been stored in the location it now occupies.

For example, if you switch from a word processing to a spreadsheet program, the instructions for the spreadsheet will replace the instructions for the word processor in your computer's RAM.

MEMORY AND SPEED

The more RAM your computer has, the faster your software will perform, and the more programs you can run at the same time. You need at least 32 megabytes (MB) of RAM. (64MB is fairly standard for a 300MHz or higher machine.)

You can also buy added RAM chips, usually in units of 32MB, that can be installed in your computer. Checking how many memory sockets are available on the add-on memory board located inside the computer will tell you how much more memory you can add. Experts suggest that you should plan for up to 128MB.

If you don't want to save it, you can erase it.

CACHE

Cache memory is the part of RAM that's set aside to hold the data and programs your CPU uses as it handles each particular task. When a task has been completed, the data that's been worked on is routed back to regular RAM and is replaced in the cache (pronounced *cash*) by data and programs for the next task.

Cache increases computer efficiency by storing frequently used data and instructions and making them instantly available for processing. The more cache you have, the quicker your computer can operate, and the more complex tasks it can perform.

All machines come with some cache installed, and you can usually add more, called secondary or level-2 cache, either on the main logic board or using an expansion slot.

ROM

ROM

Read-only memory is permanent, which is why it's used for programs that the computer needs all the time, like the **booting**, or start-up program, that tells the computer how to get itself going when it's turned on. ROM isn't lost when the computer is turned off or loses power, and you usually don't change ROM or erase it.

In most cases, information is installed on ROM chips before they're put into the PC. Then they're plugged into sockets on the motherboard, which holds all the chips that make the computer function. That way the chips can be removed and replaced if they're defective.

ALWAYS AN EXCEPTION

While most ROM in a computer is permanent, there are exceptions. The chips in newer sound cards, for example, have **erasable, programmable, read-only memory, or EPROM**. That means they can be updated rather than having to be replaced.

In that case, a technician erases the program by exposing it to ultraviolet radiation. Then the new program is written, or **burned**, onto the chip with electrical pulses.

Some chips are **electronically erasable (EEPROM)** and can be updated at home. EEPROM is built into the system and lets you update the ROM by using a driver or update disk.

PROGRAMS KEPT STORED IN ROM

A CD ROM, as the name implies, is a compact disc (CD) with read-only memory (ROM). In the past, you couldn't change what was on a CD or use it to save information. But now writable CDs are also available.

You'll need a CDR, or CD recorder, that's compatible with your computer, software such as Toast (for a Mac) or EZ CD Creator (for a PC), and writable CDs.

You can program the CDR to read files from your disk drive, a zip drive or a CD ROM. In burning or making a CD ROM, information is coded in pits and lands, or bumps, that spiral out from the center of the disc. It's then read by a miniature laser-generated light reflected off a pit or land to a photoreceptor as a series of electrical blips, or impulses.

PACKING DATA IN

Information in both RAM and ROM is stored in bytes, or sequences of eight bits of 0s and 1s. Memory capacity, describing how many bytes of information can be handled by the computer's memory, is given as kilobytes (KB, or thousands of bytes) or megabytes (MB, which is millions of bytes).

The more memory a machine has, the more programs it can run and the more jobs it can do, sometimes handling more than one at the same time. That's called **multitasking.**

RAM AT WORK

While RAM is temporary, the data that's produced doesn't have to be. If you want to have certain words, numbers, images or files available in the future, you can tell the computer to **save** them, either on your hard drive or on another storage device, such as a floppy disk.

Here's what happens, for example, if you're running a tax preparation program:

1 You insert a disk with a tax preparation program into your computer.

2 You download the program from the disk to your hard drive, and parts of it are written into RAM.

3 The numbers you input are also stored in RAM while you're working with the program. The computations themselves are kept in memory units called **registers**.

4 When the result is figured—in this case, how much you owe or is owed you—it, too, is stored in RAM.

5 If you save what you've done to your disk drive, you can turn the machine off and retrieve the information at some point in the future.

Storing Your Information

The goal is to cram more into a smaller space—electronically.

Storing information electronically takes up a lot less physical room than **hard copy**, or information that's been printed on paper. But having adequate computer storage is still a problem. If you don't have enough memory, your machine rebels. You can't run the programs you need or store the information you've produced.

There are, however, solutions. Each new generation of computers comes with more built-in storage, and you can also buy external devices for extra space. What's more, the new storage devices have a lot more **density**, which means they can store more information in a smaller amount of space.

FLOPPY DISKS

Floppy disks were once the primary way to save data and programs externally for a PC. In addition to being portable, disks have a long life. So material you saved several years ago and haven't touched since is probably still intact. Floppies can also be stored easily in a separate place for safekeeping. But they can be damaged or erased, which usually means everything you've stored on the disk is wiped out.

READING AND WRITING

Floppy disks look square rather than round and rigid rather than floppy because they are protected by a plastic case. When a disk is inserted in the disk drive, read/write heads retrieve information by detecting magnetic fields on the disk coating. The head saves data the same way a VCR or audio cassette does, by putting out magnetic impulses, thereby changing the magnetic status of the coating.

Floppies have square holes at the upper right-hand corner to indicate whether they're

"read only" or can be used to save material. If the hole is open, it's a read-only disk, though you can sometimes change it by moving a shutter from open to closed.

1 floppy disk = 1.4 megabytes

ZIPPING UP YOUR FILES

A convenient way to back up your computer files is to use a zip drive, a high-capacity disk drive that holds 94MB of information, compared to 1.4MB on a high-density floppy disk. Zip drives come installed in some new computers but can also be bought separately and added as an external device.

1 zip disk = 94 megabytes

GOOD BACKUP HELPS

Storage devices are used as insurance to back up what you've saved on your hard disk in case your computer hard disk crashes or shuts down unexpectedly. Without backup, you might have to spend hours, days or even weeks to recreate your work.

While it takes discipline, it's important to save and back up your work on a regular basis. That way, if your computer crashes, you may only lose the most recent data you're working on and not the entire file or document. Depending on how important your work is or how much you use your computer, you may want to do this on a daily or weekly basis.

Storing very important information on another device altogether, like a removable floppy disk or server, is also a good idea in case of major calamities, like fire or theft.

Random-access data-drive systems are removable cartridge drives that look like giant floppy disk drives. They're valuable for storing multimedia projects, which could take up all the available space on a hard drive. Data-drive systems are also an easy way to share information because the cartridges can be circulated and copied on different machines.

You can purchase software that automates the backup and storage of important information. Be sure it:

- **Stores selectively—only the most important files—to save space**
- **Compares its files to files on the hard drive to be sure they are the same**
- **Backs up only what has changed**
- **Restores your hard drive contents if you crash**

THE USES OF MEMORY

Memory—not filing cabinets—is the key to electronic storage. Like your memory—though hopefully without its lapses—electronic memory can function two ways. Short-term memory, including RAM, holds the data you're working on at the moment, while long-term memory **archives**, or stores, the information you want to save. Equally important, electronic memory can help you get at the information easily when you want to reuse it.

HARD DRIVES

One long-term memory device, called a **hard drive**, is installed in the computer.

A typical hard disk, which looks like a metallic phonograph record, stores programs and files internally. (*Hard disk* is often used as a synonym for *hard drive,* which is also the entire casing in which the computer's memory sits.) With some computers, you can add a removable hard drive, almost always a self-contained unit, for additional storage.

One Encyclopedia

=

1/6 of One Hard Drive

1 hard drive = 4GB or 4000 megabytes

=

1 CD ROM

1 CD ROM = 650 megabytes

A 32-volume encyclopedia = 650 megabytes

CIRCULAR FILES

CD ROMs are critical storage tools for large programs and vast amounts of information, particularly those that contain multimedia content, such as video and animation. Each disk can store up to 650 megabytes—an entire encyclopedia—and make it immediately available to anyone with a CD ROM player installed in or connected to their computer.

You can access CD ROM information quickly, though not as quickly as you can from a fast hard drive. Typical **access time**, or how long it takes to find where a particular file starts, is measured in fractions of seconds. That's so quick that you may see the material on your screen almost simultaneously with your command.

IN THE WORKS

CDs, once read-only devices, are evolving to include other capabilities:

 **WORM** disks, or **write once/read many**, let you store information you can't change

 CDRW, or **rewritable** disks, let you update information as often as needed

 Extended architecture (**XA**) drives do a better job of integrating audio and computer data and are photo CD-compatible

Conversing with Computers

Interfaces are becoming less like machines, more like people.

A few years ago, computers were considered complex machines used only by engineers, scientists and dedicated techies or hobbyists. Today, computers are even more complex machines used by almost everyone. So what happened? The answer lies, in part, in the computer's **interface**, the place where humans and computers (or any machine) meet and converse.

It's the place where you instruct and the machine responds. For instance, the key pad of your telephone is an interface. So is the key to the ignition of your car.

Today's electronic interfaces have replaced earlier human—machine interactions—such as rotary phones and crank handles on a car's engine—that were more cumbersome and less elegant.

USER-UNFRIENDLY
Early personal computers used the **command-line** interface, which required you to memorize and key in computer-language commands to get the machine to operate. For example, a simple task such as copying a file from a floppy disk to a hard drive required you to type *copy a:\filename.* c:\directory\filename.**.

For a brief period, menu-driven interfaces, which were listings of computer commands that you accessed with the arrow keys on your keyboard, reduced the burden of memorizing languages like MS-DOS, FORTRAN and PASCAL.

Still, there was a long way to go before the PC could become a household and office fixture. What was needed was an interface that would revolutionize the industry—something startling, something like...well, a mouse.

window: a rectangular on-screen frame through which you view a document, worksheet, database or application program. Windows can be moved around the desktop, and reduced or enlarged. Some windows can be viewed and run concurrently.

pointer: an on-screen symbol, usually an arrow or a hand, that shows the current position of the mouse.

toolbar: a bar across the top of a window containing buttons or icons that represent frequently used commands.

A MOUSE SHALL LEAD THEM
In the late 1970s a team of scientists in Xerox PARC, the company's research and development unit, developed a new way for humans to tell a computer what they wanted it to do. Dubbed the **graphical user interface**, or **GUI** (pronounced *gooey*), this method of interacting with computers relies on pictures or graphics called **icons** to convey instructions rather than on typewritten commands.

When Steven Jobs of Apple Computers installed a GUI on the Macintosh personal computer, he made the Mac unique because of its easy-to-use interface. By simply pointing and clicking on an icon with your mouse, you could tell your computer what to do.

While the interfaces on the PC and the Mac are increasingly similar, there are still differences in the icons, their placement, and the function they perform. But once you've learned to work with one of these interfaces, it's not very difficult to learn the other.

TALK TO YOU LATER...OR SOONER
While a GUI made it easier for humans to interact with computers, the GUI itself remains an artificial language, using pointing and clicking to signal what we want to communicate. The next step in the evolution of interfaces will allow you to communicate with computers in the most natural of ways, by talking and listening.

POINT & CLICK!

Microsoft Word

File Edit View Ins

Normal   HELVE

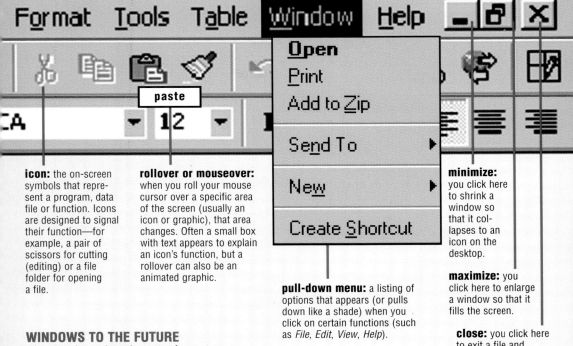

Document2

Format | Tools | Table | **Window** | Help

paste

CA ▼ 12 ▼

Window menu:
Open
Print
Add to Zip
Send To ►
New ►
Create Shortcut

icon: the on-screen symbols that represent a program, data file or function. Icons are designed to signal their function—for example, a pair of scissors for cutting (editing) or a file folder for opening a file.

rollover or mouseover: when you roll your mouse cursor over a specific area of the screen (usually an icon or graphic), that area changes. Often a small box with text appears to explain an icon's function, but a rollover can also be an animated graphic.

minimize: you click here to shrink a window so that it collapses to an icon on the desktop.

maximize: you click here to enlarge a window so that it fills the screen.

pull-down menu: a listing of options that appears (or pulls down like a shade) when you click on certain functions (such as *File*, *Edit*, *View*, *Help*).

close: you click here to exit a file and remove its window from display.

WINDOWS TO THE FUTURE

The GUI brought other significant improvements to the human–computer interface. For the first time, people saw on their screens a computer **window**, a rectangular screen framing the live document and program currently being worked on. Opening and closing windows at the click of the mouse was a vastly more appealing interface than the command-line model.

Another breakthrough was transforming the computer screen to a computer **desktop**. On the desktop you could arrange your work tools and files the way *you*, not the computer, wanted them arranged, simply by using your mouse to move, add or delete icons. Desktops brought color and fun to the once cold, blank screen of the command-line and menu-driven interfaces.

desktop: a representation of your daily work, as if you're looking at an actual desktop with folders full of work to do.

To Do List

Schedules

Notes to Mom & Dad

Add to Rolodex

Crystal Pattern

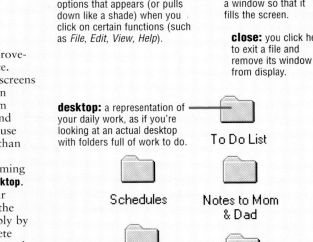

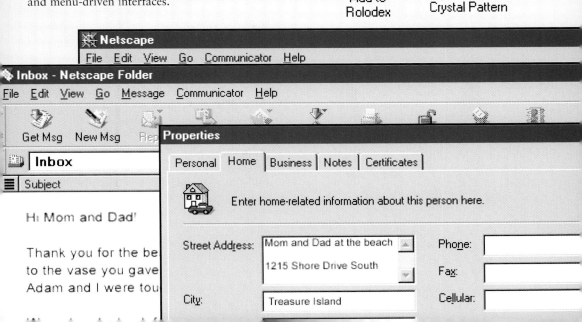

Netscape
File Edit View Go Communicator Help

Inbox - Netscape Folder
File Edit View Go Message Communicator Help

Get Msg | New Msg | Rep

Inbox

Subject

Hi Mom and Dad!

Thank you for the be
to the vase you gave
Adam and I were tou

Properties

Personal | Home | Business | Notes | Certificates

Enter home-related information about this person here.

Street Address: Mom and Dad at the beach
1215 Shore Drive South

City: Treasure Island

Phone:

Fax:

Cellular:

Computer Speak

Old dogs with new tricks.

Computers have introduced hundreds of new words to our everyday vocabulary, many of them old words with new applications. Some—like *menu*—are pretty obvious. Other derivations are more obscure and often humorous. Here are just a few of the words you will come across as you familiarize yourself with computers.

Boot To start up your computer. The term is said to be derived from the expression "pulling oneself up by the bootstraps."

Bit (**Bi**nary dig**it**) The basic unit of information in a binary numbering system.

Chip A miniaturized electronic circuit mass-produced on a tiny wafer of silicon.

Byte Eight bits, the fundamental data unit of personal computers. A byte stores the equivalent of one character (the character *m* looks like this: 0 1 0 0 1 1 0 1) and is also the basic unit of measurement for computer storage capacity.

Mouse A palm-sized device equipped with one or more control buttons and designed to be rolled about on the surface next to a computer keyboard. As it moves, circuits relay signals that correspondingly move a cursor on the screen.

Bug A programming error that can cause a computer or a program to perform erratically, produce inaccurate results, or crash.

Virus A program that replicates itself by attaching to other programs, often carrying out unwanted and sometimes damaging operations.

Port An outlet in your computer that synchronizes the flow of data between the central processing unit (CPU) and external devices like printers and modems.

Bus An internal electronic pathway along which signals are sent from one part of a computer to another.

Hardware The physical component of a computer system, including circuit boards, housing, cables, screens and peripheral equipment. Software programs tell these components what to do.

Window An on-screen frame that lets you view and work on documents, worksheets, databases, drawings or applications programs. A windowing environment lets you run multiple applications, each in its own window simultaneously.

Menu An on-screen display that lists available commands and functions.

RAM Random-access memory. The primary working memory, which stores program and data instructions so they can be directly accessed by a computer's central processing unit.

Crash A program or power failure that causes a computer to become inoperative, often resulting in a frozen keyboard. In most cases, you must restart the computer. This can result in the loss of whatever you were working on if it was not saved before the crash.

Scroll To move the contents in a window horizontally or vertically so that the position of a worksheet or document changes.

Viruses

You can stop a computer virus in its tracks.

A virus is a software program that copies itself, spreading to other programs or disks. Its **payload**, or the set of instructions it carries, can be dangerous, infecting its new host by erasing data or causing erratic behavior.

Software viruses are created by computer users, sometimes described as **virus hackers**, and then deliberately planted so they'll spread. The motives for such potentially destructive behavior are hard to understand, though one theory is that the programming challenge is too hard to resist.

IF YOUR COMPUTER SNEEZES

Dread of viruses stems in large part from their name. After all, there's no cure for that famous viral infection, the common cold. And imagining your computer coughing, sneezing and shivering is not a pretty thought, especially since the consequences can be cryptic messages and, worse still, sudden crashes.

The good news is that computer viruses are easier to prevent than human ones. Virus detection software is readily available wherever software is sold. Once you load it in your computer, it can usually find and destroy an infection easily.

Most detection programs will run every time you start your computer or insert a floppy disk, and some will automatically scan newly downloaded files. The best programs check not only for viruses but also for viral patterns, or files that appear to be replicating themselves or writing over existing data.

New viruses emerge all the time, but detection software is always being updated, too. So it's smart to be sure you're using the most current program.

HOW TO FIGHT VIRUSES

Your software should include a virus checker. It's safest to have one that runs in the background all the time. If you don't have one, you can download McAfee VirusScan (**www.mcafee.com**) or purchase Norton AntiVirus. Both programs have updates available for downloading from the Net.

WARNING SIGNS OF A VIRUS

- System slows down
- Files refuse to open
- Content is garbled
- Hard disk space keeps disappearing
- Computer restarts without being prompted to
- New files you don't recognize appear
- Repeated, inexplicable freezing or crashing occurs
- There's hard drive activity when you're not actually using the computer

NO WORK OF ART

The best-known virus, the infamous Michelangelo, threatened to destroy the data on hundreds of thousands of hard drives on March 6, 1992. Despite rumors that five million machines were infected, about 10,000 people actually reported problems on the fateful day.

EVER VIGILANT

One of the biggest myths about viruses is that shrink-wrapped, straight-from-the-factory disks are safe. Experts warn that viruses are more likely to travel hidden in commercial software than any other source.

One reason is that software posted to the Internet is routinely scanned for viruses. And consumers tend to be more cautious when downloading software from a public forum. But new disks usually aren't checked by producers and can't be checked by retailers without destroying the packaging.

Don't be fooled, either, by False Authority Syndrome. When a salesperson at your local software store or a member of your technical support staff tells you your computer's problems are caused by a virus, be skeptical. Sooner or later, anything that seems inexplicable is blamed on an invisible virus, which destroys some essential file, then deletes itself to avoid detection, never to be heard from again.

In reality, disappearing organisms don't exist. What's important is that, if you have a problem once, it can happen again. If you don't determine and resolve the real cause—a hardware malfunction, badly written software, or faulty user input—you can probably count on a return appearance.

HOAXES AND LEGENDS

Most hoaxes, also called urban legends, contain just enough technical jargon to be convincing. The very first one, reported in 1988, cautioned people not to use their 2,400-baud modems. Allegedly, a virus was programmed into the "internal bit registers," which infected all "incoming binary data" and erased the victim's hard drive.

The biggest hoax to date, introduced in 1994 as the Good Times hoax, is still in circulation (sometimes under another name, such as Deeyenda, Irina or Penpal Greetings). It warns of impending doom, with a twist: users are told not to read any e-mail message with the words *Good Times* in the subject line because opening it will allow the virus to infect the computer's hard drive, erasing all your data and sending itself to everyone in your e-mail address book.

THE BEST MEDICINE

When you receive a warning about a deadly virus, it's not necessary to forward it to the entire universe, or even to those you care about most, as Irina urges. If you're working from an office, let your technical support staff know you've received such a message.

If you're at home, contact CIAC (the Computer Incident Advisory Capability) by e-mail at **ciac@llnl.gov** or visit their Web page for a current list of legitimate viruses (**http://ciac.llnl.gov**). You can also check the Computer Virus Myths Home Page (**www.kumite.com/myths/**) for a list of circulating hoaxes.

MORE DEVIOUS STRAINS

Until recently, viruses seldom traveled in text documents, so e-mail messages, word processing documents, spreadsheets and graphics files were inherently virus-free. And documents exchanged in ASCII text-only format, for example, were, for the most part, immune to hidden viruses.

But macro viruses, small pieces of programming code designed to perform a specific destructive act or series of acts, break all the rules. They can be carried in text documents and can perform under several different operating systems. The macro travels into the underlying document template, wreaking havoc with default page margins, font size and style, and other document basics.

The good news, though, is that most virus detection software can identify and deal with a macro-infected document.

ALL CREATURES, BIG AND SMALL

A **Trojan horse** is software that, like the ancient Greek gift, carries hidden lines of code that are capable of damaging your computer. Trojan horses aren't considered viruses themselves because they don't self-replicate and can't spread. And, in fact, they're not always harmful. But if the code a Trojan horse carries is infected, it can be picked up by detection programs.

Worms don't erase data like viruses but copy themselves over and over, spreading through an entire network until its systems are clogged and no information can move.

NO LITTLE LADY

A new macro virus called Melissa arrived uninvited into Microsoft's Outlook e-mail system on March 26, 1999. No little lady, Melissa's function was to kiss and tell—using a macro to examine the recipient's address book and causing Outlook to replicate and send the same message to the first 50 people in the directory.

Because Melissa was discovered on a Friday and widely publicized over the weekend, many companies were able to contain it on Monday morning.

Modems

Your computer's handshake with the outside world.

Computers talk digital. People speak and write analog. Modems are the universal interpreters, translating between analog and digital signals so we can communicate by computer.

Technically speaking, the modem **mod**ulates, or impresses, the digital signal onto the telecom network's continuous, analog wave. At the other end, another modem **dem**odulates, or changes the electrical signal back to digital bits that the receiving machine can process.

Here's what happens: when data travels on phone lines, the binary digits have to be converted to electrical waves. A modem works by shifting the frequency, phase or amplitude of the analog wave. This process makes the flat line of the analog carrier wave rise and fall, with each peak and valley representing a binary 0 or 1.

At the receiving end, another modem interprets the rises and falls as 0s and 1s, recreates them in the proper sequence, and sends them on to the computer or fax machine that's connected to the line. The digital stream also includes error-correcting bits so that noise or other problems on the line won't damage or cloud the data session.

TEST YOUR MODEM SPEED
Your connection speed (14.4, 28.8, 56K, etc.) can vary greatly depending on network conditions like traffic, the routing path, telephone

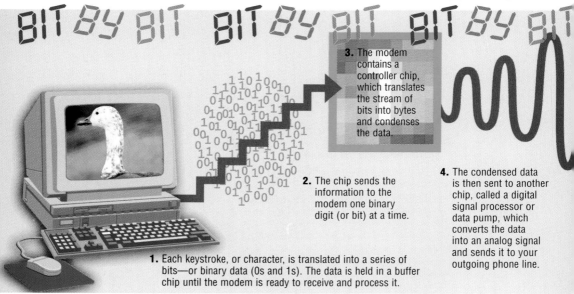

3. The modem contains a controller chip, which translates the stream of bits into bytes and condenses the data.

2. The chip sends the information to the modem one binary digit (or bit) at a time.

4. The condensed data is then sent to another chip, called a digital signal processor or data pump, which converts the data into an analog signal and sends it to your outgoing phone line.

1. Each keystroke, or character, is translated into a series of bits—or binary data (0s and 1s). The data is held in a buffer chip until the modem is ready to receive and process it.

GETTING ON BAUD
Modems are distinguished primarily by the maximum **baud rate**, or number of times a modem changes frequency, or tone, per second, though it's more accurately measured as **bits per second** (**bps**).

One baud was originally one symbol per second. The earliest modems could handle only 300 baud, while nowadays baud rates range from 75 baud up to 28,800 and beyond.

A modem's speed—typically 28,000 to 56,000 bps—describes how many bits per second of data it sends or receives. The larger the number, the faster the data moves, though the actual delivery rate is limited by the capacity of the phone lines it travels over. So it pays to check your phone lines before upgrading your modem to make sure you can take full advantage of the higher baud rate.

Advances in electronics and error-correcting software have improved the speed and reliability of transmission. The first modems used one frequency for 0 and another for 1, but modern versions transmit faster by using different pairs of frequencies, more compression and shorter codes. As a result, one baud is no longer one bit per second. For example, a 1200-bit-per-second modem actually runs at 300 baud, but it moves at 4 bits per baud (4 x 300 = 1200 bits per second).

BAUDY BEGINNING
The term *baud* was originally a unit of telegraph signaling speed, set at one Morse code dot per second. It was proposed at the International Telegraph Conference in 1927 and named after the French engineer J. M. E. Baudot, who constructed the first successful teleprinter.

line conditions, your modem settings, serial port settings, CPU speed, file compression factors, and more.

The Modem Speed Test (**http://members.aol .com/inventorr/modem/modem.html**) calculates the actual online speed of your current link to the Internet and contains helpful advice for optimizing your connection.

REPLACING YOUR MODEM

A modem may either be **internal** (built into your computer) or **external** (stand-alone), in which case it is connected to one of the computer's serial ports.

If the internal modem in your computer needs to be replaced or you want to upgrade it, you can have it done in a shop, or you can do it yourself. Few souls are brave enough to open up the computer's processor box, and you should be aware that you may violate your warranty by doing so.

However, it's fascinating to get a look inside. The internal modem is simply a card, which literally plugs into a slot. Changing it is a matter of loosening a few screws, pulling the old one out, and plugging the new one in. Of course, you have to install the drivers, or software, to let your computer know things have changed. A disk and instructions are included with your new modem.

BIT BY BIT BIT BY BIT BIT BY BIT

5. At the receiving end, a modem reconverts the analog signal to a stream of bits and bytes, and uncondenses the data.

6. The binary data is interpreted by the computer and presented as text and images on the receiving screen.

CABLE MODEMS

A **cable modem** is a device that allows high-speed data access through a cable TV (CATV) network. Cable modems allow you to download information at a speed 100 times faster than today's fastest telephone modems. In just 1.2 seconds, for example, you can download data that takes 20 minutes to transfer over a phone line. (See "Cable Able" in Chapter 2.)

SHAKING HANDS

Most modern modems support a number of different protocols or procedural languages. When first connected, two modems will automatically negotiate to find a common protocol.

Handshaking is the way modems agree on the way a transmission will be handled. The electrical connection between the two devices is called the interface. The interface, by translating the characteristics of one piece of equipment into the next, allows the devices to talk to one another.

SQUAWK BOX

When you connect to the Internet, you hear a series of squawking sounds. That's because your modem is actually "talking" to another modem. If you listen carefully, you'll notice that they run through a pattern of distinct noises that indicate testing or listening to the line, and adapting to the analog signal that will carry the transmission. These sounds loosely correspond to steps in the handshaking protocol:

1) the sending computer is ready,
2) the receiving computer is ready,
3) a request to send has been received,
4) the carrier has been detected,
5) it is now clear to send,
6) the data is transmitted, and
7) data is received.

On the Periphery

Printers, scanners, modems and other devices you attach to your computer are called peripherals.

You can scan images and text into your computer, or print them out in color or black and white.

While computers were once heralded as the dawn of the paperless society, the fact is that computers have generated even more paper. That's because people want to see in **hard copy**, or in print, what they've created on a screen.

Today, you can connect a wide range of desktop printers directly to your computer and essentially become your own publisher. And best of all, even high-quality printers are relatively inexpensive—and the prices keep coming down.

PUTTING IT ON PAPER

A printer manages the information it gets from the computer with a page description language (PDL) or with special software. The computer creates a temporary file, called a **print spool**, to hold the printing instructions. That lets you go ahead with other work while your documents are being printed.

A **printer driver** is a program that operates as an interface between the computer and the printer. It translates printing into computer code the printer can understand.

Laser printers use their own onboard RAM to process a computer file internally before actually printing it out. The more memory, the faster this translation process takes place, speeding up complicated print jobs involving lots of text and color graphics.

PUT IT IN PRINT

If you're buying a printer, the choice is between an **inkjet** and a **laser**. Inkjet printers, also known as bubble-jet printers, offer good print quality, excellent color reproduction, and relatively quiet operation at modest prices. An inkjet printer forms images by spraying ink from a matrix of tiny dots. It's also referred to as a nonimpact printer because the characters are not impressed on the paper (the way a typewriter key causes a letter to be struck against the paper).

Laser printers provide the highest-quality results, but they're more expensive than inkjets, especially the color versions. They also work differently. Using electrostatic reproduction technology (just like copy machines), the printer fuses text and graphic images to the page.

In comparing printers, you should consider the range of text, graphics and color it can

SCANNERS THAT READ

What if you've taken the ideal picture to illustrate your story about skydiving? Or find a rare shell that you'd like to show to a distant friend?

With a **scanner**, you can digitize, or reproduce an exact likeness of the images in digital form, then store them as electronic files. You can manipulate these images as you see fit, insert them into documents, turn them into post cards, put them on a Web page, or use them in dozens of other ways. (In fact, that's how the images on this page got where they are.)

If the material you scan is typed or handwritten, special software, called **Optical Character Recognition** (OCR) software, reads the text by:

- identifying all the dots in each letter
- distinguishing its outline, or shape
- comparing the shape with the shapes in its memory
- storing the letter in its ASCII value, the text-only version of letters and symbols in binary code

The scanned document, which can be edited or copied as you choose, appears as text on your screen in the same format as the original. You might scan in a recipe from a spaghetti box, for example, add a few ingredients or cooking instructions, and fax or e-mail it to a friend who volunteered to bring the main course to dinner. While not fool-

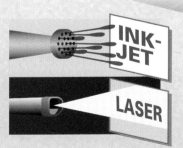

produce, the resolution—or quality—of the output, and the speed, which is measured as PPM, or pages per minute. Color printing is dramatically more time-consuming than black and white, though with increased memory, even the number of color PPMs is steadily climbing.

MEASURING QUALITY

When you talk about the quality of a scan or a print, you're talking about its resolution, or clarity. That depends on the number of **dots per square inch**, or **dpi**. The greater the dpi, the higher the resolution, and the sharper the image.

The type of resolution you need depends on what you want the scanner or printer to do. If you are using the scanner to convert documents into editable text with OCR, then you don't need the highest resolution. A 300-dpi or 400-dpi scanner will do fine. If you are scanning or printing color and grayscale halftone images, then you'll probably want a resolution of 600 dpi or more.

300 dpi

72 dpi

20 dpi

TYPES OF SCANNERS

Sheet-fed scanners work much like a plain-paper fax machine: you place a stack on a feed, and then the motor pulls the sheets through the machine and scans them one by one. Sheet-fed scanners can only accept flat sheets, so you can't scan pages bound in a book.

Flatbed scanners, while more expensive, provide the best results because they scan more precisely and don't move the original. You can scan both 2D and 3D objects, and by using a document feeder, you can scan a stack of pages without having to feed them in one at a time. Besides their cost, the chief disadvantage of flatbed scanners is that they take up a lot of space.

Hand-held scanners are moved slowly over an image or page of text and work well with irregular or curved surfaces.

There are also **slide scanners** and **film scanners** designed specifically to scan 35-millimeter slides, photographic negatives, or small 4" by 6" photographs, and scanners built to read business cards.

proof, OCR programs can translate more than 90% of the words they see correctly.

If you're going to use a lot of scanned material—especially scanned images—you'll need lots of memory. Experts estimate that a 4" by 4" black-and-white photograph scanned with an 8-bit scanner produces 5MB (megabytes) of data. For comparison, a high-density disk might hold 1.5MB.

COLOR AND GRAYSCALE

The other measure of quality is the number of shades a scanner can capture—either shades of color or shades of gray, known as the **grayscale**. Resolution is described either as the number of shades or colors, or as the number of bits required to represent them. In general, the more bits, the more precise the image you'll get.

Grayscale scanners can reproduce up to 256 shades, or 8 bits, of gray. Color scanners can provide 8-bit, 16-bit, 24-bit or 36-bit resolution. Sixteen-bit scanners offer 65,000 colors, and 24-bit scanners can reproduce the 16.7 million colors used in most color photos.

Buying a Computer

By checking around, you can find the right computer at the right price.

From the enormous variety that's available in the marketplace, you can find a computer ideally suited for handling the work you do, the games you play, or the way you use electronic communications systems.

For example, you may not need the fastest chip if you're doing primarily word processing. On the other hand, if you're a designer, you'll probably need a machine with lots of memory capacity. And if you're in constant touch with the World Wide Web, where color adds an important dimension, a higher-quality color monitor may be worth the extra money.

LAPTOP VS. PC

If you need a computer in only one place—your home office, for example—a desktop model may make the most sense. But if you want to have a computer handy wherever you are, or if space is a premium, it may pay to buy a laptop or note-book you can carry with you. You can get extra flexibility by buying a laptop with a **docking station,** which gives you access to a large monitor and a full-sized keyboard when you're at home or in the office but works as a laptop when you're on the road.

Or, if you're looking for a really compact device that you can use to send or receive e-mail, make phone calls, and get up-to-the-minute information from the Internet, you could consider hand-held equipment like AT&T's PocketNet Phone.

CHECKING IT OUT

New computer hardware and software are being introduced and evaluated all the time. So before you buy, it pays to check out how the current crop has been rated. Computer magazines are one source of information, as are feature articles in newspapers and magazines, or equipment surveys in guides like *Consumer Reports*. It also helps to talk to somebody who knows about computers, and who understands what you want your machine to do.

Some extras
Some computers come with external speakers, and a dealer may include graphics and sound cards, which are essential for enjoying multimedia programs.

Monitors
The size of the screen and clarity of the display are what you should consider when you buy a monitor. Dot pitch (or dots per inch) determines the quality of the images you're viewing. The lower the number, the higher the quality.

Processing power
A computer's processing power, or speed, determines how fast it can handle the tasks you want it to perform. The speed is measured in **megahertz (MHz)**, and generally speaking, the higher the MHz, the faster it can run programs, and the more complex tasks it can perform. Machines with an Intel Pentium II chip, which have 350MHz, are more than adequate for home use, and processors with even 225MHz can run most programs.

Hard drive capacity
The more capacity your hard drive has, the more information you can store. Currently most new machines come with a least a 4GB hard drive, and those with 6 to 10 gigabytes are becoming more common.

Memory

The more RAM you have, the faster your computer will perform. You need at least 32MB of RAM, which is fairly standard for a 200MHz machine.

Ask about the memory sockets on the motherboard or add-on memory boards to see how much more memory you can add. Experts suggest that you should plan for up to 64MB.

Cache

Cache is the part of RAM that's set aside to hold the data and program codes that your CPU uses as it handles each particular task. The current cache standard is 256K level-2 cache, one level for data and one for code, or programs.

Built-in features

Check to make sure the computer comes with a built-in CD reader. It's also helpful to have a built-in modem and, if you still have a lot of files on disk, a removable media drive.

Keyboards

Most computers come with a keyboard. But you may want to consider upgrading to an ergonomic keyboard, which is designed to let your hands rest in a more comfortable position as you type.

SOME BUYING TIPS

1. If you want a computer to send e-mail or browse the Web, virtually any new computer will work for you. You don't need a lot of power, or bells and whistles.

2. Consider buying your machine after the holiday shopping season, when prices are often reduced.

3. It may pay to buy an older machine when a new model comes out, since most existing computers can run the standard programs, such as word processing and spreadsheets.

4. If you're just getting your feet wet, or you're short on cash, look into leasing a computer. This may not be the best deal financially over the long haul, but it can get you up and running.

5. Check on the service ratings of the manufacturer so if something goes wrong, you can get the help you need. Publications like *PC Magazine* provide periodic ratings.

6. Make sure that the computer has enough processing power, memory and hard drive storage to run the software programs you want. If you're interested in games with multimedia presentations, you'll want a higher-powered machine. The package the software comes in lists the requirements.

The Internet

The merger of computing and communications has created the pipeline of plenty.

Perhaps no phenomenon better captures the unique character of the Information Age than the Internet. With its tumultuous growth and immense size, the Internet has captured the fancy of citizens and Wall Street alike, creating new businesses and new wealth as well as a new cybersociety.

Originally designed as a secure way to transmit military intelligence, the Internet has evolved into a vast global network made up of numerous smaller networks, all of which talk to each other.

Currently, the popular way to plug into this teeming cornucopia of information, commerce and entertainment is through a personal computer and phone line. But you can also get onto the Net through a box that sits on your TV connected via cable, or even through special digital phones that connect to the Net over the airwaves. Typically, you gain access to the Web through an **ISP**, or **Internet service provider**, who makes the connection from your home to a central computer, or server, which in turn connects you to the Internet. Some ISPs provide additional services, such as hosting your personal website on their computers.

> Remember, the *Internet* is a lot more than the *World Wide Web*, though the words are sometimes used to mean the same thing. The Web is only one of many networks, including e-mail, that make up the whole Net.

NET OFFERINGS

Once you're connected to the Internet, there are any number of things you can do.

Perhaps the most popular use of the Internet is **e-mail**, or electronic mail, a cyber-age postal service that lets you send messages, instead of post cards or letters, across the hall or across the world, in just moments. Not only can you can send e-mail to many people at once, but you can also attach entire documents or presentations that recipients download onto their computers.

The inherently social and populist culture of the Internet has spawned a number of **cybercommunities**, including newsgroups, mailing lists, message boards and chat rooms, that enable you to communicate with others with shared interests.

CAUGHT UP IN THE WEB

The Internet changed dramatically, and gained increasing popularity, with the advent of the **World Wide Web**—a special subset of the Internet where you can see pictures in color, animations and full-motion video as well as hear music and even converse with others. Access to the Web is provided by special software called a **browser** that lets you point to a specific website by keying in the site's unique address. The browser then displays the site's **home page** and helps you bring up and interact with the **content** of the site. By clicking on **hot links**—words, icons and images—you can move quickly to another part of the same site, or jump to another site altogether.

The Web abounds in **information tools**, such as search engines, databases and libraries. With a few clicks, you can bring to your computer screen all the works of William Shakespeare, entire dictionaries and encyclopedias, and countless collections of humor and word games. You can read any number of major newspapers every morning, follow a favorite columnist, or check on the weather anywhere in the world. You can also research a rare disease, track down a long-lost friend, or check out the ratings of local restaurants.

The Web has also spawned **e-commerce**. You'll find online retail stores, discount travel companies, and online auctions and swap meets where you can find both trash and treasures. You can configure and buy a computer, manage your finances and investments, and check on packages you've sent by overnight courier.

Entertainment on the Web ranges from movies and games to listening to the latest music, or even creating your own. You can also get your photographs over the Internet, as well as send them electronically to others.

YOU AND THE INTERNET

Of course, there's some practical knowledge you'll want to have, some tricks you'll want to learn, and some things you may want to avoid. But as you'll find out in the following pages, anyone can join and enjoy the Internet with little effort and relatively little expense. And most of all, it's fun.

THE INFORMATION YOU NEED

The Internet brings together in a highly dynamic way a number of separate but converging technologies—the increasing processing power of computers, the growing reach and sophistication of communications networks, and the evolution of multimedia as a means of presenting information in an entertaining way.

Graphics Video

Sound Animation

Buy Stocks Auctions for sale

NEW YORK STOCK EXCHANGE COMPUTER TRANSACTIONS

E. M. Ailer
0110010 Digital Way

LONDON

visit JAPAN

USENET

CULTURES

CURRENT SURFACE

4 SALE

FOR SALE

SeniorNet

CheckFree

Electronic Billing & Payment
  FINANCIAL INSTITUTIONS
  BILLERS
  CONSUMERS
Financial Services
  ACH
  COMPLIANCE
  HEALTH & FITNESS
  INVESTMENT SERVICES
  RECONCILIATION
  SBA/VAULT

About CheckFree
  News
  INVESTOR RELATIONS
  MEDIA RELATIONS
  EVENTS
  PARTNERSHIPS
  JOB OPPORTUNITIES
Contact Us

Search

THE THEORY OF LANGUAGE

An Introduction to Computer Science

THE WEATHER CHANNEL

Internet Plumbing

The Internet is a network of networks with its own connections and conventions.

The Internet is an ever-expanding amalgam of networks, software and linking devices that are seamlessly connected by physical wires, a shared computer language, and special technological and human conventions.

Each component of the Internet has a special function—whether storing information, directing the flow of messages, giving users access to the network, or keeping the different parts of the network in touch.

MILITARY INTELLIGENCE

What we've come to know as the Internet actually got its start in the US military in the 1960s. At that time, officials were concerned that a nuclear attack could completely wipe out communications between command posts. Working with university researchers and defense contractors, the military developed the **Automatic Voice Network**, or **AUTOVON**, which partially decentralized their systems so that even if one section was destroyed, the rest of the network would still function.

While the original network bears only a faint resemblance to what we think of as the Internet, several of the innovations, such as file transfer, electronic mail (or e-mail) and electronic mailing lists, are still in wide use today.

An **ISP**, or **Internet service provider**, gives you access to the Internet.

MANY NETWORKS, ONE LANGUAGE

The reason your computer can speak to someone else's on the Internet is that both machines speak a common electronic language, an agreed-upon set of procedures, or rules, called a **protocol**. The protocol used on the Internet is TCP/IP. **TCP** stands for **Transmission Control Protocol**. It manages the way data is sent and received on each computer. **IP**, or **Internet Protocol**, controls the way data is sent, or routed, across networks. This means a person in Japan using a Macintosh can send a message to someone in France using a PC—or the other way around. Neither the distance nor type of computer matters as long as the machines can communicate with each other.

HISTORY OF THE NET

1965
Hypertext, a method of preparing text that allows readers to choose their own pathways through the material, is invented by Ted Nelson. The underlined word represents a hyperlink that lets the reader click and jump to a new page. Strangely enough, it takes almost 30 years to catch on.

1969
The ARPANET is established by the Advanced Research Projects Agency (ARPA), connecting universities, the

military and defense contractors. In 1973, ARPA launches the Internetting Project to explore the possibilities of linking networks.

1976
UUCP (UNIX-to-UNIX CoPy) is developed at AT&T Bell Labs and distributed with UNIX one year later.

1979
USENET (the decentralized news group network), based on UUCP, is created by Steve Bellouin, Tom Truscott and Jim Ellis.

1986
The NSFNET, created by the National Science Foundation, is born, providing a national network. To many people, this becomes the true birth of the Internet.

1989
Quantum, formerly Q-Link online service for Atari and Commodore users, becomes AOL.

1991
Hypertext browsing software is proposed by Tim Berners-Lee, the inventor of the World Wide Web.

Information interconnected by hyperlinks is called a web. The Web is a hypertext system on a global scale. ANS, Advanced Network Systems, spins off to the NSFNET to form ANS CO_+RE and becomes the first commercial ISP. Its mission is to foster commercial and research networking opportunities.

1992
The Internet Society (ISOC) is founded, incorporating the

Internet Architecture Board. The ISOC's primary function is to foster international participation and cooperation in Internet technologies. Membership is open to all.

1993
The US envisions an Information Superhighway, formally known as the National Information Infrastructure (NII), to provide a system

SERVERS, ANYONE?

When you connect to the Internet, your computer is dialing into another computer called a **server**, which **hosts**, or contains, files, databases and other information you can access. Every network has at least one server—sometimes more. Internet servers are sometimes referred to as Internet **nodes**, hosts or hubs.

ELECTRONIC PAPER PUSHING

File Transfer Protocol, or **FTP**, lets you get hold of, or retrieve, files from remote computers. It also lets you download documents to your own computer.

CRASH!

Even if a part of the Internet were destroyed, the rest of it would live on.

ROUTERS: DIRECTING THE FLOW OF MESSAGES

With all the traffic on the Internet, some direction and control is needed. This job is handled by **routers**, which are links, or interfaces, within and between networks. Like telecom switches, they find the best routes for messages to travel over the networks, much as a traffic cop directs the flow of vehicles through busy intersections. Specialized routers, called IP (Internet Protocol) routers, connect individual networks to the Internet.

of interconnected networks linking every citizen to multiple sources of information and means of communication.

Also in 1993, Mosaic, the first navigation browser to make use of graphics and a point-and-click interface, is developed by Marc Andreessen. Internet traffic proliferates at a 341% annual growth rate.

1994
Netscape, co-founded by Marc Andreessen and James Clark, dramatically increases the popularity of the Web by incorporating video, sound and animation into their browser.

1995
Sun Microsystems introduces Java, a programming language that makes animation and other interactive features commonplace.

Also in 1995, Traditional online services (Compuserve, AOL and Prodigy) begin to provide commercial Internet access. The following year AT&T introduces its ISP.

1997
The Internet comprises an estimated 134,000 individual networks, and the number keeps growing. Competing browsers, including Microsoft's Internet Explorer, appear.

1998
The Web grows from 130 sites in 1993 to over 2 million sites, and the number keeps going up. Not only are more people using the Web, but more people, as well as companies and organizations, are launching their own sites.

Choosing an ISP

Getting on the Net is easier when you know what questions to ask.

To gain access to the Internet you need:

1. an **access device**, which is usually a computer but can also be a TV with a set-top box.

2. a **modem**, which may be stand-alone or built into your computer. The modem converts digital output from your computer to send over analog lines and also converts incoming analog signals into digital form so your computer can interpret them.

3. a **physical connection**, typically a phone line or cable, but there are also special high-performance ISDN or T-1 lines. You can also try WebTV, which uses your television as a screen for surfing the Net, or you can consider wireless connections via satellite.

4. an **Internet service provider**, or **ISP**—an organization that links you to the Internet through its own proprietary network.

INITIAL CONTACTS

ISPs usually offer an Internet software package on floppy disk or CD ROM free of charge. The installation software usually walks you through the setup process, asks you to select a password, and dials in to the ISP's network to establish your new account.

The installation software configures, or sets up, your modem and the networking controls for your computer. It also downloads an e-mail program, Web browser, newsreader or other software, depending on which programs your ISP includes in its introductory package.

Once the installation is completed, your ISP's number is programmed into your computer's software. The next time you click the Internet icon on your screen, your modem automatically dials the number and establishes contact.

When the connection is made, you identify yourself by typing your user name and password, a process called **logging on**. Once you're logged on, you have access to all the far-reaching parts of the Internet. You can surf the Web, read newsgroups, send and receive e-mail, chat with others, or download files.

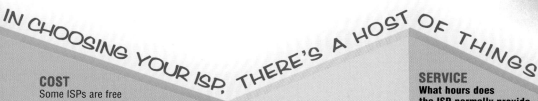

IN CHOOSING YOUR ISP, THERE'S A HOST OF THINGS

COST
Some ISPs are free for members of a sponsoring organization, such as a university or a corporation. Or you may be able to use freenet connections through your public library.

Is there a setup fee?
Most ISPs no longer charge a setup fee, so be sure to check if there is one.

Does the ISP provide a flat rate account?
If the ISP doesn't charge a flat rate per month for unlimited usage, ask how many hours per week or month are included. Remember, while you may start out using the Internet only occasionally, chances are your usage will increase over time.

PHONE LINES
Does the ISP provide dial-up numbers in your local area?
Check your White Pages or phone company to be sure the number you call is local.

Is there an 800 number you can use?
This is useful if you travel a lot and want to check your e-mail from the road. Many large ISPs provide local dial-up numbers in heavily populated areas.

SOFTWARE
Is the software for connecting to the Internet included in the price?
It should be, at no extra cost.

Will customer support guide you through the process of installing the software?
If not, you may want a friendlier provider.

Does the ISP provide its own browser?
Some ISPs require you to use their software, not allowing the use of Netscape, for example. You probably want a choice of browsers.

Does the ISP mail you the software or can you access it through a dial-up connection?
Once you have chosen your ISP, you may be able to enroll, install the necessary software, and connect to the Internet simply by using your telephone.

SERVICE
What hours does the ISP normally provide technical support?
You may find yourself frustrated and seeking support on weekends or late at night, particularly if you are connecting at home rather than at your place of business.

How difficult is it to get through to the technical support line?
You can test this out by calling the support line number for yourself before you sign up. And check to see if the support line is an 800 number, which can save you money on a call, especially if the lines are busy and you're put on hold.

Is there an alternative dial-up number?
The main number may sometimes be out of service.

WHAT INTERNET SERVICE PROVIDERS PROVIDE

ISPs offer a range of software programs and varying levels of service, technical advice and support. Since competition is intense in many areas, you often have a wide range of choices.

BASIC LOCAL PROVIDERS

Basic-service ISPs tend to be smaller local companies that offer direct access to the Internet. Most of the reputable ones have local dial-up numbers, provide the software for connecting you to the Internet, and offer technical support.

FULL-SERVICE PROVIDERS

Full-service ISPs, such as AT&T's Worldnet or America Online, offer more to their members than basic connection and support. For example, they typically provide:

- Free Web hosting services that let you maintain your own website
- Several phone numbers you can call in case one is out of service (this type of backup is also known as multiple POPs—points of presence)
- National and often international local access so that, if you travel, your connection to your ISP is always a local call
- Extensive technical support if you need help—the level and type of service provided is often the main differentiator among full-service providers

TO CONSIDER:

RELIABILITY
What is the average connection rate?
The connect success rate measures how many customers successfully connect to the Internet on their first try. The industry average is 93.1%.

What is the ISP's connection speed?
The higher the speed of the transmission between the ISP and your computer, the quicker the access you'll have to the Internet, and the faster you'll be able to move around it. Speed is measured in kilobytes per second, or Kbps—for example 28Kbps, 56Kbps, etc.

PRIVACY
Will the ISP give out personal information?
Some service providers do this. Make sure they won't do so without your permission.

WHO'S IN CHARGE?
Every ISP has a **systems administrator**, a person responsible for making sure the network is operating properly. Usually, the systems administrator will send you a welcoming message when you sign up and e-mails about downtimes, upgrades and potentially harmful viruses.

WHERE TO FIND AN ISP
To find an ISP, watch the ads in computer and Internet magazines, such as *Wired* or *Internet World*. Your phone company is also likely to offer Internet service. There are ads in newspapers as well. Ask your friends if they would recommend their ISP to you.

And if your local library has Internet access, you can go online and do some comparison shopping at **www.thelist.com**. This site maintains comprehensive listings of ISPs all over the world and will lead you through the process of finding an ISP best suited to your needs.

Internet Traffic

The quickest route isn't necessarily the shortest.

When you key in an e-mail address to send someone e-mail, you are initiating an electronic race to get your message delivered as quickly as possible.

By way of analogy, think of your message as the pages of a document that are being sent across town by bicycle messenger. Each page of the document is taken by a different messenger. Given potential traffic congestion and other delays along the way, each messenger may take a different route and arrive at a different time, so the document does not arrive in the same order it was sent. However, since each page has a unique identification, the document can be easily reassembled in

the right order when it reaches its destination.

In actual practice, your message travels across a number of relay points, controlled by **routers**, whose job it is to find the most efficient path across any number of interconnected networks. Rather than sticking with one path from start to finish, routers may switch the data packets from one path to another to complete the circuit in the most efficient way.

Each race—and there are multimillions of them going on simultaneously—is completed in a matter of seconds, or less.

1. Your computer creates digital data packets that contain both your message and the unique address you're sending it to—think of it as a postal address and zip code. Your computer doesn't recognize the address—only that it's another computer on the network. The packets are transmitted through your Internet connection—for example, by phone line or cable—to your ISP (Internet service provider), which may be local, national or even international.

2. Each router, either at your local ISP or at a major network, reads the address and selects the most efficient physical pathway—over the phone and cable lines operated by telecommunications companies—for the packet to travel. The router sends the packet along and then hands it off to the next router along the way.

3. The packets may get routed to a large network interchange—think of it as a major traffic circle—where a number of different networks come together. There the packet may get switched from one ISP's network router to another router operated by a different ISP.

4. Eventually, the packet is handed off to another router, located at the destination server site. (Many companies that receive a large number of messages—think of a large mailroom in a major corporation—maintain their own routers to better regulate the traffic flow.)

5. Finally, the packet arrives at its destination, where the digital data is reconverted into text, graphics and images that appear on your computer screen.

The Client-Server Model

You need special software and setups to send or retrieve files over the Internet.

Moving data from one place to another—a process known as **file transfer**—is a way of life in the Information Age.

When you load software onto your computer, for example, you transfer files from a diskette or CD ROM to your hard drive. If you copy a document from your computer to a diskette, you transfer the file through your floppy disk drive.

You can also transfer files directly between computers or systems as well as over the Internet. This kind of file transfer is called **downloading** when the files are moved to your computer and **uploading** when you transfer files from your computer to a server.

FOLLOWING PROTOCOLS

Transferring files between systems involves accessing a remote computer called the **server**. The server may be a mainframe computer that stores vast amounts of data and files, or an **application server** that stands between a mainframe and your computer, making it easier to access and manipulate the data.

Many businesses have at least one and sometimes multiple servers that store their corporate records and let their employees share this information. The server usually has a special name, such as Poke or SRV1120, and is typically accessed by clicking an icon on the computer's desktop or main screen.

Your own computer is called the **client**, and the entire setup is called the client-server model. The model can only work, however, if there's a common language and procedures for getting the information from one place to another. That's where the protocol comes in.

A **protocol** is an agreed-upon set of standards, or rules, for preparing data to be sent from one computer to another. Protocols handle how the information is compressed, sent, and then decompressed, and how the transmission is checked for accuracy—a process known as **error detection**.

YOUR COMPUTER   **YOUR ISP**

THE KEYS TO THE FILE

An **FTP** (or **File Transfer Protocol**) server can, and usually does, store a huge array of files, some of which are available to the public and some that are not. A university, for example, might maintain a site with both public and private directories.

Students and professors are assigned individual user names and given a password that identifies them to the system, allowing them access to specified private files—test scores, for example, or lecture transcripts.

When users outside the university access the network, however, the computer needs a way to identify them. The solution is Anonymous FTP. That means your user name is *anonymous* and your password is your e-mail address. That combination

identifies you to the system as a member of the Internet-using public.

The system automatically routes you to its public directories but doesn't give you access to the rest. However, it may sometimes be hard to connect to the site you're looking for because there may be a limit on the number of connections permitted at any one time or during peak user hours.

FTP USER
Anonymous
me@mysite.com

SERVERS

VIRUS CHECKING

You run the risk of getting **viruses** if you download software programs. Every year virus writers get more clever and make it more difficult to avoid picking up their viruses. If you've installed antiviral software—always a smart move—it will detect the problem and take care of it. (See "Viruses" in Chapter 3.)

If you've downloaded a virus from an FTP site on the Internet, you should notify the **system administrator** at your ISP so the virus can be wiped out at the source.

COMPRESSION

Since most files stored on a server are **compressed** to save space, you'll need a program to **decompress** these files when you download them to restore their full form and content.

You can use a file decompression utility, like WINZIP for Windows PCs or Stuffit Expander for Macintosh.

These programs are available via FTP in numerous locations on the Internet. You can visit the newsgroup **comp.compression** (see "Usenet" in this chapter) or use a search engine to look for *compression utilities* for suggestions on where to find the files you need.

WINZIP

File compression programs like this one combine groups of similar files and compress them simultaneously. This not only frees up storage space on host computers and speeds up transmission times but keeps related material together.

Stuffit

A program for Macintosh that compresses files before transferring them and decompresses them automatically when you download, restoring them to useable format.

DOWNLOADING FILES

There are two ways to access files: using your Web browser or using special software, called an **FTP client program**, like Fetch. In either case, downloading the files is simply a matter of clicking your mouse to start the process. There are two types of files that you can download:

- **ASCII files**, which are text only
- **Binary files**, which include software programs, sound files and graphics files

ASCII (American Standard Code for Information Interchange) is the worldwide standard for the binary code numbers used by computers to represent all upper- and lower-case Latin letters, numbers and punctuation.

Sometimes you need to tell the FTP server to switch from ASCII to binary if you want to download programs or multimedia files.

UPLOADING FILES

Although your Web browser can handle most downloading functions, you will probably need to use special client software for uploading, especially if you want to transfer large files, like Web pages with sound or graphics.

Some sites set aside space for the public to use for uploaded files—which is useful if you want to exchange a large file with a friend, for example, or post the Great American Novel you've written to a public forum. Keep in mind, though, that FTP sites are run by real people. Overuse or misuse of public space can prompt a site administrator to close down the public directories.

E-mail Is the Way to Go

The first thing most people do on the Internet is send e-mail.

E-mail, one of the most common uses of the Internet, is an electronic mail service that lets you send messages to anyone else on the Net. There are tens of millions of users of e-mail who transmit trillions of messages a year. The Internet is growing so rapidly that it's become difficult to calculate exactly how many users there are today.

For many people, using e-mail is as easy as—or easier than—dashing off a post card or sending a letter by "snail mail." You can send messages any time of the day or night and usually get them through right away. You can also send the same message simultaneously to several people in different locations.

Lets you include the text of a message you are replying to.

Allows you to attach any file to your e-mail. Simply click on the icon and then select the file you want to send from your file menu.

Send

Send Quote Address Attach Sp

To ▼ bdoe@add

Cc ▼ cdoe@add

Subject: Hello

Hi Mom,

I heard from Sis about Dad'

Speaking of Sis, IMHO she r

BTW, loved the fruitcake,

TTFN,

Anne

Through sleet and snow and gloom of Net

Recipients can often retrieve their e-mail no matter where they are, as long as they have access to the Internet.

E-mail lets you communicate when you don't want to talk to someone directly, or when you want your message to provide instructions, back-up information or other details that a listener might miss or ignore. In addition to the message, you can attach documents or other files to your e-mail and send them over the Internet as well.

E-MAIL CARRIERS

Once you're connected to the Net with an account and an e-mail address, all you need is an e-mail software program like Eudora, Outlook Express or Claris Works to get started. In addition, browsers such as Netscape Communicator or Microsoft Internet Explorer include an e-mail program as part of their package, and you can get e-mail accounts on **portals**, or gateways, to various services, such as Yahoo, Excite or Lycos, or through Juno (**www.juno.com**), for free. Internet services like America Online (AOL) and AT&T's Worldnet provide e-mail for their subscribers, and many people use an e-mail address provided by their ISP.

E-MAIL (IL)LITERACY

Some experts maintain that e-mail is good for literacy since it has people writing again. But not everyone is convinced that literacy is the right term for the hasty, often endless outpourings that find their way into e-mail.

E-MAIL QUICKSPEAK

If you're looking for a way to save space in your messages, try an acronym.

AFAIK	as far as I know
BTW	by the way
FWIW	for what it's worth
FYI	for your information
IMHO	in my humble opinion
LOL	laughing out loud
ROTFL	rolling on the floor laughing
SEMA	some exceptions may apply
TTFN	ta-ta for now
TIA	thanks in advance
WRT	with regard to
WTG	way to go
WB	welcome back

Every e-mail address contains the same basic sections

All e-mail addresses follow the same convention: **user@domain**. The user can be a simple name such as *jdoe*, or more complicated, like *Jonathan_DoeHR* for some corporate users. The domain can be any set of names separated by a dot, such as *internetcorp.employees.forms.com*. Domain names must be registered—you can't simply invent one. You can check on the availability of an address and register it at **www.register.com** or at InterNic (**www.internicregistrations.com**).

Every part of an e-mail address is essential and must be exact: extra spaces, typos or abbreviations will mean the message can't be delivered.

Fortunately, you don't have to retype an e-mail address each time you use it. Most programs provide a mini-database, called an **address book**, that lets you store the addresses of incoming mail. Most programs also let you assign an alias, or name, to each address so you can click on *Jane* instead of typing out *jane@worldnet.att.net* when you're ready to send Jane a message.

And if you use the *Reply* command, the e-mail address is automatically filled in.

WHAT YOU SEE

E-mail messages always appear on your screen in the **default font**, or typeface, for your system. So options such as bold or italic text may be converted into unintelligible symbols (like > or •) at the other end. And lines of text may break differently on your screen than they do on someone else's, so don't depend on stylistic options to enhance the meaning of your text.

That's not the case with attached files, though. They carry their own formatting information with them, so what you send should look the same on your recipient's screen, provided he or she has the necessary software to read them.

DAEMONS

A **daemon** is not a devil but (on certain systems) a helpful piece of software that runs constantly in the background—announcing, for example, when new e-mail arrives in your mailbox.

WHAT'S IN A DOMAIN NAME?
The abbreviation at the far right of the @ sign in an e-mail address is called the **domain** name. It may include the name of the ISP you're using, your company's name, or a name you've created and registered yourself. In addition, in the United States, there are a number of top-level domains that work like Internet zip codes. The most common are:

.com business and commercial organizations (editor@lightbulbpress.com)

.edu educational institutions (provost@harvard.edu)

.gov government bureaus and agencies (president@whitehouse.gov)

.mil military agencies and installations (general@pentagon.mil)

.net network resources, like an ISP (majordomo@att.net)

.org other organizations, usually nonprofit (producer@pbs.org)

There are also a number of international domains, the equivalent of including a country name at the bottom of a conventional street address. For example, **.jp** stands for Japan, **.uk** for the United Kingdom, **.au** for Australia.

Usenet
Looking for a perfect soapbox? Try the electronic version.

Usenet makes it possible to communicate with people around the world who are interested in the same things you are. You can ask questions, provide answers, follow a discussion, or join a debate any time of the day or night from wherever you are, as long as you have a computer link that lets you send and read messages through special software called a **newsreader**.

HEY! I'M LOOKING TO FIND LEONBERGERS— ANY LEADS?

MAKING THE LINK
Usenet is a worldwide network of **host** computers that store and forward all the messages that have been posted, or e-mailed, to the various individual newsgroups—about 30,000 of them in late 1998. Each host gets and passes on messages, which are also called **articles** or **netnews**, to other hosts.

Some people have compared the process to a chain letter or a telephone chain. The host lets you, and anyone else who's interested, read what's posted and then respond with comments or questions. Those contributions are then forwarded through the network so other users can read and react to them.

CHECK OUT THE LEONBERGER CLUB OF AMERICA AT WWW.LEONBERGER.COM.

MY LEONBERGER PLAYS WITH BOWLING BALLS, IF YOU CAN BELIEVE IT!

POSTING NOTES IN CYBERSPACE
The newsreader software you need to access Usenet is generally included in your ISP's introductory package. A helpful place to start is the Usenet Info Center Launch Pad at **http://metalab.unc.edu/usenet-i**.

All newsreaders contain three basic sections: the **newsgroup listing**, the **message listing**, which lets you find a specific article, and the **message text**. To participate in a particular newsgroup regularly, you subscribe to it, or add the name to your personal list of newsgroups. There's no fee or official registry, and you can drop out at any time simply by not keeping up. And you don't have to subscribe to go **lurking**, or browsing without posting your own messages.

To add a specific newsgroup, you need to know its name. To locate newsgroups that interest you, use a Web search engine such as Dejanews at **www.dejanews.com**. If you type your topic into the interest box, Dejanews presents a list of newsgroups that discuss that issue. Portals such as Yahoo!, Excite or Lycos can also be set to search through Usenet, providing lists of specific postings on a topic.

IS IT FOR REAL?
One criticism leveled against Usenet is that it allows people—including quacks and those with specific agendas—to spread rumors that others accept as gospel. It's not the only forum for misinformation—just the most recent.

DON'T FORGET MAILING LISTS
Mailing lists, like newsgroups, are sources of information posted by experts or enthusiastic amateurs. Instead of using a specialized program, however, mailing lists use e-mail for communicating. To join, you simply subscribe, and each time you send e-mail it's automatically forwarded to every other subscriber on the list.

To find a list that is likely to have the information that you want, try looking through the Publicly Accessible Mailing Lists site at **www.neosoft.com/internet/paml**. Most lists have a **FAQ** (**Frequently Asked Questions**) that provides answers to common questions.

FOLLOWING THE THREAD
A series, or string, of related Usenet postings is called a **thread**. Threads can be simple, such as a single question and a response, or complex, such as debate involving numerous participants from around the world and lasting several weeks or even months.

A single newsgroup, say one devoted to American music, might contain a number of different threads—one for Duke Ellington and another for Louis Armstrong, for example—covering narrower aspects of a broader subject.

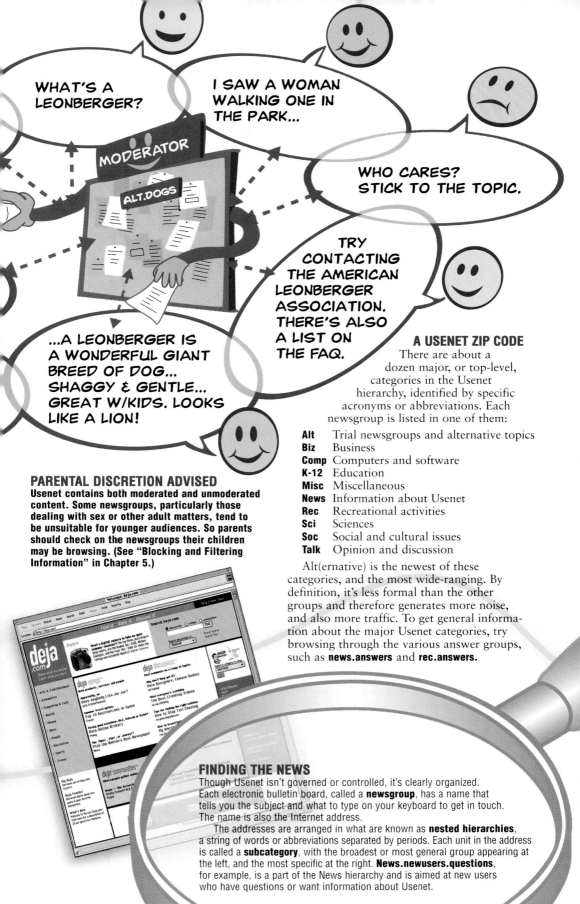

A USENET ZIP CODE

There are about a dozen major, or top-level, categories in the Usenet hierarchy, identified by specific acronyms or abbreviations. Each newsgroup is listed in one of them:

Alt   Trial newsgroups and alternative topics
Biz   Business
Comp Computers and software
K-12 Education
Misc Miscellaneous
News Information about Usenet
Rec   Recreational activities
Sci   Sciences
Soc   Social and cultural issues
Talk Opinion and discussion

Alt(ernative) is the newest of these categories, and the most wide-ranging. By definition, it's less formal than the other groups and therefore generates more noise, and also more traffic. To get general information about the major Usenet categories, try browsing through the various answer groups, such as **news.answers** and **rec.answers**.

PARENTAL DISCRETION ADVISED

Usenet contains both moderated and unmoderated content. Some newsgroups, particularly those dealing with sex or other adult matters, tend to be unsuitable for younger audiences. So parents should check on the newsgroups their children may be browsing. (See "Blocking and Filtering Information" in Chapter 5.)

FINDING THE NEWS

Though Usenet isn't governed or controlled, it's clearly organized. Each electronic bulletin board, called a **newsgroup**, has a name that tells you the subject and what to type on your keyboard to get in touch. The name is also the Internet address.

The addresses are arranged in what are known as **nested hierarchies**, a string of words or abbreviations separated by periods. Each unit in the address is called a **subcategory**, with the broadest or most general group appearing at the left, and the most specific at the right. **News.newusers.questions**, for example, is a part of the News hierarchy and is aimed at new users who have questions or want information about Usenet.

The Chat Room

People are getting together online as members of Internet communities.

A community usually refers to a geographical area where people live or work. But groups with common interests also form communities, and the Net, with its diversity of users, has been a natural spawning ground for newly formed Information Age communities.

Sometimes dubbed **cyberhoods**, these Net-based communities provide places to socialize and pass the time. They also provide an important bonding experience for their **netizens**, whose interactions range from businesslike communications to frivolous conversation.

HOW COMMUNITIES COMMUNICATE

Cyberhoods often provide both a **message board** system and opportunities for **real-time chat**. A message board allows you to post a query, state an opinion, or simply leave an essay for the consideration of others. Events like this are described as occurring **asynchronously**. As other users find the **post**, they may or may not add to it, establishing a line of conversation known as a **thread**.

In real-time chat situations, or **RTC**, you converse much as you would in person or on the phone. You say something, people hear it and respond, and you hear their responses, all nearly simultaneously. Of course, your conversation is typed and not spoken.

RTC is often like being at a crowded party. There are any number of people present, and many threads of conversation occurring all at once. As a result, the conversation may be much more random than the content you find in a message board system.

HOME, HOME ON THE NET

Net-based communities don't develop by accident. They're generally initiated by an individual or organization, either as a commercial venture aimed at a specific audience or as a way to build on or respond to a particular interest. For example, Tripod has created a community for twentysomethings, while iVillage's Parent Soup enables parents of small children to share experiences and advice. SeniorNet lets older adults participate in a community without having to leave home.

Internet pundits maintain that adding a chat forum boosts traffic on a website as much as 50%. They also say that chat visitors stay longer during each site visit as well. Website communities attract advertising dollars because they provide an ideal audience for targeted messages, or what is known as **narrowcasting**.

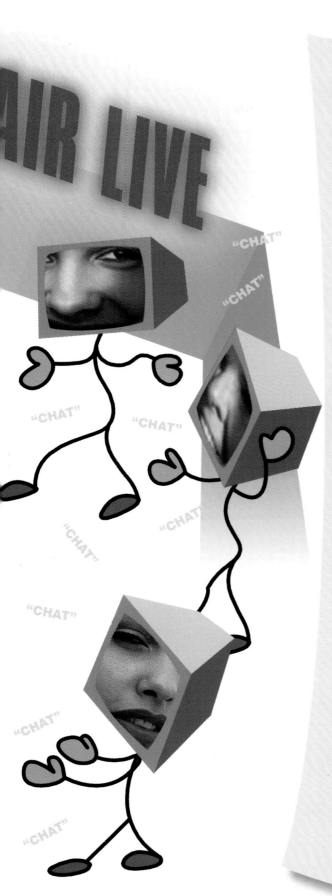

"CHAT" "CHAT" "CHAT" "CHAT" "CHAT" "CHAT" "CHAT" "CHAT" "CHAT"

CHATTING IT UP

Internet Relay Chat, or **IRC**, is one of the most popular chat facilities on the Net. Getting onto and using IRC, however, involves more than using your browser to access a message board system or chat room.

IRC allows people to get together on various channels—which are basically virtual rooms for conversation. You need a chat client, such as the Windows-based mIRC, which can be downloaded for free, and you need to know a little about the command protocols, or language, to participate. There are thousands of pages of "help" about IRC on the Net. A good starting place is the IRC help archive at **www.irchelp.org**.

Freenets, or community-based **bulletin board systems** (**BBS**), are a blend of cyber- and real communities. Like message boards, they are organized and updated by actual communities, like a college or a city. BBS provide access to a range of computer databases that you can dial up for information about political and cultural events, medical services and other information about a particular place.

GETTING IN TOUCH

Online chat has gotten very personalized. There are a number of simple programs you can easily download that let you communicate one-to-one with someone you know. These programs inform you when a friend is online and allow you to converse with them in real time. In some cases, you can even hear your friend's voice while you're in the chat room. And it's free. You can visit the following websites and download the program and instructions there:

AT&T I M Here at **www.att.net/comm__center**

AOL Instant Messenger at **www.aol.com**

ICQ at **www.mirabilis.com**

PAL Personal Access List at **www.excite.com**

PeopleLink at **www.peoplelink.com**

Pager at **www.ichat.com**

Yahoo Pager at **http://pager.yahoo.com**

The World Wide Web

For many people, surfin' the Web is what being online is all about.

After e-mail, visiting sites on the World Wide Web is the most popular use of the Internet. The main difference between the Web and other parts of the Internet is the way it looks on your screen and how you navigate within it.

For example, if you were reading this book on your computer screen, you could click on the word **hypertext** in this sentence and go directly to a definition. You could click on a different word in that definition and get another definition, a piece of related information, or a graphic image. You could then click back to the original screen or go somewhere else. You can go on linking from one page to another literally without end, making the Web a boundless system.

Technically, the Web consists of a **protocol**, or set of rules for exchanging information, called **HTTP (HyperText Transfer Protocol)** and a data format that determines what gets displayed on your screen, called **HTML (HyperText Markup Language)**.

AT&T has created a prototype service using their own **Phone Markup Language**, which allows you to use your phone as a browser if you don't have a computer.

GRAPHICS GALORE

Not too long ago, the Web was a collection of static documents, comprised of text and a few pictures. Now websites routinely feature photographs, interactive forms and tables, marquee-like animations, and blinking headlines.

The catch is, the higher the graphic content, the longer the Web page takes to load onto your screen. But new formats are being developed, along with quicker speeds and wider bandwidths, to allow faster loading as well as richer, more varied graphic content.

HITTING THE LINKS

If you want to visit a site you have read about, you type in an address called the **URL**, or **Universal Resource Locator**. The URL is a string of characters that describes—without ambiguity—the location of a discrete piece of information anywhere on the Internet. Each part of the URL has a specific meaning. For example, **http://www.lightbulbpress.com/custom/index .html** would translate like this:

http:// means HyperText Transfer Protocol, which is the agreed-on set of procedures used on the World Wide Web.

WEBSITES

A **website** can be a Web page, a collection of related Web pages, or the physical location of a Web server that hosts a particular site.

For example, Paris's Catacombs website provides historical and structural information about the underground network of rooms and passages but isn't physically located under the streets of Paris. In contrast, the website of the University of Colorado in Boulder is actually located within the University.

Websites also range from the very simple to the extremely complex. A personal site might consist of a single page, called a **home page** or welcome page, and have many links to other sites. A large commercial site, on the other hand, might contain hundreds of pages linked to each other but have few, if any, external links.

FINANCES ONLINE

The Web is fast becoming the haven for personal finance and investing. You can keep up on the latest news and financial analyses, or open a brokerage account and buy stocks, bonds and mutual funds online.

You can also bank electronically through virtual and online banks, which let you pay bills, transfer funds and do a host of other banking transactions from any computer with an Internet connection and a Web browser.

In 1995, approximately 250,000 people in the United States used some form of online banking. Less than two years later, that number had grown to 2.5 million, a 1,000% increase. Today, 25% of the population banks online.

www.lightbulbpress.com is the host name, or server administering the site. (**www** identifies the World Wide Web, **lightbulbpress** is the name of the host, and **.com** is the top-level domain, indicating that Lightbulb Press is a business or organization.)

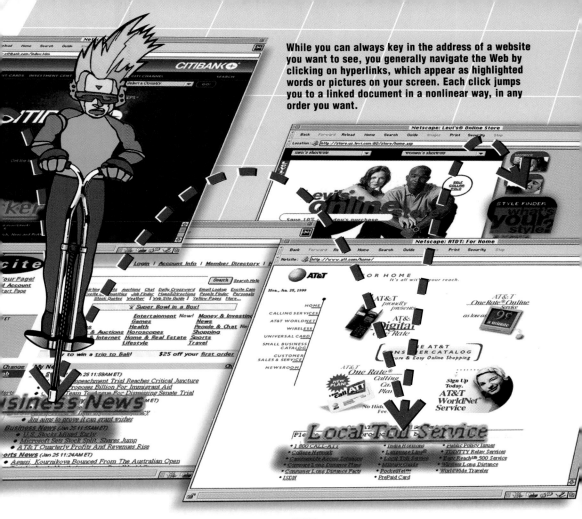

While you can always key in the address of a website you want to see, you generally navigate the Web by clicking on hyperlinks, which appear as highlighted words or pictures on your screen. Each click jumps you to a linked document in a nonlinear way, in any order you want.

RETAIL SERVICES

Online shopping is becoming big business. You can purchase just about anything—from cars to blue jeans to airline tickets. And you can use **intelligent agents** (software that keeps track of your preferences) to comparison shop the products or services you want to purchase. Best of all, online stores never close, so you can always shop at your own convenience.

Though electronic retailing is in its infancy, Forrester Research reported $530 million in transactions in 1996 and predicts $7 billion by 2000.

ENTERTAINMENT

You can play games online, from chess to bridge, and you can find thousands of crossword puzzles and word games. You can visit virtual art galleries and listen to music. You can read the paper, check local TV listings, and watch a music video.

JAVA

Programming languages like Java are contributing to the graphic richness of the Web, providing such features as animations, moving banners and automatically scrolling text boxes.

When you reach a Web page that has an embedded **Java applet** (an applet is a small program embedded in a Web document), the program is transmitted to your computer, and the browser runs the program. The program may be a game of some sort, a multimedia display, a financial calculator or detailed maps.

Examples of helpful, well-designed Java programs can be found on Microsoft's travel site, Expedia, at **www.expedia.com** and MapQuest at **www.mapquest.com**. These programs let you select an area and then zoom in from a state or county to a street address.

Somewhat easier for developers to use than Java is JavaScript. There are many JavaScript programs available at **www.developer.com**.

/custom tells the host or server exactly which of the directories you need to retrieve a file from.

/index.html is the specific file you are requesting.

s.com/custom/index.htm

Browsers

Your browser lets you focus on the websites you want to see.

You can easily access all parts of the World Wide Web through special software called a **browser**. You can point your browser to a specific site by keying in the unique address or selecting a site you've already "book-marked," or stored. The browser will then display the website on your screen, giving you direct access to the information and other functions there.

WHICH MODEL?

If your ISP provides a browser as part of its installation package, it's probably simplest to start with that one. New computers generally come loaded with a browser as well. Netscape Communicator and Microsoft Internet Explorer are two of the most popular, and you'll find that they both do the job of getting you around the Web. One of the nice things about Web browsers is that, like cars, they all look and act similarly, so if you know how to operate one, you can operate them all.

STARTING FROM HOME

When you start up your browser, the first thing you see is your **home page** or **start page**. A good start page can have links that take you to sites you want to visit frequently, such as the day's news headlines, stock quotes, weather reports and search engines.

Many ISPs arrange to have their own start page displayed as a part of the installation process. But you can custom create your own start page using one of the new customizing systems both Netscape and Explorer offer in their browsers (**www.netscape.com/custom/index.html** and **www.microsoft.com/windows/ie**). You can select exactly what links you'll use most often, include a notepad for reminders, and create your own headline or greeting.

A similar but more comprehensive service is provided by My Excite, My Yahoo and My Netscape. These online services collect data about the information you want to see frequently and then create a personalized page as the start or **default** page. The default page can contain a wide range of items, such as specific types of news, local and national weather forecasts, sports scores, stock quotations, horoscopes and state lottery results.

Personalized pages may also feature links to favorite sites, daily health tips, travel alerts and reminders of specific occasions, such as birthdays and anniversaries.

TRAVERSING THE LABYRINTH

Jumping from link to link on the Web is fun, but it's really easy to get lost. Imagine yourself on a highway with no signs. You turn off onto an exit, only to find yourself at an intersection. You turn one way or another, look around and find yet another intersection. Soon you have no idea how to return to your starting point, or where your starting point was to begin with.

File   Edit   View   Go

Back   Forward   Reload   Home

Back moves you to a previous page or site.

Forward lets you revisit a page you have just returned from.

If the page you are loading appears garbled or is stalled in transmission, press **Reload** to retrieve it again.

Click **Home** or **Start** to return all the way back to your start page.

SEEING IS BELIEVING

Your browser can download and display short video segments on-screen—for example, a clip from an athletic or news event. Until quite recently, these video files had to be small to be practical. Assuming that your computer had the memory to handle it, a music video would take the better part of a day to download, even over a fast modem. But television and motion-picture companies are joining with technology companies to develop new compression technologies, and more efficient and flexible video formats are already appearing on the market.

Fortunately, browsers come with navigational aids. Located at the top of your browser screen are features that will help you move around, keeping track of where you've been and where you want to go.

SHORTCUTS

If you are using a PC and you click on your right mouse button, you can reach many of the functions on your browser's toolbar. You'll find a pop-up menu displaying choices such as *Back*, *Forward*, *Stop* and *Reload*.

PLUG-INS

Originally, browsers were limited in the sort of data they could display. Many graphic images, as well as video and audio files, were just too complicated for most browsers to handle. External applications, called plug-ins, had to be downloaded to display files the browsers couldn't handle.

Nowadays browsers have gotten very smart. If you encounter a file your browser can't process, and there is a plug-in that will help, your browser will ask you if you want it. If you do, the browser will then walk you through the downloading process.

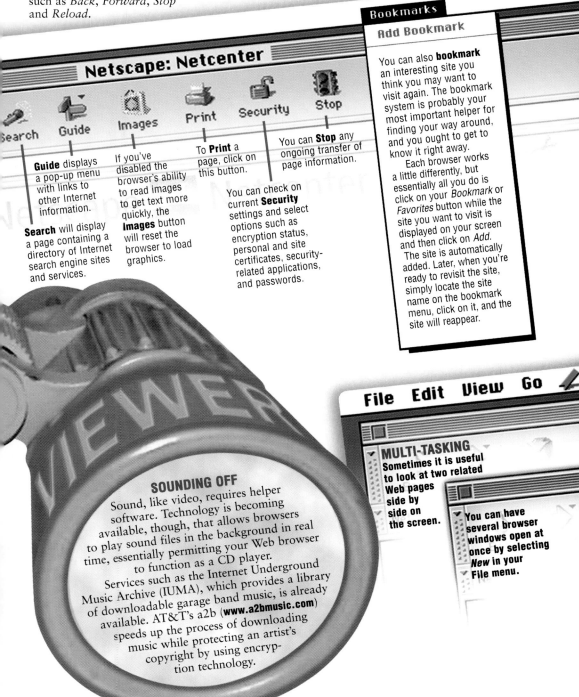

Netscape: Netcenter

Search | **Guide** | **Images** | **Print** | **Security** | **Stop**

Guide displays a pop-up menu with links to other Internet information.

Search will display a page containing a directory of Internet search engine sites and services.

If you've disabled the browser's ability to read images to get text more quickly, the **Images** button will reset the browser to load graphics.

To **Print** a page, click on this button.

You can check on current **Security** settings and select options such as encryption status, personal and site certificates, security-related applications, and passwords.

You can **Stop** any ongoing transfer of page information.

Bookmarks
Add Bookmark

You can also **bookmark** an interesting site you think you may want to visit again. The bookmark system is probably your most important helper for finding your way around, and you ought to get to know it right away.

Each browser works a little differently, but essentially all you do is click on your *Bookmark* or *Favorites* button while the site you want to visit is displayed on your screen and then click on *Add*. The site is automatically added. Later, when you're ready to revisit the site, simply locate the site name on the bookmark menu, click on it, and the site will reappear.

SOUNDING OFF

Sound, like video, requires helper software. Technology is becoming available, though, that allows browsers to play sound files in the background in real time, essentially permitting your Web browser to function as a CD player. Services such as the Internet Underground Music Archive (IUMA), which provides a library of downloadable garage band music, is already available. AT&T's a2b (**www.a2bmusic.com**) speeds up the process of downloading music while protecting an artist's copyright by using encryption technology.

File   Edit   View   Go

MULTI-TASKING
Sometimes it is useful to look at two related Web pages side by side on the screen.

You can have several browser windows open at once by selecting *New* in your File menu.

Searching for Information

You can find virtually anything you want on the Web—if you know how to look.

With millions of websites on the Internet covering virtually every topic from Aardvarks to Zygotes (not to mention all the newsgroup postings and bulletin boards available), how do you find what you're looking for? The solution is a special kind of website called a **search engine**.

Search engines allow you to use words or phrases, called search criteria, to define the information you want. The engine responds with a list of matches, with hyperlinks to take you to them.

HOW SEARCH ENGINES WORK

Some engines search by **keyword**, or title subject words. Others check the complete text of websites and Usenet postings for matching words. And still others are self-contained databases, compiled and indexed by human beings.

FROM ENGINE TO PORTAL

Search engines have gotten much more sophisticated and now function as **portals**, or gateways, to a vast store of information and services. In the past, search engines and Web directories were different—a search engine let you use a program to search databases of Web pages, and a directory allowed you to select from a hierarchy of catagories.

Now most portals offer both services as well as daily news, weather and stock reports, and e-mail services. When you pull up Excite, for instance, you can type in keywords, drill down through categories to find information, or check your daily horoscope.

Popular portals include:

AltaVista
www.altavista
.digital.com

Excite
www.excite.com

HotBot
www.hotbot.com

InfoSeek
www.infoseek.com

Lycos
www.lycos.com

WebCrawler
www.webcrawler.com

Yahoo
www.yahoo.com

FINDING PEOPLE

One of the most complicated search tasks is finding people on the Internet. There are millions of users and no single directory. A good place to start is at Netscape's People Finder, located on their home page at **www.netscape.com**. Another useful directory is Yahoo!'s People Search (**www.yahoo.com/search/ people/**). AT&T's AnyWho (**www.anywho.com**) provides an inclusive directory containing telephone and fax numbers, street and e-mail addresses, and URLs for home pages.

A good way to look up businesses is through the Yellow Pages. There are a number of them, and you can start with Big Yellow (**www.bigyellow.com**) or simply type *yellow pages* into a search engine for a comprehensive selection.

There are White Pages, too, and a helpful overall listing can be found at Microviet (**www.firstexplorer .com/onestop/directoryemail.html**).

NARROWING THE SEARCH

Sometimes a search turns up nothing, which can mean the search engine is having a problem, that your search criteria are too limiting, or that you're not using the appropriate keywords.

Usually, though, the problem is the reverse: a simple search can turn up thousands, sometimes millions, of matches. In that case you'll need to narrow your search. Here are some things you can try:

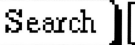

- Use more criteria: try *car repair* rather than simply *car*.
- Be more specific: search for *collie* instead of *dog*.
- Use synonyms or close words: if *stable* doesn't provide what you're looking for, try *barn*, *ranch* or *corral*.
- Include acronyms where appropriate: *NASA* may yield better results than *National Aeronautics and Space Administration*.

Some search engines also give weighted results, indicating the subjects or articles that have a higher probability (starting at 100%) of meeting the criteria you provide.

SPIDERS

A spider is a computer program that searches through websites, newsgroups, online news services and library catalogs, identifying and indexing at the rate of 5,000 or more new topics per day. Large search engines stay up to date by using spiders (also sometimes referred to as robots).

Each engine has some strengths that others may not have, so you usually get the best results using two or three different engines as part of your search. You can also try a **metasearcher**, which submits your criteria to several search engines simultaneously. One of the most popular is MetaCrawler, located at **www.metacrawler.com**.

BOOLEAN OPERATORS

Boolean operators were developed by George Boole, a 19th-century Scottish mathematician and doctor of philosophy. Using a set of algebraic rules, the logical concepts expressed by *and*, *or* and *not* let you specify the relationship between your search words.

AND will locate only sources that include both words.

OR will find all sources that include either word.

NOT will yield sources that discuss one but not the other.

If you were looking for the Guide Dog Foundation, keying in *Guide* AND *Dog* AND *Foundation*—which will look for documents containing all three words—will yield better results than *Guide* OR *Dog* OR *Foundation*—which will get you any document with the words *Guide* or *Dog* or *Foundation* in them.

While not every search engine supports Boolean searches, Boolean operators can help you find exactly what you're looking for.

DID YOU KNOW?

You can also search directly from your browser's *Location* text box. Simply type in the words you are looking for, and the browser will chose a search engine for you. Netscape requires two words, such as *retirement annuities* (if you only want *annuities*, type it in twice), and Microsoft Internet Explorer requires the word *find* before your keyword.

MARK YOUR PLACE

Not only do different search engines produce different results—sometimes the same search engine returns different results on different days. That's because the Web is constantly growing and changing. So, once you've found the site you're looking for, don't forget to bookmark it. Otherwise, you might spend a lot of time finding it again.

And if you think you may want to check back for updated information later, you can bookmark the actual search result page. Each time you return, your browser will display new search results.

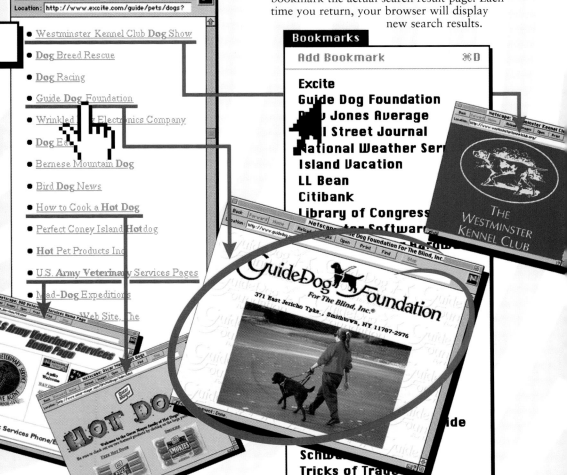

Building a Home Page

You don't need a permit to build a home page on the Web.

The Web is not just made up of sites created by large companies and professionals; it's at your disposal, too. You can create your own home page, complete with pictures of your pets, family and friends, your observations about life, or anything you choose. And many budding writers, artists and musicians deciding to bypass publishers, galleries and recording companies are now delivering their work directly to the public via the Web.

DETERMINE THE PURPOSE

The first task is deciding your website's purpose. Will it be about you, about your hobbies and interests, about a subject that interests you, or a

cause you care about? Or will it be a site for your small business? Whatever the subject, it's important to consider both the content of the page and the layout, or how it will appear on the computer screen.

FINDING A HOME

You'll find that most **Internet service providers**, or **ISPs**, offer a set amount of free Web space to their subscribers. These ISPs will often allow you to buy additional space fairly cheaply, especially if you are planning a very large site.

PICKING A DOMAIN NAME

If you don't mind paying for it, you can register your own domain name—for example, recipesgalore.com—so people can find it.

You register through InterNIC (**www.InterNIC.net**) or through your ISP, if that is where your site is hosted. InterNIC needs your domain name and address as well as the **name server**, or computer, that knows your address. In most cases, when you create a personal site, your name server is run by your ISP.

It costs about $70 to register for the first two years and $35 each year to renew.

DESIGN DECISIONS

Almost always, a simpler Web page is better. That doesn't mean you can't use graphics, sounds, animations, tables, forms or even Java applets if you want. They're lively and help to get your points across. Many of the design files are available on the Web for free, usually in exchange for including a design credit or a link to the creator's website.

You can also try searching **clip art** databases, available on the Web or commercially on CD ROM. You'll have to get permission to use them, as Web publishing is subject to many of the same regulations as book publishing. But permission is usually granted.

FORGING YOUR OWN LINKS

You may also want to include hyperlinks on your page that will jump your readers to other websites. You don't need to get permission to link to someone else's website, but it doesn't hurt to let them know. After all, they may want to reciprocate by adding a hyperlink back to you.

If your subject matter is limited, you may be able to fit it easily on one Web page. But if you have a lot of information, you might create a group of small pages hyperlinked together. Then users can jump quickly to the information they're interested in. Since small, compact pages tend to load more quickly than long, scrollable ones, a site with many interwoven hyperlinks can be easier to navigate than a single, large home page.

TEXT À LA WEB

Writing for the Web has become an art in itself. Rather than creating a script from beginning to end, it's often more effective to "layer" the material. That means starting with a broad topic and building hyperlinks to more specific subjects. A breezy, informal style and a sense of humor can also help to keep your visitors engaged.

For an overall guide to everything Web-oriented, including downloadable art, try the Nuthin' but Links metapage at **http://pages.prodigy.net/bombadil**.

For a downloadable HTML editor, try:

Hot Dog at **www.sausage.com**
HoTMetaL at **www.sq.com**
HTML Assistant at **www.brooknorth.com**

BUILD YOUR WEB PAGE

However you go about the actual creation of your page, the end result will be a site written in **HTML**, the **HyperText Markup Language**.

For starters, you can purchase software programs, such as PageMill 2.0 from Adobe Systems, Inc. and Home Page 3.0 from Allaire. These programs walk you through the process, so you don't need a lot of technical knowledge to get started.

There are also sites on the Web, such as Tripod (**www.tripod.com**) and GeoCities (**www.geocities.com**), that provide basic tools for building a home page from scratch.

These applications range from HTML editors, which help you write the source code for Web pages, to full WYSIWYG—what you see is what you get—Web page makers, which handle all the coding in the background. HTML editors simplify the process by inserting the appropriate HTML tags for you when you click on buttons or select menu items.

HTML

If you decide to work directly with HTML code, you can get a good general tutorial at the Maricopa Center for Learning and Instruction pages at **http://hakatai.mcli.dist.mari copa.edu/tut/index.html**. Creating an HTML document consists of inserting **tags** into a text file to format the text and define the hypertext links. A tag is the actual coding command that specifies headings, paragraphs and bulleted lists as well as text styles like bold and italic, or color. Tags also enable you to insert graphics into your document.

SAMPLE HTML

```
<font size="2"
face="Arial,Helvetica"><b>
How accessible is your
money? </b>
<img src="money.gif">
```

You can learn about techniques for creating features you like by using the *View Source* command on your browser. This function makes the hidden code visible so you can study the HTML in detail.

TOOLS

Netiquette

It's no tea party if you flout the Web's conventions.

While it's hard to be rude to a Web page, you may unintentionally offend the people reading an e-mail message you send or the information you submit to a newsgroup or mailing list. What's more, you can unknowingly violate the unspoken rules and guidelines that have been established for the Web community.

Netiquette (or Internet etiquette) is based on two basic rules of thumb: (1) Never say anything you wouldn't be willing to say face to face, and (2) Don't waste other people's time. These principles may seem obvious, but **newbies**, or new Internet users, can easily err if they're not careful. And even old hands risk offending others if they send e-mail or post things to a group in anger or say things they may later regret.

PLAYING BY THE RULES

Every newsgroup, mailing list or message board has its own set of rules of conduct. If you don't agree with them, you don't have to join. But if you do participate, you're expected to play along. Poor netiquette isn't just frowned on. It's punishable by public humiliation in the form of retaliatory postings called **flames**, expulsion from the group, or even termination of your Internet account.

Although some groups are **moderated**, which means the members of the group have appointed a monitor to review all new postings, most are self-regulating. It's up to the users of a group to decide what is and is not appropriate behavior.

To determine the norms for a specific community, check its **Frequently Asked Questions (FAQs)**. Most groups make a point of posting FAQs so new readers will have access to them. For a more complete (and humorous) guide to netiquette, go to the newsgroup **news.answers** and locate the message "Emily PostNews."

NOT SO FUNNY

Since humor varies from culture to culture, between genders, and within the scope of socio-economic experience, remember that just because you think something is funny doesn't mean that everyone else will.

There are right ways—

Things to Avoid

CONDUCT UNBECOMING

Here are some guidelines to help you avoid the most flagrant faux pas on the Net:

- Using all capital letters is equivalent to SHOUTING, and it's considered rude. Save caps for emphasis, and use **emoticons** (visual symbols created with keyboard characters) to indicate sarcasm or irony.

- Sending sloppy messages, full of spelling and grammatical errors, is also taboo. So is criticizing others for these errors. Remember that, while English is the primary vehicle of communication, the Internet is an international community.

- Cross-posting, or sending Usenet or e-mail messages to multiple groups, is an easy way to notify several groups of an important event or issue. But inappropriate cross-posting is one of the most serious breaches of netiquette.

- Sending e-mail messages with unnecessary or graphically laden attachments that can take a long time to download is inconsiderate.

- Posting off-topic contributions may also leave you open to criticism. Offering your grandmother's recipe for meat loaf is appropriate for a cooking group, unless that group is for vegetarians, in which case you've committed a serious blunder.

- Neglecting to remove addresses of previous recipients when forwarding a message takes up lots of space and violates privacy. It's best to "remove header" (a control bar option).

A thread that's a series of flames

and wrong ways— to share information on the Web.

Things to Do

LAW-ABIDING NETIZENS

Netiquette spells out what you ought to do as well as what you should avoid.

- Providing a pertinent subject line, both in Usenet postings and e-mail messages, can make the difference between a message that's read and one that's passed by. On the other hand, misleading subject lines can result in **public flames**—a scathing response to your message posted to the entire group.

- Using a signature, preferably your real name followed by your e-mail address, is important. Some users also include poetry quotations or even keyboard art, which is pictures made by using the punctuation keys of your keyboard. But other users consider this extraneous text a waste of bandwidth.

- Replying **off-list** (that is, sending an e-mail directly to the person seeking information) is appropriate if you're asked to. In fact, it's the preferable, and more efficient, response, especially if there's a question or comment you'd like to address to a specific person.

DON'T LOSE THE THREAD

When you reply to a posting, it's helpful to quote the relevant portion of the message you're responding to. This saves other readers from having to travel back through the **thread** to discover the original subject.

Most newsreaders and e-mail readers have an automatic quoting function, which places the entire text of the original message in your outgoing response. It's helpful to edit the text to include just the comments you wish to address.

SPAM

Spam is repeated postings or advertising that disrupts Internet discourse, and is highly frowned upon, if not illegal. The term comes from a Monty Python skit in which customers in a restaurant are unable to converse due to the constant repetition of "Spam, spam, eggs and spam, spam, spam (etc.)" by a group of Vikings in the background.

TESTING THE WATERS

You can learn the ropes before launching into a debate with seasoned Usenet denizens by sending test messages. There's even a special newsgroup called *alt.test* that you can use. When you're experimenting, you use *Testing: please ignore* on the subject line to let other readers know what you're doing.

is called a flame war.

111

Intranets

Companies can share organizational knowledge with employees on their own secure network.

An **Intranet** is an internal Internet, a private network of linked computers that's becoming a powerful resource in organizations and groups of all sizes.

When a company builds a public website, the point is to make selected information available to customers, investors and other interested parties. An Intranet, on the other hand, is an internal business tool: it functions as a keeper of proprietary information that helps the company operate more efficiently, and enables employees to share knowledge to do their jobs more professionally.

ONE FOR ALL

Organizations are increasingly turning to Intranets because of their flexibility, speed, cost savings and ability to facilitate collaboration across different locations, usually in real time.

In many organizations, an Intranet serves as a repository for documents, which is less costly and more accessible than a file room or company library. These documents may include a policy manual and benefits, an employee directory, project and research reports, or works in progress. When the information is updated, the change takes place instantly and universally, so there's no need to distribute the information on paper—like copying and distributing new internal telephone directories each time there's been an update.

Another popular Intranet function involves both accessing and processing online forms, such as those used for expense reports, applications for benefits, timesheets and requests for supplies. And employee communications, such as newsletters and major announcements, increasingly appear on Intranets.

ONLINE COLLABORATION

Intranets also help an entire company stay in touch, even when front offices and manufacturing sites are in different places. And since information on an Intranet can be accessed by many employees at once, colleagues in different locales can work collaboratively on a project, sharing their ideas in real time.

Intranets can help resolve problems with language and cultural differences as well. An international organization with offices all over the world, for example, might set up an Intranet home page with links to subsites in the appropriate languages.

Security

Administrative files

LIMITED ACCESS

LIMITED ACCESS

Virtual offices

Investors

Employee access to the Internet

WHAT IS A FIREWALL?

In an Intranet, a **firewall** is a device that prevents unwanted access into a corporate network. While the firewall allows authorized users to move freely within the Intranet—except for certain sensitive areas, like financial reports or employee payroll information, which might require special access—the security

SPEED

Accessing an Intranet is usually faster, at least for in-house users, than accessing the Internet. That's because Intranets work on a **LAN** (a **local area network**), which directly links the computers in the Intranet system. This means the speed of transmission is greatly accelerated since the network is not dependent on modems or the connections to **Internet service providers** (**ISPs**). However, telecommuters and other remote users connect to the Intranet network at ordinary modem speeds.

FLEXIBILITY

Intranets are platform-independent, which means that different types of computers—Windows and DOS-based machines, Macintoshes and UNIX workstations—can all access the same information. Since many organizations use a variety of computers, this cross-platform capability means all workstations, from accounting to the art department, can access and share the same information. No special software is needed to translate it.

Employee benefits

Online forms

E-mail

LIMITED ACCESS

LIMITED ACCESS

Vendors and supplies

EXTRANETS: LETTING THE OUTSIDERS IN

Some companies want to provide limited Intranet access to outsiders who work closely with them, such as suppliers, marketing agencies and technology partners. In these cases, companies have set up **Extranets**, which allow these groups to quickly and conveniently get the information they need to do their jobs more effectively. Extranets are especially popular for routine transactions, such as purchasing.

features make it difficult or impossible for unauthorized visitors to gain entrance to the network.

The firewall itself consists of two parts: a gate, which passes data between the Intranet and Internet networks, and a choke, which forces all data packets flowing between the two networks to pass through the gate. The gate authenticates users, enforces security, searches for viruses, and then allows data or users into the system.

Since Intranet users can access the Internet—but not the other way around—an Intranet can include hyperlinks to key sites on the Net, which is always accessible to employees.

Webspeak

Getting to know the jargon of the Web can be as important as getting around the Web itself.

The 20th century has produced hundreds of thousands of acronyms—many of them scientific, technical and computer-related terms. Often they create more confusion than they clear up, but they've steadily made their way into common use.

The computer industry, in fact, is currently responsible for a large percentage of all new words, and the Internet can seem like a minefield of mumbo-jumbo to the novice. Knowing the following terms will help.

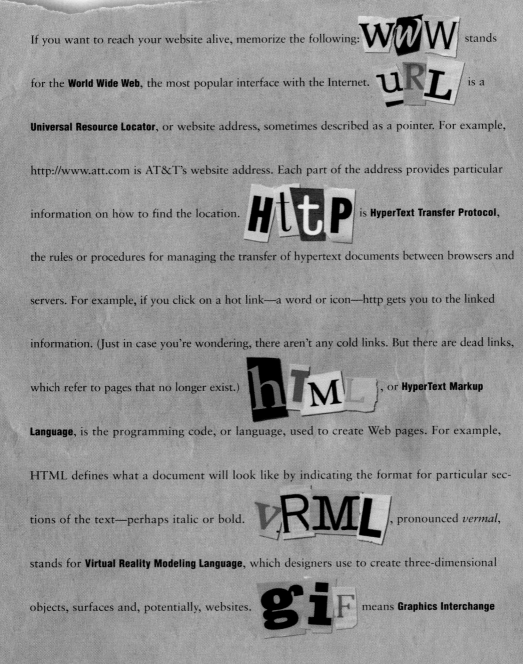

If you want to reach your website alive, memorize the following: **WWW** stands for the **World Wide Web**, the most popular interface with the Internet. **uRL** is a **Universal Resource Locator**, or website address, sometimes described as a pointer. For example, http://www.att.com is AT&T's website address. Each part of the address provides particular information on how to find the location. **HttP** is **HyperText Transfer Protocol**, the rules or procedures for managing the transfer of hypertext documents between browsers and servers. For example, if you click on a hot link—a word or icon—http gets you to the linked information. (Just in case you're wondering, there aren't any cold links. But there are dead links, which refer to pages that no longer exist.) **hTML**, or **HyperText Markup Language**, is the programming code, or language, used to create Web pages. For example, HTML defines what a document will look like by indicating the format for particular sec-tions of the text—perhaps italic or bold. **vRML**, pronounced *vermal*, stands for **Virtual Reality Modeling Language**, which designers use to create three-dimensional objects, surfaces and, potentially, websites. **giF** means **Graphics Interchange**

Format. It's the one format that all graphical browsers can read. Inline images, which appear on Web pages and are loaded when you load the page, are customarily in GIF format. Files that end in **.ZIP** are compressed files that have to be unzipped or decompressed with special software. **mPEg**, which stands for **Moving Picture Experts Group**, is a cross-platform data compression format that delivers audio and video images. An MPEG audio file can provide high-quality sound. MPEG video, on the other hand, plays at only about the quality of a VCR—far below today's digital standards. **JPeG**, or **Joint Photographic Experts Group**, is an efficient image file format that compresses graphic images and lets you download them. For example, a JPEG color image can be downloaded directly into a newspaper article as it is going is to press. **JAVA** is a programming language for the Internet. The mini-applications written in Java are called applets. A **FAQ** is a **Frequently Asked Question** and an **RFC** is a **Request for Comment**. (These are ways to get help or give feedback when you're surfing the Net.) **PdF**, or **Portable Document Format**, allows you to view a file exactly as the author intended—even if you don't own the application software. A **HackeR** is an expert computer user who enjoys solving technical challenges, while a **CRackeR** is a criminal whose primary purpose is to create destruction. And **RL**, or **Real Life**, is whatever it is you do when you're not busy browsing the Web.

A Digital Day in the Life

Digital communication keeps us going and in touch.

GOING DIGITAL

From the time our radio alarm goes off in the morning until we reset it later that night, our Information Age lives are becoming increasingly digital.

Virtually all of our familiar activities—working in the office, shopping in a store, visiting the library, or going to the movies—are being transformed by the combination of computer processing, intelligent networks and multimedia communications.

Things we once had to do in person we can now do remotely, anywhere, anytime, from a variety of digital devices that are no longer just phones, or televisions, or number-crunching computers, but hybrid versions of these.

And while there is untold excitement about the convenience, economics and personal choices of doing things online and in cyberspace, there are also new issues about privacy and security, and filtering unwanted information for our children.

For all we can do in the digital world today, we are just glimpsing the beginning, the harbinger of things we'll be able to do tomorrow... or sooner.

6:30 AM
THE DAY STARTS

- Digital alarm clock rings
- Preprogrammed timer and microprocessor start coffee maker
- Turn on computer
- Check e-mail
- Check weather report
- Receive faxes
- Grab laptop

1:00 PM IN THE AIR

- Finish writing presentation using laptop
- Use onboard phone to make a rental car reservation and check e-mail
- Play solitaire on the laptop

6:30 PM
AND IT JUST DOESN'T STOP

- Check into hotel using electronic key kiosk
- Connect laptop and make notes about presentation
- Check e-mail
- Message light blinking on hotel phone
- Voicemail from boss requests presence at emergency meeting first thing in the morning
- Check available flights on Internet and book ticket for last flight out

3:00 PM ARRIVAL

- Rental car shuttle bus shows reservation on screen
- Consult hand-held computer for directions to meeting and who will be present

0011110101001

4:00 PM THE MEETING

- Make presentation using laptop and digital projector
- Participate in video conference call
- Alpha-numeric pager shows message from kids
- Phone boss from cell phone before leaving for the hotel

8:00 AM THE COMMUTE

- Open garage door with remote control
- Drive to gas station and use debit card to fill up, stop by ATM machine for cash
- Pager goes off—call business associate from cellular phone while on the road
- Breeze through toll station with E-Z Pass

8:45 AM HOTELING AT THE OFFICE

- Check in for office assignment
- Set up laptop
- Log on and confirm seat assignment for 1:00 p.m. flight today
- Answer the morning's e-mail
- Check voice messages and return calls
- Call assistant and confirm conference call at 11:00 a.m. as well as out-of-town presentation at 4:00 p.m.
- Fax project report to boss

11:30 AM TO THE AIRPORT

- Area map on dashboard shows best route to airport
- Overhead electronic signs on highway warn "congestion for the next ten miles"
- Cellular phone rings—afternoon meeting is confirmed
- Use kiosk at gate to print out boarding pass for electronic ticket

9:00 PM UP IN THE AIR AGAIN

- Use onboard phone to call home with change of plans
- Play solitaire again
- Try to sleep

11:00 PM HOME AGAIN

- Consider checking voice- and e-mail, but don't
- Set alarm
- Zzzzzzzzzzz

117

Card Smarts

A little plastic can pack a storehouse of information.

When you swipe your credit card to make a phone call, or slip your ATM card in a bank machine, the magnetic tape on the back of the card contains coded information that identifies you and initiates the transaction. But these cards are considered to be **passive**—if you change your PIN (personal identification number) or account number, you'll usually need a new card. That's because the magnetic strip is not programmable, so the bank or issuing organization will need to print a new card.

Smart cards, on the other hand, are actually tiny computers that have a microprocessor, or intelligent chip, built in. Their **PROM**, or **programmable read-only memory**, allows personal data to be stored

permanently in what is known as the "secret zone" of the memory, as well as to be changed or updated, if needed. Smart cards are capable of carrying public and private information. Personal information can be stored in the secret zone and can not be accessed unless the a PIN number is used. Nonpersonal information, such as how often one has made a phone call or traveled on public transportation, can be stored in the public zone and accessed without a PIN.

Because the PROM can hold both types of information, it is possible that one day a single card may contain all of the information you need to get around.

ELECTRONIC TRAILS

Some smart cards are anonymous. If you buy an over-the-counter phone card to make calls, there'll be a record of where the call originated but no way to know who made it. The same is true of a transit system pass, or any card you buy without identifying yourself.

But if your card is personalized—whether it's a traditional credit or debit card or a smarter cousin—there is a record of what you do with it.

SIMPLE BUT SMART

Smart cards with microprocessors are not only capable of carrying information but acting on it as well. For example, smart cards can:

- **Store large amounts of personal information.** Your medical history, for example, can be encoded on a smart card. It would be available if you were taken ill away from home, or you were unable to alert nurses and doctors about a pre-existing condition or medication you were taking.

  While it's easy enough to record your blood type or major allergies on a card in your wallet, health care providers may need a more extensive set of information to treat you, especially in an emergency.

- **Provide financial value.** A phone card, for example, starts out with a specific value—say $20. As you use it, the cost of your calls is debited electronically from the value of the card. When you've used up the total, you can replenish or restore value to the card, or discard it and buy another.

- **Be upgraded.** Upgradable smart cards let you subscribe to new services or update information. For example, you can add value to your transit or phone card, or you can update medical information by adding data about new medications or allergies.

1st Bank
3322 1171 3311 1773
VALID DATES
03/96 30SEP99
MR. CARL S MOORE

MTA MetroC

← Insert this way

SMARTER AND SAFER

An experimental test to prevent the illegal modification of smart cards is being conducted by Schlumberger Test and Transactions. By coating the chips inside the card with a compound that makes them so brittle they self-destruct if tampered with, they hope to prevent smart card hackers from reading or changing the recorded information or the monetary value on the card.

CHARGING AND RECHARGING

If you're using a smart card to make a purchase, you insert the card in a receptor that debits the correct amount and credits it to the merchant's account.

When you've used up the value of the card, you can refill it and spend it down again. All you have to do is go back to the issuer and pay the amount you're loading on the card.

You can also arrange to maintain a continuing balance by having the amounts you spend replenished by charging them to a card or debiting your bank account.

Before long, experts predict you'll be able to use your smart card for electronic commerce over the Internet, perhaps by using a reader built into your computer.

THE NEW MONEY?

Some say smart cards may turn out to be the common currency of the 21st century, replacing not only pocket change but bills as well. By some estimates, there will be 100 million electronic cash cards, such as the Mondex e-purse, in use by 2000, accounting for $300 million in spending worldwide.

But in a 1998 pilot program in New York City, cards designed to replace cash for the purchase of goods did not fare well. Many businesses refused to install the terminals needed, and there were some problems with the programming in the cards themselves.

There are also some practical issues to resolve, including what happens if you lose your card. And enough retailers will have to install terminals to make it practical to use the card.

Behind Bars

To get the data, you need to read between the lines.

If you wanted, you could trace the route of the corn or wheat that ends up in a box of cereal on your breakfast table by following the **bar codes** on the containers that hold them, from the field to your shopping cart.

A bar code or, more accurately, a **Universal Product Code** (**UPC**), is a set of dark bars and white spaces that appears on millions of manufactured and processed products available for sale, identifying each one by its producer and its distinguishing features. In some, but not all, cases, it also includes the price at which the product is to be sold.

A SHOPPER'S VIEW

From your perspective, bar codes have some real advantages, most obviously checking out faster and more accurately. There's no wait if you buy one can of cat food marked 3/79¢. The computer knows it's 27¢—and that the next two are 26¢ each—long before a clerk could do the division. When the items are totaled and you get your receipt, the product name and price are there. The receipt can also tell you how much you saved that day (and in some stores, that year) by buying on-sale merchandise.

The efficiencies of the system mean that the store is more likely to have the product you want, and the inventory is apt to be fresher since warehousing time has been cut.

BREAKING THE CODE

In reading a bar code, a scanner looks at the lines and spaces, matching the data to a product it's been programmed to understand.

There's always a start code at the left and a stop code at the right. A scanner can read a UPC backwards or forwards and at any angle, as long as it has the start/stop information.

The start code can be any one of seven numbers: 0, 6 and 7 indicate a national brand, 2 means products to be weighed, 3 indicates drugs and similar products, 4 is for items that retailers price themselves, and 5 is for coupons.

The first five-digit number identifies the manufacturer of the product and is the same on the range of products produced by the company. It's assigned by the Uniform Code Council.

The second five-digit number is a product code assigned by the company that manufactures it. Each product has its own number, and differences in size, color or flavor are indicated in the code.

The final element, a single number, is the stop sign. It's also used for error checking, to insure that the scanner picked up the correct information.

HOW SCANNING WORKS

When you check out, a clerk moves the bar code over a window above a laser scanner or points a hand-held device at the code or touches it with a wand. The scanner emits a beam of infrared light. The white spaces on the bar code reflect the infrared rays, sending pulses or signals back to a detector, or reader, which converts the pulses and the absences of pulses (where the lines are) into binary code

that is relayed to a computer. Wide bars and spaces represents 1s and thin bars and spaces represent 0s.

The computer matches the code it receives with the data in its memory, supplies the price and relays the information to the clerk's register. The price appears almost instantaneously on the screen, and the item name and cost are printed the receipt.

TRACKING INFORMATION

Today, bar codes are name plates, or passive labels that scanners use to identify a product. But experts point out that if the codes had a power source, such as sunlight or a small battery, they could be digitally active, identifying themselves or saying where they were.

Once it's in the system:

THE SUPPLY SIDE

Using UPC-coded merchandise means retailers, and the entire supply chain—wholesalers, shippers and producers—can streamline the way business is done.

In a grocery store, for example, the computer keeps up-to-the-minute inventory and reorders when supplies of a product run low. That's possible because the store's computers can communicate directly with the wholesaler's.

UPC-coded products make retailers part of a network

The computer can also keep track of what sells and what doesn't—and even of who buys what and when if you've handed the cashier your membership or discount card. Those records enable a retailer to make effective use of shelf space, track changing customer demands and even do fine-tuned targeted marketing if they want.

Since coupons, too, have bar codes, the computer can check the code on the coupon against the list of purchases to be sure the customer bought the product the discount is being offered on.

Electronic data interchange (EDI) standards are common protocols, or formats, that computers in specific industries follow to send orders, invoices and other information directly between purchasers and suppliers. Using bar codes has simplified the supply chain by increasing the speed and accuracy of placing, recording and filling orders.

that provides reliable and up-to-the-minute information

on every phase of the supply chain.

AN INFORMATION AGE IDEA

The Uniform Code Council, a not-for-profit organization, sets the standards for identifying millions of products, sharing information about them and the system in which they move, and handling electronic communications for ordering, tracking and supplying them. Since 1971, when the idea of a uniform identification code originated in the grocery business, digital technology and interlocking, networked systems have altered every phase of the way that retail businesses and their supply systems operate.

STAYING IN LINE

Bar codes can appear in a variety of colors—though never in red or any colors containing red because the color of the laser is red—and must meet specific printing standards. The key is getting enough contrast between the bars and the spaces so that light areas reflect accurately when they are scanned. The size of the bar code has to meet UCC specifications as well to be sure it's readable.

THE SCOPE OF THE SYSTEM

Almost 200,000 producers in North America use the UPC code and 350,000 more around the world use the EAN (European Article Numbering System) code that was adapted from it.

And it's not only the 20,000 or more items in your local grocery store that carry the code. All of the containers in which UPC-marked products are packed and shipped have a bar code themselves, or a more extensive version of the UPC, with additional information, known as SCC-14 and SCC-18 codes.

Telecommuting

If you're connected, you can do office work from anywhere.

"I'm going to work" once meant going to an office, lab, factory or store. But workplaces no longer need to be fixed locations where a group of employees gather. With the growing intelligence of phones, computers, modems and fax machines, and the networks that connect them, many workers are now **telecommuting**—doing many of the same things away from the office that they could do if they were there.

THE GOING PERCENTAGES

By some estimates, more than 11 million people telecommuted in 1998, according to a survey from FIND/SVP. Over 75% of them use a PC, and 31% access the Internet. About 62% of all telecommuters travel for business, averaging nine travel days a month. Gil Gordon Associates reports a 10% to 15% annual growth in the number of tele-commuters and an increasing diversity in the types of employers and job types involved.

VIRTUAL MEETINGS

Before ISDN lines and other network innovations, people could save the time and money of business travel by conferring face-to-face through **videoconferencing**. One disadvantage of videoconferencing is that it always requires special equipment and conference rooms, dedicated lines or reservations made well in advance. But you can now confer with people without these inconveniences—and at a fraction of the cost—by attaching video cameras to PCs and using the PC as your conference table.

SPAWNING NEW BUSINESS

England's Oakmoor Telecentres Ltd. is marketing modular telecenter units that range in size from 150 to 250 square feet.

STAYING CONNECTED

Employees on the go can increasingly do their work whenever they want, wherever they are. Laptop computers can be plugged into phone lines on planes and trains as well as hotel rooms and airport lounges. Amtrak's Metroliner has both electrical outlets and phone service, but the phone service does not yet support Internet connection. Many hotel rooms are equipped with fax machines that double as copiers and printers.

With a cellular phone, a client or colleague doesn't have to know where you are to get in touch—just your phone number. Even if your phone is off, or you're using it when a call comes through, digital phone networks can record a message and store it until you're ready to hear it.

To make the virtual workplace a reality, many companies are investing large sums to help employees keep in touch with their offices **transparently**—that is, with simple direct access to the company Intranet from any location.

VIRTUALLY CLEAN

Telecommuting may be good for the environment, too. The Clean Air Act mandates that employers in many states reduce the number of cars entering their parking lots by 25%, a reduction that's unlikely to be achieved by car pooling or mass transit alone. But as more people work at home or on the road, the more realistic that goal becomes.

You can visit On The Road at **www.road news.com** for travel tips for laptop users.

HOTELING

OFFICE WITHOUT WALLS

Many businesses are taking an innovative approach to the virtual office by totally restructuring their workspaces. When employees arrive in the morning, they pick up a telephone and a portable computer and work at the desk or in the cubicle they choose. There are no assigned spaces. This concept is called **hoteling** and is used for employees who spend most of their time out of the office.

To meet worker needs on in-office days, the company makes available private workstations, while a "hotel coordinator" orchestrates the process of taking reservations for the workstations, assigning space, providing office support, and programming phone numbers.

Sweden has introduced the "office train," with managers working for half-pay during an 80-minute train ride in and out of Stockholm.

A Japanese innovation, the "creative office," combines telecommuting with a resort setting designed to help employees recover from fatigue. During an average two-week stay, employees perform their normal tasks but do so in a vacationlike atmosphere.

IT'S NOT FOR EVERYONE

In their 1995 analysis of virtual offices, Kelly and McGraw came up with a list of traits that seem to make successful telecommuters. Employees who thrive on this free-form style of working tend to be flexible, strongly organized, highly communicative and independent, with a low need for daily social interaction. Many highly competent employees, on the other hand, find themselves feeling isolated and dispirited in a telecommuter job. Many companies now use full-time, temporary, contract, part-time and freelance employees simultaneously. The trick is to figure out which employees will make good telecommuters.

THE PROS AND CONS OF TELECOMMUTING

Company rules for telecommuting vary significantly. In some places, there's a trade-off—some days at home and some at the office. In others, certain people work primarily at home, while others spend most of their time in the office.

For employees:

Advantages
- More economical than commuting
- Easier to juggle personal and work schedules
- Increased productivity and fewer distractions
- Portability—work can be taken anywhere
- Flexible working hours

Potential problems
- Dependence on connectivity and technology working reliably
- Distractions—at home and on the road
- Working longer hours
- Difficulty in qualifying for promotion
- Feeling isolated

For employers:

Advantages
- Reduced overhead cost of providing office space
- Ability to hire people who live in remote locations from the office
- Greater competitive advantage in global markets
- Potential for increased productivity

Potential problems
- Identifying self-reliant workers
- Difficulty in evaluating work
- Potential loss of group spirit and collaborative solutions
- Increased cost and maintenance of network connections

TELECENTERS

Somewhat of a hybrid between the home office and the traditional one, **telecenters** provide office space, equipment and support staff that tenants can share instead of maintaining their own space.

Telecenters are convenient and economical for people who have to meet clients or handle other business only occasionally, or who are just starting a business and want to keep their overhead costs down. Telecenters are also ideal for organizations that want to maintain a presence in a particular locale but staff it primarily with people from the central office to keep operating costs at a minimum.

The Hands-off Office

You're always tuned in without having to log on.

Office life a century ago was a lot simpler. When you arrived, you hung up your coat, sharpened your pencils and maybe your quill pen, threw some coal on the fire, and sat down to the paperwork where you left off.

While this picture may be a bit idyllic, it's nevertheless a far cry from office life today, where the day often begins with turning on your computer. When the computer is ready, it asks your identification and password. You also need to identify yourself to access e-mail, and maybe key in another code to open other programs. Then, at last, you're ready to bring up the work you carefully closed down the last time you used the computer.

Much of this tedium may soon disappear thanks to an innovative technology called **sentient computing**, which is designed to bring back the simplicity of yesteryear by helping your computer keep up with you.

THE MOBILE DESKTOP

With sentient computing, the network always knows who you are, where you are, and what you've been doing on your computer. So, for example, when you walk into your office each day, your computer automatically displays the desktop that was last on your screen. You can just pick up where you left off.

And if you walk next door or down the hall, or go anyplace else that is connected to the network, the very same desktop will just follow you wherever you go. You are continuously in contact with the network, so you never have to go through start-up procedures to access your computer desktop.

You walk down the hall to a conference room to show colleagues what you've just been working on. Your active badge triggers the system to present your most recent desktop on a large screen.

When you get to your office, your badge signals that you're there.

The lights go on, the temperature adjusts to your comfort level...

and your computer brings up the screen where you left off.

ACTIVE BADGES

To tell the network where you are, you use a miniature electronic tag called an **active badge**, which can be worn like an identification card. The very latest tags transmit ultrasonic pulses to sensors in the ceiling, which can then locate the wearer to the nearest two inches in 3D space. The tags are attached to equipment, too, so that it can also be located.

The sentient computing system uses this location information to build a detailed 3D model of the office environment. Programs then use this information to adapt the environment to your desires, making your desktop follow you around, turning lights on and off, and even adjusting the temperature and humidity to your liking. All you have to do is show up. The network handles the rest.

ALWAYS IN TOUCH

Sentient computing can tell the system not just where you are but who you are with. For example, if you and other badge wearers are holding a meeting, and a call comes through to you, the operator can detect that you're with others and decide to hold the call or put it through to your voicemail.

But if the sensors indicate that you are alone when the call comes through, it can be routed to the phone nearest you, whether you're in the office or on the move.

That's because the sensors are creating a communications context that recognizes your environment. So the network can respond intelligently—deciding, for example, where and how to route calls, and when.

VIRTUALLY ALWAYS THERE

Because the sentient computing system maintains an up-to-date 3D model of the environment, it can display a 3D image of the whole building showing exactly where everybody is and who they are with. So, if your colleague at the other end of the building wants to drop in on you, they can bring up a virtual view of the building to see if the time is right. They can see immediately whether you are sitting alone in your office or running down the corridor to get to an important meeting.

By using active badges, you can be seen without losing your privacy. There are no cameras to show exactly what you're doing, so all your colleagues see is your **avatar**, or digital representation, in the virtual building. And if you don't want people to see where you are, you can simply take off your badge.

Of course, sometimes you do want people to see you on camera, like when you're in a videoconference. Using the data from your active badge, the conferencing software can detect when you move around and select a suitable camera to keep you in the shot wherever you go. Rather than compelling people to sit frozen in one spot, sentient computing enables people to act and communicate more naturally.

VIRTUAL NETWORK COMPUTING

The reason you can move seamlessly from one computer terminal to another, and pick up where you left off without having to sign on again, is that all the active equipment in the system is connected by a special protocol called **virtual network computing**, or **VNC**. In the VNC environment, the ultimate laptop is actually no laptop at all. You travel, and the information follows you. For example, if you're viewing a document on one screen and move to another office, the document is automatically transmitted to a screen in that room when it senses your active badge.

Later, you take part in a video conference. As you walk around the room, the sensors track your movement so the viewers at the other end can always see you.

You and your colleagues are deep in conversation when a call comes through. The system senses other people with you and decides to route the call to your voicemail.

Because the system is platform-independent—each viewing device can have a different kind of screen (computer, TV, picture phone) and use a different operating system. The information can be transferred from one device to another without your ever needing to use a mouse or a keyboard. With virtual computing, you're always on, always connected, and can access your desktop virtually anytime from anywhere.

Home, Home on the Job

What do you really need?

If you're one of millions of Americans who have set up shop in your home, the right technology and equipment can transform your office into a sophisticated, as well as cozy, workplace. Because you can rely on networking to maintain phone, fax and data connections to colleagues and customers—just as in a conventional office—you have everything you need to do your job, except maybe a water cooler.

While no two home offices are alike, there are some basics you should always consider.

The Basics

1. Your workspace: Set up a place separate from your other home activities. If you don't have a separate room, reserve a corner or nook for work.

2. Phone lines: Set up at least one separate phone line in addition to your home line. Two is better—one for business calls and one for your computer and fax. Ideal, but more expensive, are separate lines for your computer and Internet access, your fax machine, and your business calls.

3. Equipment: This will vary according to your budget and your needs. If you'll be working mostly from your home, the choices are easier and less costly. If you'll be traveling frequently, they'll be more complex—and more expensive.

Buying Equipment

To the chagrin of every business owner, office equipment is constantly upgraded or replaced entirely. By the time this book goes to press, the latest and fastest machines will undoubtedly be superseded by yet newer and faster ones. But don't let this throw you. Most of the equipment that's already out there is more than adequate to run your business effectively.

PERSONAL COMPUTERS

Solid research is the key to finding and purchasing the right computer. You can start by looking in the newspapers, PC catalogs and stores. And don't forget to check the websites of computer manufacturers.

If you find equipment on sale, or at a greatly reduced price, it may mean the next model has become available. So look at all the features on the latest equipment and compare them with what's on sale. But remember—today's bargains were probably state-of-the-art six months ago, so they may be all you need to get started.

Here's what to look for:

CPU—This is the power of the machine to perform tasks. In 1999, 450MHz is common and 333 is on the way out. This is a good barometer to go by when understanding power.

RAM—64MB, or megabytes (which measure the active memory capacity of the machine), is common now, but you can purchase systems with 96MB. Your software will run faster with more RAM, so you'll want to purchase as much as you can afford.

Hard drive space—This is one of the most critical components. Get as much as you can. Anything below 4GB (gigabytes) may be a problem

because business and office software, multimedia files and business documents, such as e-mail, presentations and proposals, will use up hard drive space very quickly.

Quality laser printer

Dedicated phone line

Phone line w/ 3-way calling

THE FREQUENT TRAVELER

If you'll be doing a lot of traveling as part of your business, you may need some extra office equipment.

Peripherals

1. Printers: Black-and-white laser printers deliver the highest quality at an affordable price. Color inkjet printers are versatile, cost slightly less than laser printers, and are very useful for presentations and graphics.

2. Fax machines: Your PC may have software that lets your computer receive and send faxes. Unfortunately, this feature doesn't work when your computer is turned off, so it pays to buy a separate fax machine. Plain-paper machines are preferable to those requiring special paper that may have a waxy finish that is hard to write on. Some fax machines also function as a copier and printer for your computer.

3. External storage: Zip drives, tape backup and rewritable CD ROMs are all useful storage devices and necessary if you keep filling up your hard drive.

Laptop computer: If you want to purchase a laptop, consider using a port replicator bar, which connects your laptop to a stand-alone monitor, a keyboard, a zip drive or other peripherals. You'll have the advantage of portability without having to buy a separate PC.

Cellular phone: If you're away, and you don't want to miss important messages, it probably pays to buy a digital cellular phone. This device can save voicemail and even text messages, and lets you store a lot of other reference information.

Hand-held computer: These devices have many advantages. They're small, portable and can hold lots of information all in one place—calendar, phone numbers, addresses and calculators.

Modem—Buy the fastest one available that will hook up to a regular phone line. At the moment, that's 56K and may remain as such for a while.

Scanner—You can often save time by scanning paper documents and graphics. Once they're digitized, you can work on them on your PC.

CD ROM drive and floppy drive—Make sure these are included since you'll probably be using both these features at one point or another.

Monitor—Good resolution is important. A minimum of 800x600 pixels is good, and 1028x768 is better. Screen size is also important, especially when you're running multiple applications or want to see full-screen representations at a comfortable size.

PHONE SERVICES

Installing custom calling services and buying phones with special features, such as teleconferencing, can make your business seem more sophisticated. For example, call waiting and voicemail are ideal for making sure you get all your calls, and a speaker phone is essential for freeing you up to use your computer or letting another person join the conversation.

HOME NETWORK

To make your home office hum, you can now purchase equipment that lets you connect several computers so that they can talk to each other and share a single Internet connection. For more information, check out Home Phoneline Networking Alliance at **www.homepna.org**.

Distance Learning

Online education is for everyone.

The Internet offers a wide spectrum of learning opportunities, from virtual universities and classrooms to certification and refresher courses for professionals. And companies are offering training seminars and information briefings for their employees—in the office and at home as well as in remote locations.

Some online education programs—or **distance learning**, as it's becoming known—let you work at your own pace, whenever it's convenient for you. Other "live" learning programs are scheduled at specific times and often involve direct interaction with an instructor through audio, video and e-mail channels.

VIRTUAL CAMPUSES

As a nontraditional college student—for example, a working adult, homemaker, single parent or retired person—you can use distance learning to enhance your education on a broad variety of subjects.

You may, for example, attend electronic lectures at scheduled times or read materials posted on a website. You can also join chat room-like discussion groups with your "classmates," use online libraries 24 hours a day, and send e-mail to your instructor rather than attend conferences or raise a hand to ask a question. You can even submit papers and exams electronically and get your grades the same way.

Virtual campuses operate in a **virtual education environment**, or **VEE**, where instructors can create a virtual lab or lecture hall. This environment lets a large number of participants interact with each another simultaneously, though lines can get overloaded, causing a slowdown. And while

ON THE JOB...ONLINE

Corporate training departments and professional associations have graduated from videotaped lectures and paper manuals to distance learning as a low-cost, effective way of providing training and information to employees. A survey by The American Society for Training and Development predicts that by the year 2000, only an estimated 55% of training will be instructor-led, compared to 80% in 1996.

Companies like Horizon Live Distance Learning, PlaceWare and Centra have been creating highly interactive programs that deliver live presentations and training to employees anywhere in the world. Horizon has developed software applications that allow companies using ordinary computers and phone lines to deliver specially tailored training workshops.

The presenter can speak directly to participants as well as send Web pages, slide shows or video clips to their screens. Participants can type in their responses or questions, receiving feedback much like the give-and-take of a real classroom. You can see a demonstration at **www.horizonlive.com**.

most VEEs are currently text-based, software companies are beginning to produce graphical interfaces to make the online learning experience visually more stimulating.

BEST BUYS FOR CAREER CHANGES

Distance learning can also help working people renew their certifications or accreditations, keep up with professional practices, or take part in training seminars—all without leaving their home or office.

If you've been considering changing careers, for example, you might look into distance learning certificates. To earn a certificate, you need to complete a preset number of courses, all related to your career field.

For instance, the University of California Extension, at **www-cmil.unex.berkeley.edu**, offers home-study certificates in business by using mail, fax, video and electronic mail. Certificates can also be earned in specialized business areas, including accounting, real estate, database management, economics, systems analysis and human resources management.

You can also check out degree and certificate programs at **www.petersons.com/dlearn** and **www.geteducated.com/dlsites.htm**.

GETTING FULL CREDIT

If you want your degree or certification to be recognized and accepted by employers, professional associations and other educational institutions, you'll want to be sure that your online college courses are accredited. You can check the accreditation of a class or program at the Council for Higher Education's directory at **www.detc.org**.

NEW DAY DAWNING

Distance learning dates as far back as Sunrise Semester of the 1950s, which replaced correspondence courses with early-morning television lectures. The advantage of interactive education in a virtual classroom is the ability to offer two-way communication and immediate response.

IT'S A SMALL WORLD

Classes that are electronically connected, sometimes called **networked classrooms**, enable students in one locale to participate in a curriculum being taught somewhere else entirely. For example, a classroom in the US can visit with a student in France. Or high school students from many locations can participate in a single honors English class.

AT&T has a number of educational programs and resources available through their Learning Network at **www.att.com/learningnetwork/index2.html**. Their Virtual Academy helps teachers meet their professional development requirements.

AT&T's Virtual Classroom is a successful online program targeted at primary and secondary schools around the world. Currently, it offers three programs open to any school with Internet access.

The popular International Web authoring contest is in its third year and gives students an opportunity to compete against other students as they learn to create a Web page for their classrooms or schools. The newly introduced Virtual Classroom Clubhouse allows classrooms to meet and collaborate on specific projects. Also new is a program called Race Across Time, developed by the Powerhouse Museum in Australia. You can visit them at **www.vc.attjens.co.jp/e/index**.

Cyberlibraries

Checking out your books takes on new meaning in an electronic library.

You probably think of a library as a quiet place to do research or simply to check out books, tapes or CDs. While not as comprehensive as a traditional library, online libraries make some books, periodicals and reference materials easily available, and are accessible to anyone, anywhere, anytime.

Traditional and virtual libraries aren't in competition with each other. In fact, libraries are in the process of putting their catalogs online. And because many old texts are out of print or irreplaceable, they're converting many of their holdings into digital form, creating the substance of electronic libraries.

ADVANTAGES OF CYBERLIBRARIES

Though you can't actually thumb through the books, cyberlibraries have many advantages. For example, a text once available in a single location can be accessed in electronic form from anywhere in the world. And an unlimited number of people can use an electronic book simultaneously rather than waiting for a single copy to be returned to the reserve desk.

Another advantage is that **e-texts** aren't subject to the same wear and tear as hardbound and paperback books, so you can view historically significant documents in their original state. For instance, works as diverse as Egyptian cryptography, the Magna Carta or the Declaration of Independence can be reproduced faithfully in every visual detail.

The Reference Desk

Cyberlibraries help you find information. For instance, if you visit Bibliomania at **www.bibliomania.com**, you'll find a search screen. You can type in your query and select from different book categories— Reference, Literature and Language, Fiction, Nonfiction (Biography, Science, Economics and ancient texts) and Poetry. A list of "hits" will appear and you can browse through them.

Homework Central, at **www.home workcentral.com**, is designed to answer students' questions. It lays out information categories such as Science, History and Math. If you want to know something about online libraries, for example, you'd start by clicking on the Libraries and Archives section. From there you can progressively narrow your search, choosing electronic libraries, then selecting a specific library. Or if you can't find what you need, you can e-mail your question in.

Homework Central is one of a number of sites targeting students. Try these other sites as well:

Ask Adam at **http://remus.rut gers.edu/~adamj/askadam.html**
Homework Help at **www.star tribune.com/stonline/html/ special/homework**
Schoolwork Ugh! at **www.schoolwork.org**

A-C D-F G-I J-L M

V I R T U A L

While public domain laws limit the number of digital books available online, information about almost any book is easy to find. Nearly every volume ever published is listed on the Internet. It's just a matter of locating it.

The easiest way to find a book is to use a searchable catalog—an electronic version of a card catalog. Most major public and university library catalogs are available to Internet users via **Telnet** (short for **Telephone** or **Telecommunications Network**). Telnet lets you log on as a guest on a remote computer network so that you can search the databases at a university, government agency or, in this case, a library.

Project Gutenberg

In 1971, a computer operator named Michael Hart was given a console and a mission: find a way to use $100,000,000 of computer time on the mainframe computer in the Materials Research Lab at the University of Illinois. He figured he had only one option—so he typed in the Declaration of Independence and sent it to everyone he could think of.

He narrowly missed crashing the network but provided the first posting of an electronic text in a public forum. Since then, Project Gutenberg has slowly but steadily built the single largest collection of public domain electronic documents, working toward a goal of a 10,000-book electronic library by the end of 2001.

Project Gutenberg can be found at **www.promo.net/pg** and via FTP at **ftp://uiarchive.cso.uiuc. edu/pub/etext/gutenberg**. The collection includes the Gutenberg Bible, Webster's Unabridged Dictionary, *Gulliver's Travels* and thousands more.

E-BOOKS

Electronic or **e-books** blend commerce, computer wizardry and the experience of holding a book in your hands. They are stand-alone devices that typically look like a tablet with a single screen. And since e-books are portable and easy to hold—most weigh about one to three pounds—they are becoming increasingly popular with students, who have lots of books to carry and are comfortable reading texts on screen.

Electronic books do not use keyboards but rely on touch-screen technology. To "turn pages" you touch one of the outside corners. To find the index or table of contents you touch another area of the screen—each manufacturer has designed them slightly differently.

Each e-book is a comprehensive library, but it's not free. To buy a new book, you simply connect your e-book to a bookstore by phone line and do your shopping. Once you pay for your selections with your debit or credit card, or with an e-cash account, your new books are downloaded onto your e-book.

You can look at e-books at these sites:

Everybook, Inc. at **www.everybk.com**
Librius, Inc. at **www.librius.com**
Rocket eBook at **www.rocketbook.com**

Scanning the Stacks

Scanning is one way libraries can make their materials available to a wider audience. But the process does have limitations. Converting printed material to electronic text is time-consuming because each page has to be scanned. Plus, only works in the public domain—a book in print for 73 years or for 50 years after the death of the copyright owner—can be duplicated by libraries (or anyone) for the Internet for free public access.

The Library of Congress's National Digital Library (NDL) Program makes digitized versions of millions of books and other records from the Library available for free on the Internet. The library's entire card catalog is now available online, as is THOMAS, the Library's congressional database. Library of Congress exhibitions with text and images, as well as hundreds of thousands of images from the Library's map, photographic, manuscript and film collections, have also been scanned into the system. The Library's home page is **www.loc.gov.**

O   P-R   S-T   U-V   W-Z

C A T A L O G S

For more information, you can visit:
Library Spot **www.libraryspot.com**
The On-line Books Page **www.cs.cmu.edu/books**
Libraries and Online Catalogues
http://history.hanover.edu/libcat.html
Internet Public Library **www.ipl.org**

Fairrosa Cyber Library
www.users.interport.net/~fairrosa
Sunsite **http://sunsite.berkeley.edu**
Dartmouth College **www.dartmouth.edu/~library**
Smithsonian Institution **www.sil.si.edu/newstart.htm**

E-Commerce

Doing business in cyberspace opens new worlds of opportunity.

The explosion of Internet commerce is giving us greater choice of products (often at lower cost) and letting us shop around the clock from the comfort of our homes. It has created new businesses—and new millionaires—overnight and forced established companies to develop innovative strategies for their newest outlet—the World Wide Web.

The electronic marketplace is also a business equalizer. Since size and location are not an issue, and creating an online presence is fairly inexpensive, the Web offers entrepreneurs an ideal environment to develop and market entirely new services, from virtual bookstores and music shops to online auctions and discount ticket outlets.

RETHINKING OPPORTUNITIES

Pioneers in **electronic commerce** are rethinking the way conventional business is handled. Some companies have explored charging membership fees or selling subscriptions for access, following the model of magazines or research services.

Others have turned to advertising as a source of revenue and receive fees for adding "banner ads" to their pages or to websites they host for others. The appeal, from the advertiser's perspective, is the guarantee of an interested audience, potentially longer exposure, and the ability to customize messages for different viewers.

For example, Microsoft's Sidewalk site (**www.sidewalk.com**) relies on advertising to provide free information on over 65 cities in the US. You can check traffic reports and local weather as well as movie listings. You can also use their Expedia site to check on inexpensive flights and their Carpoint site to look for good deals on cars. There's a local Yellow Pages for each city as well.

E-MBAS

Recognizing the changes being wrought by the Internet, business schools across the country are offering MBAs in electronic commerce. The theory is that the Internet is spawning an entirely new way of doing business. Not only will successful entrepreneurs and managers need technological skills, but they'll need to study innovative approaches to marketing and finance. These disciplines don't work the same way in a Web-based business culture as they do in more traditional marketplaces.

A NATURAL ALLIANCE

The Web and the telephone—two primary channels to e-commerce—appear to be working hand-in-hand. Most commercial websites, for example, provide 800 numbers that let you talk directly to a representative. And AT&T's InteractiveAnswers (**www.ipservices.att.com/wss.interactiveanswers**) lets customers click on a phone number to automatically dial a merchant's 800 number on a second phone line. The merchants can "push" or display their Web pages onto the consumer's computer screen while talking to that consumer over the phone.

THE HARD AND THE SOFT OF IT

Despite its great variety, retail commerce on the Web can be divided into two broad categories: **hard goods**, like clothes and computers, which you can view, compare and purchase online—but which must be sent to you through the mail—and **soft goods**, like newspapers, music and software, which you can actually download to your site and then print or incorporate into a program.

Companies like Beyond.com (**www.beyond.com**) specialize in marketing software over the Web and allow customers to download their selections directly to their site. And Canon (**www.canon.com**) and other office equipment manufacturers let you download software developed for their products.

GOING, GOING...GONE

Even auctions have gone online. For example, eBay (**www.ebay.com**), founded in 1995, provides a meeting place, like a town square, where members hold a cyber-auction 24 hours a day, 7 days a week. In fact, eBay has close to two million items listed for sale, including antiques, books, movies, coins, stamps and other collectibles, with more than 100,000 new items added daily.

For a comprehensive list of auctions online, visit the Internet Auction list at **www.internetauctionlist.com**.

BUSINESS TO BUSINESS, AND THEN SOME

The electronic sale, or exchange, of goods and services between companies is predicted to grow even more rapidly than online retailing. For one, the opportunities are extremely broad, encompassing such diverse activities as purchasing used industrial material, selling closed-out items or overruns, providing wholesale price lists, displaying current inventories, or itemizing shipping regulations and costs for certain locales.

Courier services like FedEx and UPS have even made their internal tracking systems available to customers, who can visit their websites and determine where a package is at any particular time. Providing easy access to this information has saved these companies huge sums by reducing customer phone inquiries.

By some estimates, business-to-business electronic commerce is projected to represent $66 billion in US-related Internet revenues by the year 2000, according to Forrester Research.

DISSING THE MIDDLEMAN
Since Internet-based services are offered directly to consumers, the traditional middlemen, such as sales staff and agents, are being squeezed out. If you hear the unpronounceable word **disintermediation**, that's what it's all about.

Virtual Storefronts

There are few things you can't buy on the Net.

The electronic marketplace emerging on the World Wide Web is rapidly and radically changing the world of retailing. For plugged-in consumers, the Web has become an expansive, 24-hour virtual bazaar with offerings that range from cars and clothing to computers and books, and from online supermarkets to online auctions.

MAKING AN ONLINE PURCHASE

Besides being a multibillion-dollar industry—with no ceiling in sight—online purchasing can also be a lot of fun. Say you want to buy the current hot novel everyone's talking about and the latest CD from your favorite musician—and you want to do it online. What do you do? Here's a brief guide to purchasing online:

1. Shopping online is similar to shopping in a store you visit—if you're not sure where to go, check the store directory. Using built-in search engines, you can quickly find the titles you're interested in.

2. Next, you type in the name of the author or the title of the book you're looking for. (If you don't know the exact name or spelling, the search will show you all similar names and titles.)

By clicking on the name of the book, you can often read reviews posted by other people who have read it, and maybe even the author or publisher.

3. If you decide to buy the book, you can add it to your "shopping cart." (You can always change your mind later.)

4. Next, you go to the music department and, again using the search engine, type in the name of the musician or the CD you're looking for. When you find it, just add it to your shopping cart.

5. Now you're ready to buy. Your shopping cart will show the items you've selected, and if discounts are offered, you'll see how much you'll save.

6. Your next stop is the "checkout"—or cash register. You'll be asked to provide your e-mail address and payment method, such as a credit card. You also provide basic account information, and where and how you'd like your purchases sent.

If you enjoyed your online buying spree, you may be able to set up a special ordering account. The next time you want to buy something, all you have to do is make your selection. The company will keep your billing and shipping information on file, and you can always confirm or change it.

And if you decide that you really don't want to read the book or listen to the CD after you receive it, most stores have a very generous return policy.

CYBEROUTLETS

Many catalog retailers and stores now merchandise their wares in virtual stores you can visit online. For instance, retailers like L.L. Bean use their website as an enhanced outlet—a cyberbranch—to market products they also sell by mail-order catalog. Companies like Bean also add special, personalized features—such as Bean's "Address Book," which allows you to store addresses and shopping lists for gift purchases—which are designed to appeal to individual customers and to keep them coming back to their site.

The Web has also spawned exclusively Internet companies, like CDnow (**www.cdnow.com**), which offer comprehensive listings of CDs along with discounted prices, reviews of new releases, and special shopping services such as help in researching titles.

These companies have replaced bricks-and-mortar stores with access to extensive inventories, so they can fill orders for rare or hard-to-find items in relatively short order.

Some innovative marketers are even offering groceries on the Internet. In addition to providing online shopping lists, automatic billing and home delivery, they offer helpful information, like nutritional analysis or menu ideas, as well as incentives for splurging.

YourGrocer (**www.YourGrocer.com**), a regional company in the Northeast, is one example. You can find online grocery stores in your area by using a search engine.

And for real do-it-your-selfers, computer manufacturers like Dell have taken retailing online one step further by letting customers configure a PC or laptop computer to their own specifications and then place the order electronically.

In a virtual showroom, no item seems too big. An Internet firm called Autobytel (**www.autobytel.com**), for example, lets you buy a car without the hassle of showrooms and salespeople. After viewing different makes and models, you can submit a purchase order for a particular car at a specific price. Interested dealers, who pay to advertise on the site, can then respond and negotiate the deal.

ONLINE MALLS

If you hate shopping in crowded malls, you might try the virtual version, which is actually a series of hot-linked retailers. For instance, iMall (**www.imall.com**), a pioneer in electronic commerce services, provides small- and medium-sized businesses the opportunity to market their wares using the electronic mall's proprietary e-commerce tools and services.

Go Shopping Online can be found at **www.goshoppingonline.com** and Shop Internet at **http://shopinternet.ro.com**.

SAFETY TIPS FOR INTERNET SHOPPERS

The Better Business Bureau (**www.bbb.org**) offers the following tips when cybershopping:

- Think about security, starting with your connection. Be sure to look for the little "padlock" (on the lower left corner of your browser screen) that tells you whether or not the server the online store is using is secure. If the lock is open, it's not. If the site doesn't offer a secure server or a phone number to complete your order, consider going elsewhere.

- Don't give out your Internet password. If the site asks you to create an account with a password, never use the same password you use for other accounts or sites.

- Request a catalog or brochure, if available, to get a better idea of the merchant's products and services. These pieces should supply you with the permanent business information you'll need if you have to contact the company again.

- Determine the company's refund and return policies. This will make your purchasing decision easier, since it may demonstrate that the company stands behind its products.

- If you can, print a copy of your order and confirmation number for your records. This information could be useful if you need to contact the business in case of error.

- Know your rights. The same laws that protect you when you shop by phone or mail apply when you shop in cyberspace. Under the law, a company must ship your order within the time stated in its advertisements.

ANOTHER WAY TO SHOP SAFELY

Another way to shop—or sell—safely on the Web is by using AT&T's SecureBuy Service (**www.securebuy.com**), which guarantees the security of your transaction.

When you make a purchase from a SecureBuy merchant, AT&T adds the item to the online order form, computes the shipping charges and taxes for the merchant, securely completes the credit card transaction, and sends the order to the merchant.

One of the many advantages to becoming a SecureBuy member—it's free—is that you don't have to re-enter personal information when buying online.

Online Banking

Your computer can be a 24-hour teller.

Banker's hours—once strictly 10 a.m. to 3 p.m.—are now a thing of the past. ATMs extended teller's hours around the clock so that the banking business you could once do only in a branch—paying bills, transferring funds and checking your balance—can now be done any time of the night or day. And **electronic banking** lets you do even more, whether you're at home or on the road.

There are two kinds of electronic banks: **virtual banks**, which reside exclusively on the World Wide Web, and **online banks**, which are institutions that offer private, or dedicated, networks in addition to conventional banking services. You can do most of the same things—bill paying, money transfers and investment transactions, for example—with either.

VIRTUAL BANKS

Since virtual banks are Web-based, you can access your account from any computer with an Internet connection and a Web browser. There's no special software involved, and enhancements are added at the bank's end, so you don't have to upgrade your equipment.

Since your virtual bank doesn't have a neighborhood branch, you can usually withdraw money from any ATM network linked to the bank. But deposits must be made electronically—online, direct-deposited or wire-transferred from another bank.

Some Internet banks will also let you complete transactions in **real time**. For example, that means if you transfer money from a money market fund to your checking account, that money is immediately available for use in your checking account. With regular online banking, it might take overnight or several days to complete this transaction.

CHOOSING A BANK

Probably the best way to choose a virtual or online bank is to concentrate on the basics: service, cost and ease of use. Whatever your choice, location is one thing you won't have to consider since the bank brings the service to you. A good way to look for an electronic bank is by visiting the Banking and Financial Services Web Directory at **www.orcc.com/banking**.

Cost can be an issue, so comparative shopping

pays. In addition to fees for basic banking services, you may want to check to see if the bank has any additional fees for online service.

Some banks may also charge extra for transactions like direct payments if you request more than their monthly limit, often 10. And some banks require five or more days' notice to pay bills and then debit your account several days before they credit the money to the payee. This procedure gives banks the benefit of the float, or free use of your money.

ONLINE BANKING

Online banks are generally an electronic branch of the bank you use in person. To get started, here's all you have to do:

1. Speak to an account representative at your local branch and fill out an application to receive your online banking package. (You can sometimes find a kiosk within the bank that will explain the process.)

2. Provide personal background information. You'll probably be asked about your PC and modem type. This information is on your computer's Control Panel or in the material that came with it.

3. You'll then receive an introductory package with a detailed explanation of the process, as well as an 800-number help line, just in case.

4. Before you sign up, check the cost of PC banking, since each bank is different.

5. If the bank offers a trial period, you may want to select this option so you can decide if the system works for you.

PAYING ONLINE

One of the most appealing features of electronic banking is that you can pay your bills—such as rent or mortgage, car leases or loans, insurance or utility bills—without writing checks, licking envelopes or buying stamps. You simply authorize the bank, usually five to seven days before the due date, to make the payment. If the company you're paying accepts electronic payments, your bank debits your account and transfers the money. If not, your bank writes a check against your account and puts it in the mail.

Another way to pay bills electronically—at less cost—is to authorize the organizations you pay to deduct the correct amount from your account every month. The amount is simply debited from your account as if you wrote a check or told the bank to pay the bill. Usually, a payee will let you name the payment date, so you can be sure there's money to cover the amount.

TAKE YOUR BANKING WITH YOU

BANKING FOR LESS, FOR BANKS

According to industry statistics, the average payment transaction on the Internet is only about 4¢. This compares with 26¢ for a transaction done through a typical personal computer banking service where you use the bank's own software, 54¢ for a telephone banking service, and $1.44 for a bank branch.

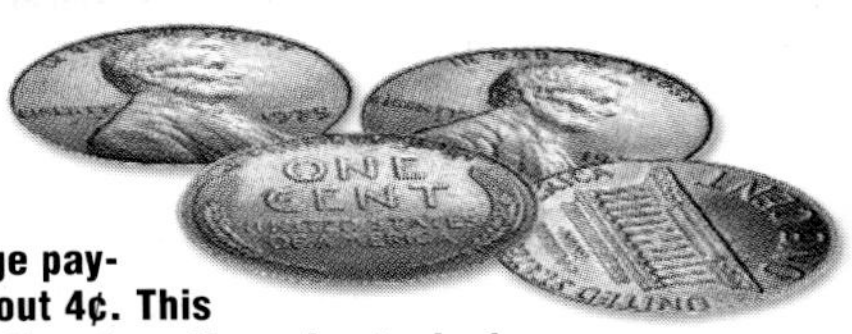

YOUR ONLINE TELLER
WHAT KIND OF TRANSACTION WOULD YOU LIKE TO DO TODAY?
PIN#
SEE ACCOUNT BALANCE
TRANSFER FUNDS
ABOUT OUR SERVICES
PAY BILLS

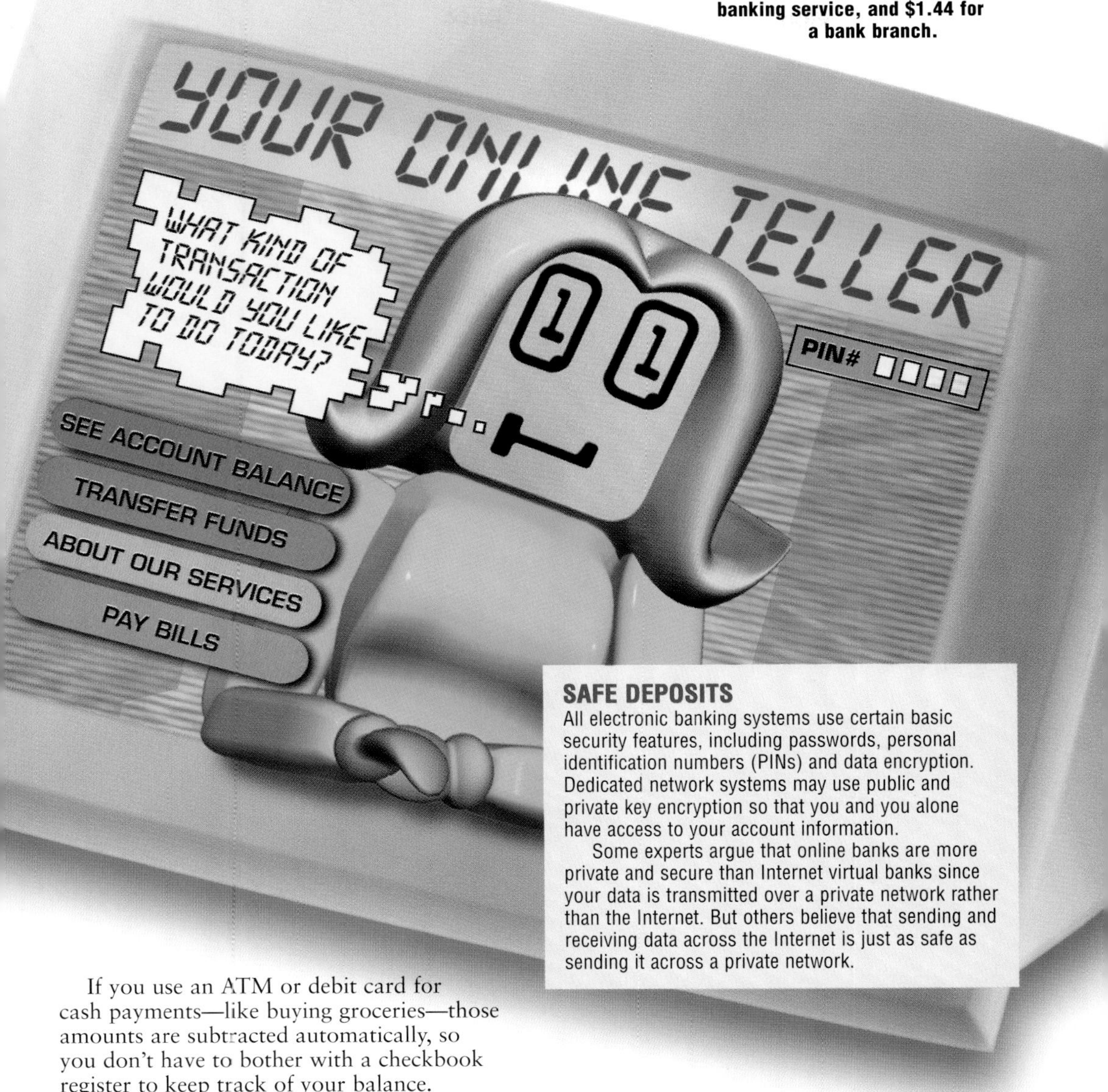

SAFE DEPOSITS

All electronic banking systems use certain basic security features, including passwords, personal identification numbers (PINs) and data encryption. Dedicated network systems may use public and private key encryption so that you and you alone have access to your account information.

Some experts argue that online banks are more private and secure than Internet virtual banks since your data is transmitted over a private network rather than the Internet. But others believe that sending and receiving data across the Internet is just as safe as sending it across a private network.

If you use an ATM or debit card for cash payments—like buying groceries—those amounts are subtracted automatically, so you don't have to bother with a checkbook register to keep track of your balance.

You can also handle occasional payments, such as charitable donations, or payments where the amount varies each month—like your credit card bill—electronically. Once you've set up the payee in the bank's system, you simply notify the bank of the amount, by e-mail or telephone connection, whenever it's time to make a payment.

SOFTWARE BANKING

Software products like Intuit's Quicken or Microsoft Money also let you do electronic banking, either using your own bank account online or a service such as Checkfree, which allows you to pay bills online from any checking account even if your bank doesn't offer electronic banking.

You can use this software to do much more than banking—for example, to keep track of your investments, loan payments and business expenses. And at year's end you can produce the records you need to prepare your taxes. Most programs also have planning capabilities, so you can create budgets, check loan amortization tables, and figure your net worth. You can even convert your data into pie charts or bar graphs so you can see exactly how you spend your money.

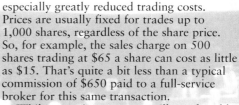

Investing Online

Stock prices, analysts' reports and initiating your own trades are just a click away.

Traditionally, individual investors relied on their brokers and financial experts—not to mention hot tips from family and acquaintances—for investment information and advice.

But the emergence of **electronic trading** has dramatically changed investing by putting a wealth of financial information—formerly available only to professionals—into the hands of anyone wanting to trade online.

LESS COST, MORE INFORMATION

Online brokerages offer many advantages, especially greatly reduced trading costs. Prices are usually fixed for trades up to 1,000 shares, regardless of the share price. So, for example, the sales charge on 500 shares trading at $65 a share can cost as little as $15. That's quite a bit less than a typical commission of $650 paid to a full-service broker for this same transaction.

While many investors are still comfortable with their brokers, some are experimenting with online brokerages by making limited investments just to get the hang of electronic trading and what it offers.

Recognizing this trend, some brokerage firms are offering reduced commissions to investors who book the trade online. And even full-service brokerages are exploring ways to attract online investors without alienating their sales force.

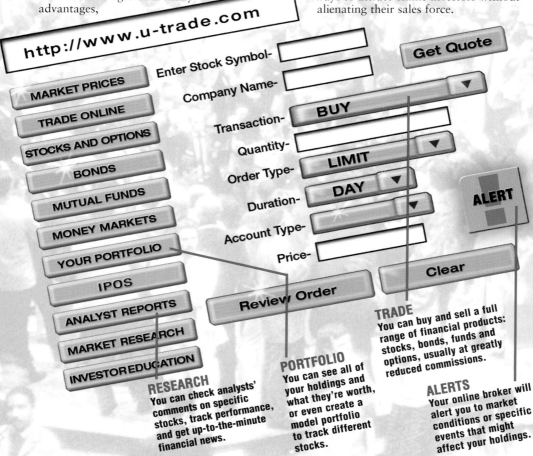

http://www.u-trade.com

Enter Stock Symbol-
Company Name-
Transaction- BUY
Quantity-
Order Type- LIMIT
Duration- DAY
Account Type-
Price-

Get Quote

MARKET PRICES
TRADE ONLINE
STOCKS AND OPTIONS
BONDS
MUTUAL FUNDS
MONEY MARKETS
YOUR PORTFOLIO
IPOS
ANALYST REPORTS
MARKET RESEARCH
INVESTOR EDUCATION

ALERT

Review Order

Clear

RESEARCH
You can check analysts' comments on specific stocks, track performance, and get up-to-the-minute financial news.

PORTFOLIO
You can see all of your holdings and what they're worth, or even create a model portfolio to track different stocks.

TRADE
You can buy and sell a full range of financial products: stocks, bonds, funds and options, usually at greatly reduced commissions.

ALERTS
Your online broker will alert you to market conditions or specific events that might affect your holdings.

MAKING THE TRADE

To buy a stock you enter the stock symbol (which you can look up on the site), the number of shares you want to buy, and the price you're willing to pay. You can also research the stock to check current price and past performance, and what analysts have to say. "Market" price means you'll buy the stock at the going price when the trade is negotiated. Most services will reconfirm your order before executing the trade.

You pay an online broker by sending a check, wiring money, or having the broker deduct the payment from your cash or management account.

INSTANT FINANCIAL INFORMATION

Online trading sites provide a wealth of information, including financial research and commentary, the latest price quotations and price histories, market indexes, and even access to IPOs, or initial public offerings, of new companies. These sites also alert you to events that may affect your portfolio.

Online trading gives you 24-hour access to your own portfolio, including all of your holdings, a history of completed and pending transactions, and the price you paid for each security. You can even create a model portfolio of stocks you're interested in and then trace their performance over time, without any risk.

In addition to dedicated online brokerages, websites supported by financial services companies and Internet portals (general access sites) also provide investment information.

If you're especially interested in mutual funds, you might check Brill's Mutual Funds Interactive (**www.fundsinteractive.com**), The Armchair Millionaire featuring Charles Schwab (**www.armchairmillionaire.com/schwab/gettingstarted**), or Vanguard (**www.vanguard.com**).

GETTING STARTED

Don't send your broker packing just because you've discovered online investing. The array of information on the Web can be dizzying to the newcomer, and it's important to learn how to evaluate the quality of your sources and information.

If you feel you need basic knowledge of investing online or off, there are several websites devoted to teaching you how. Concepts of Investing (**http://tqd.advanced.org/3096/1concept.htm**) discusses the world of investing in simple basic terms. Investtrek (**www.investtrek.com**) contains a page for beginners as well as many resources for learning about the stock market.

A good way to choose an online broker is to visit Gomez Advisors (**www.gomez.com**). Gomez ranks online services according to cost, ease of use, customer satisfaction and resources (such as quotes, news,

advice, recommendations and screening tools). And some brokerage sites, like Discover Brokerage (**www.discoverbrokerage.com**), walk you through a demo so you can see how an actual transaction works.

If you're familiar with the stock market but unsure of negotiating transactions online, there's an excellent step-by-step walk-through available at Gomez's Broker Selection 101 (**www.gomez.com/finance/tools/brokerselection.cfm?tid-1173782**).

DAY TRADERS

Electronic trading has also spawned a new breed of investor, many of them amateurs, who actively (some say overactively) moves in and out of stocks at cyberspeeds. The result is that many Internet stocks followed by day traders show dramatic price swings, or spikes, that increase the volatility of the markets. Day trading, by the way, is not for the faint-hearted.

AFTER HOURS

Already on the drawing boards are plans for 24-hour trading, even when the exchanges are closed. And new services will allow individuals to trade directly with other investors, bypassing the broker altogether.

THE YOUNG INVESTOR

A very impressive program for children was designed by three teenagers in California. The site, called Investing for Kids (**http://tqd.advanced.org/3096**), explains complicated financial concepts in an easy-to-grasp style and examines stocks, bonds and mutual funds while teaching the principles of saving and investing. It also includes a stock game.

Liberty Financial Companies offers The Young Investor Website, found at **www.younginvestor.com**.

THE NUMBERS

As of 1998 there were an estimated 7.1 million online accounts, with 35% of all retail trades being processed online. The number of online brokers has grown from 27 in 1997 to 140 in 1999.

Travel

The Web's your ticket.

Using the World Wide Web, you can plan an entire trip, from laying out your itinerary to making reservations and purchasing tickets.

The list of travel sites on the Web is huge and ranges from travel guides, books, magazines and maps to flight selection, online ticketing and hotel reservations.

If you want to use the Internet to plan your trip, you might start with a portal, such as Yahoo!, Lycos or Excite, and go to their travel section. Usually, the information is arranged in categories such as air travel, automotive, business, lodgings, resorts, train travel, etc., so you can just click through the topics until you find what you're looking for.

THE NUMBERS

Forrester Research reports nearly 3 billion online bookings in 1998, while NPD Online Research estimates that 70% of Web users (and there are 70 million users in the US) have visited a travel site.

E-FARES

If you're flexible there are excellent savings to be found through the Web. Most of the major airlines offer last-minute savings to fill empty seats on flights, and they send fare information to you by e-mail at your request. To sign up, just visit the websites of the airlines you're interested in and register.

E-TICKETING

Many airlines are using new technologies to eliminate printing tickets and speed airport departures. When you purchase an e-ticket, you merely present your identification and credit card at the ticketing counter or at the gate, where you'll receive your boarding card. Some airlines have e-ticket kiosks that let you select your seat assignment.

To confirm your e-ticket, many airlines still send a fax with your itinerary included. While you can't lose an e-ticket, you do have to remember what flight you're on.

ONLINE TRAVEL AGENTS

There are several advantages to making plane reservations online. To begin with, you can usually get through immediately—there's no waiting for "the next available service representative." And all the information you want, from flight times and availability to price comparisons, is at your fingertips.

Sites that work like cyber travel agents scan all airline schedules for flights to and from your destination as well as search for the cheapest fare or the fastest connection. They also offer deep discounts on same-day or next-day flights that still have seats available. Check out The Trip at **www.thetrip.com**, Biztravel at **www.biztravel.com**, Travelocity at **www.travelocity.com**, or Expedia at **www.expedia.com.**

GETTING THE LOCAL LOWDOWN

The Net can quickly profile an area you plan to visit, including local customs, weather, exchange rates, inoculations and visa requirements. The State Department operates a site (**http://travel.state.gov/travel_warnings.html**) that alerts you about any travel warnings, sometimes accompanied by a description of any unstable conditions.

Consular Information Sheets are available for every country of the world. They tell you the location of the US Embassy or Consulate, unusual immigration practices, health conditions, unusual currency and entry regulations, crime and security information, and drug penalties.

GETTING AROUND BY CAR

All of the major automobile rental companies also have websites that let you book cars in advance, so you might do some comparison shopping. Many airline ticketing sites also offer deals on car rentals, though you may pay a little more for this service than you would by dealing directly with the car rental service. For many, the convenience of taking care of both plane and auto travel at once is worth the extra cost.

MAPPING YOUR JOURNEY

If you are planning a driving tour, there are a wealth of map sites to be found, including those on portals such as Yahoo!, Excite, Lycos and Webcrawler. Expedia (**www.expedia.com**) lets you zoom in on the area you are interested in. Maps On Us (**www.mapsonus .com/index.cgi**) has a route planner. Cyber Router (**www .delorme.com/cybermaps/route .asp**) offers a similar service.

You can also purchase detailed maps on CD ROM. Visit Street Atlas USA (**www .delorme.com/StreetAtlasUSA**) for an example of how comprehensive these maps can be.

THE DIGITAL MAP

Some cars now come equipped with a **GPS (Global Positioning Satellite)** system, which can pinpoint your location and guide you turn by turn to your destination. You can also purchase GPS software for a palm-sized PC to use in your car or anywhere else. To learn more about the software, visit Teletype GPS at **www.teletype.com/gps**.

HOTEL RESERVATIONS

If you're planning your own itinerary, you can find a hotel in the area you'll be visiting through a search engine or one of the many other travel guides. You simply key in the country and region, narrowing the search until you locate the specific town or locale you're interested in. You'll find many listings for lodgings as well as information about the area and nearby tourist attractions.

TRAVEL TIPS ONLINE

Here are some special travel sites to keep in mind.

- Web Travel Secrets (**www.web-travel-secrets.com**) helps you create an itinerary, making reservations and purchasing tickets online.
- The Universal Packing List (**www.henricson.se/mats/upl**) focuses on travel essentials and cuts out the items you'll regret carrying around.
- Travlang (**www.travlang.com**) provides foreign language information, including the award-winning "Foreign Languages for Travelers." It also provides information on hotels worldwide, exchange rates, and links to translating dictionaries.
- On The Road (**www.roadnews.com**) offers help to travelers with a laptop computer, including going online in a foreign country and getting technical support.
- Dan's Travel Page (**www.mindspring.com/~paschal/travel/ index.html**) links you to maps, information on road and traffic conditions, weather information sites, automobile rental, toll-free phone numbers, state tourism information, and US newspapers online.

Digital Photography

You don't need film to get the picture.

Digital technology is not only opening new vistas on the Internet, it's affecting how we take and develop pictures. While film processing has become quicker and more convenient than ever, the ability to see our pictures instantly, and then edit them on our home computers, has triggered the growing popularity of digital photography.

Take a photo

Preview the image before downloading to your PC

Store the image

View it on your monitor

Pick an image you like

THE BIG PICTURE

At first glance, digital cameras share many features with traditional film cameras. Lenses, shutters and exposures are relatively the same, though digital camera shutters can be electronic as well as mechanical.

The difference is primarily how the images are stored and retrieved. With traditional cameras, the lens focuses light on the film, which is then developed as negatives or transparencies (slides). When you take a digital picture, however, the camera memorizes or stores the image flashed upon the chip as a computer file. In some cameras, this file is stored directly on a removable card or disk. In other models, the image file can be transferred to your computer through a cable.

WHY DIGITAL PIX

There are many advantages to digital cameras. They work especially well for screen-oriented applications such as desktop publishing, e-mail attachments, and Web page design. And digital cameras let you immediately see the image that you've captured.

Operating a digital camera is also inexpensive because the only recurring cost is batteries. The camera's storage is reusable once you download a batch of images. And since you don't have to pay for film processing, you can experiment with as many angles or compositions as you like.

Despite their advantages, digital cameras still lag behind film cameras in image quality. For example, pictures from film cameras have resolutions of many thousands of **dpi**, or **dots per inch**, while most digital cameras deliver resolutions under 100 dpi. So if your application requires the highest possible image quality, your best bet is to use a conventional camera and then have the prints scanned.

ZOOM

In a digital camera, a light-sensing computer chip—either the popular **charge-coupled device** (**CCD**) or the newer CMOS image sensor—takes the place of film. The image sensor operates by converting refracted rays of light that strike the camera lens into digital data in the form of electrical charges. The charges are then interpreted by a microprocessor and stored in RAM or on a hard drive.

SOME SITES TO SEE

If you're interested in digital cameras, or in reworking images you've taken with a conventional camera, there's lots of information on the Web. Check out:

www.dcresource.com
www.fujifilm.net
www.kodak.com
www.filmworks.com

DIGITAL ORIGINS

Digital photography processes originated within the Defense Department during the Cold War. Powerful cameras mounted on satellites could photograph objects anywhere in the world and instantly relay the image to a waiting satellite dish.

CREATING A DIGITAL DARKROOM

Another major advantage of digital cameras is that you can download the images to your computer via a cable or disk that comes with the camera. Once the photo is in your computer, you can crop, enhance or recolor it, create a collage, or manipulate the image in ways formerly available only to expert film developers.

Kodak maintains a "how-to" page at **www.kodak.com/global/en/consumer/digitization**, which includes templates for creating electronic post cards and birth announcements, tips for attaching your images to e-mail, and graphically illustrated help on getting your image onto a Web page.

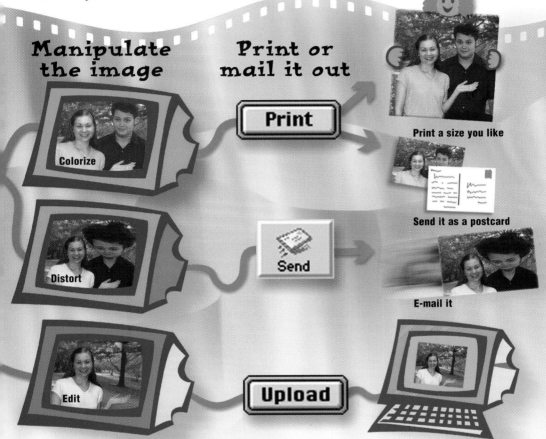

Manipulate the image

Print or mail it out

Print

Colorize

Distort

Edit

Send

Upload

Print a size you like

Send it as a postcard

E-mail it

Put it on your website

FEATURES OF DIGITAL CAMERAS

Image quality. In general, the less-expensive cameras work well for photos you plan to use on your screen—for Web pages and e-mail—rather than on your printer. More-expensive cameras provide higher resolutions and better images, making them better suited for applications where you want to include photos in printed documents.

Capacity. If you have ready access to a computer, you can get by with less internal storage. But if you want to take vacation snapshots, your camera will need enough capacity to last the entire trip. In that case, consider a camera with some type of removable storage that you can swap out when it is full.

Previewing. Many digital cameras come with a small LCD viewfinder that doubles as a playback screen, letting you see the pictures you've taken before you download them to your computer. This can be a great memory saver because you can delete the images you don't want to save.

CONVERTING FROM FILM TO DIGITAL

Imagek is developing an add-on device to convert your film camera to digital. The EFS-1, or Electronic Film System, looks like a roll of film that you'd pop into your camera. The device holds up to 30 photos and hooks into your computer using a parallel cable for PCs and SCSI cable for Macs.

FILM GOES DIGITAL

Even if you are using a conventional camera, you can have your processed prints scanned to a CD ROM or disk. Some film processors will even post your developed film on the Web for you to download.

That's Entertainment

It's easy to get immersed in Information Age games.

WATCHING THE WORLD GO BY

Perhaps the most popular form of entertainment on the Net is simply watching the world go by—and staying in touch with other people. Whether it's through e-mail, a bulletin board, a chat room, or an online forum, many people check in on a daily basis to catch up with online friends and just to see what might be new.

MAKING THE MIGRATION

If you're looking for entertainment, much of what you'll find on the Web is a migration of the old into the new— well-known forms of entertainment that are simply moving to a new medium.

Many of the games you can play online will be very familiar if you've spent any time in an arcade. You'll find that radio has appeared as **RealAudio**, a streaming technology that allows you to begin hearing an audio file as soon as you begin to download it. The quality is about the same as an AM radio broadcast. Television is slower to make the move because the moving images require greater bandwidth.

What makes the entertainment on the Web different is interactivity: you can be a participant rather than just an observer.

COMPUTER GAMES

Since the introduction of the PC, computers have been used for playing games. These include both electronic versions of traditional match-ups, like chess, and fantasy games in which each participant assumes a fictional personality and plays a role in an imaginary world, sometimes, though not always, a violent one. In either case, your decisions trigger responses in the program to which you in turn react.

Replete with rich graphics and dramatic sound effects, games can have a spellbinding effect. Some, like MYST—which has sold more than 3 million copies—and its successor, Riven, are semi-solitary, with each player moving through the complex plot and reacting to its challenges alone.

Games like SimCity or SimAnt allow the players to immerse themselves in a world with its own rules and logic that parallel real-world situations. In SimCity, for example, you are responsible for the well-being of the city you create. You make decisions about industry, transportation, recreation facilities and taxes. If you don't balance the various needs of the community, your ratings go down and people begin to move away.

Many players—especially children—prefer games that allow them to change the rules or modify the situations they find themselves in. There are some who feel that this disparity between the rules of the game and real life is problematic—after all, there is no *Undo* button in real life when you get killed, even though it may work for your game character.

r:Welcome to RealPlayer!

The SimCity Exchange Is Now Open!
Over 100 SC3K Cities and Terrains
Browse more than a dozen categories ...
Submit your City & see how it ranks ...

SIMCITY HOME | register | support | sitemap | contact

ORDER NOW!

LOVE THOSE MOVIES

If playing games or chatting isn't your idea of a good time, what about movies? Imagine being able to see any film you want at any hour of the day or night. With access to stored multimedia information, either on the Internet, CD ROM or the new **digital versatile disks** (**DVDs**), that's not only possible but practical.

New technology means you'll be able to select not only the film but the format you see it in, and the language you want to hear or read as subtitles. Sometimes you can even choose among alternative endings, so you have a hand in determining the film's outcome.

DVD: IT AIN'T JUST MOVIES

A DVD, the newest storage medium, looks like a CD but holds up to 17 gigabytes of information, enough for a full-length feature movie. DVD has lots of advantages over videotape, including higher-quality images and sound, plus the ability to add special features.

You can plug a DVD playback device into your TV, replace the CD ROM drive in your computer, or, if you buy a new PC, you may be able to get a DVD player as standard equipment. DVD players will soon offer write-once recording and, later, full read/write capabilities. This means you'll be able to store whatever you like and later record new data over old, if you wish.

And while DVDs are being used primarily for movies at present, their huge storage capacity will make them ideal for the creation of education and training tools and sophisticated games.

PERSONAL PERFORMANCES

Live-action events are another form of entertainment that seem destined to be changed by the power of online multimedia delivery channels. The ability to **narrowcast**, or provide programming directly for an interested few, means that many more special events—musical, theatrical or sporting—will be available to those interested in them.

It also means producers can make the experience even more appealing by combining a real-time broadcast with a chat environment, or website links to related materials, such as earlier sports events or interviews with participants.

And the Band Played On(line)

Tickling the virtual ivories.

Words are an important way to create and communicate, but they're not the only way. That's true in traditional media, such as books, magazines and television. And it's increasingly the case online as well, as text-based Internet communication evolves into a real-time multimedia experience.

Music and sounds can be created using special software programs. Then they can be stored as computer files, produced on tape or CD, or uploaded to a website.

MAKING DIGITAL MUSIC

Today most computers come equipped with a sound card or sound board that lets you play—and create—music. The sound card functions as a built-in synthesizer by sending electrical signals to the computer's speakers.

Using music software, you can manipulate the signals to alter the sound quality. For example, you might go from a high-pitched reedy sound to a hollow flute tone or a scratchy percussive noise. You can also control the pitch and volume of sounds, creating simple songs or complex compositions. Most programs come with preprogrammed settings that allow the sound card to mimic conventional musical instruments, such as a piano, violin, flute or trumpet.

You can convert an analog recording to a digital format and then play it back on your computer or CD player. The sound quality is indistinguishable from the original, and the digital version can be copied over and over with no loss of integrity.

INTELLECTUAL PROPERTY

While the Web can provide an enormous audience for an artist's or composer's work, there is a down side. There's limited ability to control what happens to your intellectual property, and so far no real way to reap any potential financial rewards when people access it online or make themselves a copy. However, coding and encryption technologies will solve that problem, so that writers, artists and musicians may be able to bypass publishers, galleries and recording companies.

The International Federation of the Phonographic Industry (IFPI) is completing listening tests and will recommend a specific watermarking technology to control unauthorized music copying and trace pirated digital music. The Secure Digital Music Initiative (SDMI) is working on a set of standards that will allow the public to access music in all forms while protecting the copyrights held by artists and recording companies.

THE WORLD'S LARGEST JUKEBOX

Using an online jukebox, such as AT&T's a2b music (**www.a2bmusic.com**), lets you download high-quality music. One of the big drawbacks to downloading music over the Internet has been that it can take a long, long time—typically four hours for a five-minute song. The a2b service solves that problem using advanced compression technology. The music file is reduced to about 7% of its original size without loss of sound quality. So a five-minute song downloads in about 16 minutes as opposed to four hours.

Live Online (**www.live-online.com**) provides online music events and cybercasts. The Digital Jukebox spins some of the best new music out there, and the Almost Live Archives lets you listen to thousands of past cybercasts.

To enjoy music on the Web, you may want to download audio and voice plug-ins. RealAudio (**www.real.com**), TrueSpeech and StreamWorks all play sounds as they are being transferred and are used by radio stations and music libraries, for example, so you can listen to the news from National Public Radio (**www.npr.org**) or music from the Internet Underground Music Archives (**www.iuma.com**).

THE MIDI CONNECTION

Through **MIDI**, or **Musical Instrument Digital Interface**, a computer can control a synthesizer, electronic keyboard, drum machine and other electronic devices. The interface allows the computer and electronic instruments to send information back and forth to each other.

For example, a computer can act as the conductor or bandleader, telling the other instruments what notes to play, how loudly, or when to bang the drum and when to bring in the brass.

MIDI also lets the instruments send information to the computer. For example, you can sit down at an electronic keyboard, improvise a song, and the computer will capture all the notes and display them on the screen, producing a musical score. You can even edit the score and have the computer play back your finished masterpiece. Once your piece is finished, you can save it as a file on your hard drive. You can play it back whenever you want—even e-mail it to fans and friends around the world.

If you choose this route to make music, you'll be in good company. Former Beatle Paul McCartney (who doesn't read music) used an electronic keyboard, computer, MIDI and composition software to write his classical hit, "Standing Stone." In fact, many professional composers now use computers, MIDI devices and composition software to write their music.

DOWNLOAD MUSIC FROM THE WEB

MP3 stands for **MPEG 1 layer 3**, which is a way to store music files on a computer disk in such a way that the file size is relatively small, but the song sounds quite good. MP3 stores files in a digital format, but ordinarily such information takes up quite a bit of space. So MP3 compresses it into a smaller package to move and store it. MP3 is popular right now because you can store compressed sound in a sound file and get great sound back out. Before MP3 you could use the popular Windows **.wav** format, which gave good sound but could not be compressed like MP3.

It is important to realize that, while it is legal if you encode MP3s from your own CDs and keep them to yourself, it's illegal to encode MP3s and trade them with others unless you have the permission of the copyright holder of the music.

TAKE IT WITH YOU

The Rio player is a compact portable music player capable of playing MP3 files downloaded from the Internet or from CDs. The player is about the size of a deck of cards and roughly the same weight. Even better, it has no moving parts, so it won't skip. It holds about 30-35 minutes of music (30MG). Included with the Rio player is a bonus MP3.com CD with over 100 songs and other software and music files.

SOME SITES WORTH VISITING:

- Broadcast.com (**www.broadcast.com/music**) specializes in streaming hundreds of live and on-demand audio and video programs over the Internet to hundreds of thousands of users.
- The Classical MIDI Archives (**www.prs.net/midi.html**) contains thousands of classical music files you can listen to at the click of your mouse. Most composers are represented. A search engine is included.
- Exploding Art (**www.explodingart.com.au**)
- Digital Music Media (**www.xs4all.nl/~hanuman/index.html**)
- Digital Music Corporation (**www.voodoolab.com**)

Virtual Reality

Experiencing the real world
without its perils.

1850s
Stereoscope

If you've ever played a video game in
an arcade, participated in an interactive
computer game at home, seen a movie
wearing 3D glasses, or taken an imaginary
ride in a spaceship in a theme park, you've
experienced **virtual reality**, or **VR**.

Virtual reality is an attempt to recreate,
or simulate, through computer-imaging
technology and other sensory stimulations,
something that approximates a real-world
experience. Mentally, viscerally and emotion-
ally, you are transported into another world,
where you see and feel something even
though it's not actually happening. Your
response is a physical one—turning your
head, for example—just as it would be in
real life.

Because the computer is monitoring your
reactions, it can adjust its response, changing
what you see and making you feel as if you
are controlling what's happening. The more
continuous and seamless the stream of images
is, and the more sensations you experience—
sight, sound, movement—the more real the
situation seems.

Sophisticated virtual reality experiences are
still equipment-intensive. You use a helmet,
called a head-mounted display (HMD), with
sensor-equipped gloves, body suits and
footwear to send messages to a computer.
The HMD is equipped with tiny screens and
speakers that display computer-generated
images, immersing you in the simulated
experience by presenting a computerized
representation of what something looks like
from your particular vantage point.

EXTREME BUT SAFE
One of the values—and enjoyments—of
virtual reality is that you can experience
exciting, even hazardous, situations without
risk of injury. For example, you can ski
down steep mountains and over formidable
moguls, drive a race car at ridiculous
speeds, hang glide off a cliff, or, if you're
so inclined, engage in martial arts and

other contests of prowess and
power—and never leave your room.

But virtual reality is more than just
animated good times. Visual flight simulators,
for example, give pilots a physical sense of
flying—including forcing them to respond to
in-flight disasters, such as severe weather or
aircraft malfunctions.

In fact, virtual reality can be a valuable
tool in many fields, including teaching people
how to drive cars, retraining physically disabled people to control their body movement,
or giving control room personnel "practical"
experience in operating a nuclear power
plant. And a virtual reality operation can
allow medical students to practice difficult
medical procedures on virtual patients. In
fact, the possibilities are virtually limitless.

FRASCA
NB0-105

Today
Virtual Reality
Simulators

SEEING IS BELIEVING
Virtual reality is a booming entertainment industry.
Portrayed in films like *TRON* (where a programmer
finds himself a character in one of his own games)
and *Star Trek* (where characters enter into and play
out virtual reality scenarios in a holodeck), VR has
titillated our desires to experience what would
otherwise be impossible.

VRML

The World Wide Web is a new frontier for virtual reality. VRML (pronounced either as the letters V-R-M-L or *verm'l*), which stands for Virtual Reality Modeling Language, is a coding language that allows you to create a 3D space on a website. By piecing together a number of contiguous pictures and superimposing sound and other visual effects, VRML lets you enter an environment through the eyes of a character who is virtually present in that world. As the character moves, or turns her head, you see what the character sees as if you were there.

Some chat rooms on the Web also have avatars, or representations of people in the chat room. People who have been in chats using avatars sometimes find the experience disconcerting, since they are actually communicating by e-mail, though they want to converse as if the person they're talking to is physically beside them.

VIRTUAL REAL ESTATE

Virtual reality technology is also simplifying buying and selling property. Three-dimensional walk-throughs of several homes or commercial buildings can give prospective buyers a first-hand look at the property—from the inside out.

And while you might hesitate to buy a place you'd never actually set foot in, you'd probably have fewer qualms about renting that way, especially if you could save yourself the time and expense of a house-hunting trip.

1950s 3D Movies

1970s Arcade Video Games

1980s Home Video Games

1990s Arcade Video Simulators

GOGGLE-EYED

Virtual reality is perhaps the most exotic interface. Already found in arcade games, VR could move into the PC, permitting you to don sensory-mimicking equipment like helmet and gloves. You could then, in effect, get inside your data by viewing images in depth, changing your position and perspective, and feeling surfaces and textures. It's the next best thing to being there.

Eventually, speech recognition, intelligent agents and VR will become standard components in the operating systems of personal computers. You'll no longer need to learn computer languages, since the computers will have learned yours.

Security

There is safety in numbers—particularly the ones that encode your personal information.

ONLINE TRANSACTIONS

Many people have fears about giving out their credit card numbers or other sensitive information over the Net, perhaps with good reason. If the information is not protected or coded—the technical term is **encrypted**—it can be intercepted and manipulated by cyber-intruders.

This situation is somewhat akin to buying mail-order goods by phone. You want to be sure that no one but the mail-order company hears and uses your credit card number.

BEEFING UP SECURITY

A method commonly used by many merchants to provide security is to host their Web page on a secure server that uses **SSL** (**Secure Socket Layer**) or **S-HTTP** (**Secure HyperText Transfer Protocol**). These protocols, or procedures, encrypt or code the data being transmitted, so when you submit your credit card number on their electronic form, it can't be deciphered by anyone who doesn't know the code.

THE KEY TO SECURITY

By convention, sites using SSL begin with **https://** instead of **http://**. Also, both Netscape Navigator and Microsoft Internet Explorer use a padlock symbol, usually located in the lower left corner of your screen, to indicate whether or not your transaction is secure.

If your browser does not have this symbol, you may want to download a more current version. You can find free downloads at Netscape's home page (**www.netscape.com**) and Microsoft's home page (**www.microsoft.com**).

CYBER HIEROGLYPHICS

Encryption is the translation of data—in this case, all of your private information—into a secret code. The key is simply a table used both to encrypt and then to decipher the encoded information. The most basic system is known as symmetric encryption and uses only one key to encode and decode messages.

SSL verifies that you are who you say you are by **authenticating** that you are the account user. After you enter a user ID and a password, SSL uses **public key encryption** (which allows you to keep a private key) as well as **certificates** to establish your identity. A certificate is supplied by the card-issuing bank to the merchant and verifies that your identification is in order.

SECURE ELECTRONIC TRANSACTIONS

Although the SSL system is widely used, **SET** (**Secure Electronic Transmissions**) is a new standard being developed for credit card transactions over the Net. Initiated by Visa and MasterCard, with technical assistance from various Internet and information technology companies, such as Netscape, IBM, Verisign and recently Microsoft, SET may well be the dominant method for paying by credit card in the future.

SERIAL HACKERS

Many hackers use the technique of breaking into a chain of computers (for instance, break into A, use A to break into B, B to break into C, etc.). This technique allows them to cover their tracks more efficiently.

SET is a bigger and more complicated system than SSL but will not compete with or supersede it because the encryption process will utilize the SSL protocol. The most significant difference is that merchants will not have access to your credit card number—that information will remain between you and your card-issuing bank.

DRAGNET: ONLINE POLICE

To keep up with security issues, the government has funded **CERT** (**Computer Emergency Response Team**), an organization that investigates security problems and works to solve them. CERT also produces aids that allow people to assess the security of their computers. CERT prefers to work directly with site security personnel but will field questions from anyone in an emergency. They can be reached by e-mail at **cert@cert.sei.cmu.edu**.

SECURITY CONSCIOUSNESS

If you're connected to the Net, you may run the risk of a break-in—that is, an outsider, or hacker, gaining access to your computer and removing or destroying information. Fortunately, most break-ins happen on machines that are continuously connected to the Net, such as machines supporting an office Intranet, or owners of mailing lists. But it is still a wise idea to understand how break-ins occur and to guard against them.

PREVENTING A BREAK-IN

Primary ways that computers become vulnerable to security breaches include:
- Bad passwords
- Downloading corrupt software
- Operating system flaws

PASSWORDS

Passwords are the most important line of defense in preventing people from illegally accessing your computer. You can usually configure your computer's operating system to require a password when you start up the program. Your ISP requires a password when you log on to the Net. You may also need a password to access e-mail.

Some passwords can be "remembered" by your computer, while others will have to be entered each time they are needed.

Most people choose passwords because they're easy to recall. But remember—what's obvious to you may be obvious to a hacker.

CERT reports that 80% of computer break-ins are due to poor password choice. A hacking program can spend all day trying passwords, and most of these programs don't pick random letters—they pick common names and words from the dictionary.

It's a good habit to change your password every week if you're dealing with sensitive information. Otherwise, every few months should suffice. Also, consider picking a password that:
- Is at least six characters long
- Has a mix of upper-case, lower-case, and numbers
- Is not a word
- Is not a set of adjacent keyboard keys (like qwerty)

WHAT TO AVOID

Don't choose a password easily guessed by others—such as your birthday or your child's name. And don't store your password anywhere near your computer. Leaving a note to remind yourself is a common practice. Remember, not all security problems come from outside.

DOWNLOADING CORRUPT SOFTWARE

Sharing software can be a great benefit, but if you don't know where it's been, you don't know what sort of virus it may have contracted. Buying software from reputable vendors is the most secure. Downloading from the Internet can be risky. Protect yourself by following these guidelines:
- Use official sources. If you are looking for a patch to fix a bug in an operating system, it's better to get the program from a site supported by the company that manufactured the system.
- Back up all your files before using new software.
- Use a virus checker to test the software you download from the Net. If you don't have one, there are many available, including McAfee VirusScan (**www.mcafee.com**), which you can download from the Net, and Norton Utilities, which you can purchase where software is sold.

SYSTEM SOFTWARE FLAWS

Sometimes the software you use will have a flaw that allows access into your system. Manufacturers will provide updates or patches, and your job is to know about both the flaw and the remedy.

For security reasons, manufacturers don't like to announce that a system has a hole in it, so the best way to keep up is by staying in touch with your manufacturer's or employer's support services.

You can also watch newsgroups that discuss your system. For instance, you can find a number of Windows95 newsgroups in the listing **comp.os.ms-windows.win95**.

INTERNAL SECURITY

How do you know if your computer has been broken into? One way is to check the size of file directories: if you see directories that look too big, seem to have changed, or which have strange modification dates, you should investigate further.

If you do notice anything suspicious, don't ignore it and don't act on your own. Get help immediately from either your employer's security department or from the manufacturer of your computer.

FACE TIME, ELECTRONICALLY

Biometrics is the science of identifying you electronically by encoding details such as fingerprints, hand geometry, retina prints, and voice and signature analysis on a smart card. That way, your identity can be verified when you use it, providing proof that you're the owner.

One of the simplest biometric techniques uses a digital photograph of your face, converting the distinguishing features to data that can be stored in a bar code on your card and in a related database.

Privacy

The information you disclose, especially on the Net, can go almost anywhere.

As consumers, we often relinquish all sorts of personal data each time we apply for a credit card, enroll in a frequent flier program, or sign up for a grocery store discount card. We assume that the information will be held in confidence.

The Net, however, is a very efficient collector, as well as distributor, of information. The personal data you supply may eventually be seen by parties you have no intention of sharing it with.

The Web has many sites that offer free information if you enroll and fill out a survey. While information may be used to provide you with personalized information, such as the weather in a particular city, it can also be shared with advertisers. And search engines routinely note the topics you are looking up to determine which advertisements would be most suitable to display to you.

Cookies

Even if you don't register for a particular website, remote servers gather information about your activities using **cookies**. A cookie is a piece of information shared between your browser and certain servers—and lets the server know that you're visiting.

Here's how it works: The first time you connect to a site that utilizes cookies, the server sends a small text file to your browser. Each time you return, your browser sends it back. In this way, the server tracks your visits.

The information in a cookie is encoded and is generally used for helpful reasons. For example, when you go to a retail site, the shopping basket you use depends on cookies to remember who you are and what you've placed in your basket.

But cookies can also tell someone about your interests, since they provide a record of the sites you visit. This use of cookies raises some concerns, since your spending or surfing habits may become available to hackers or unscrupulous businesses.

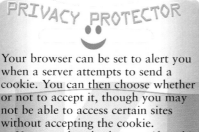

PRIVACY PROTECTOR

Your browser can be set to alert you when a server attempts to send a cookie. You can then choose whether or not to accept it, though you may not be able to access certain sites without accepting the cookie.

You can also check to see if cookie files have been left on your computer. Netscape users can use a file called *cookies.txt*. If you use Explorer, look for the directory c:*windows\cookies*. Mac users can search a file called *magic cookies*. You can then remove the cookies from your hard drive.

E-mail privacy

E-mail is not very private. If you actively participate in newsgroups or mailing lists, you have made your e-mail address public. You might be registered with an online service that makes your address a matter of public record, or even sells their subscriber list.

A common breach of privacy occurs when an e-mail recipient passes your e-mail on to someone else, whether deliberately or not. And messages you send from your workplace are typically saved on a backup system—so they can be read by someone else. Your employer, for example, has the legal right to read your mail. Less likely, but still possible, is that your e-mail can be intercepted by a knowledgeable hacker.

PRIVACY PROTECTOR

If you're worried about e-mail privacy for business or personal reasons, there are some precautions you can take. First, carefully consider what you're sending out. It's easy to avoid putting sensitive or embarrassing information in e-mail.

A more technical solution is to encrypt your e-mail by installing a package like PGP (Pretty Good Privacy), which uses **public key cryptography** to encode and decode messages. With PGP, you have both a public and a private secret key. You can distribute your public key to friends and colleagues, who use that key to encrypt messages to you. You then use your secret key to decrypt a message that was encrypted with your public key. Only those who have your private key can read the message.

Electronic spam is also canned

Your privacy on the Internet can also be intruded upon in the form of unwanted junk e-mail, popularly called **spam**. Spam refers to messages you find valueless and annoying, particularly those sent to a large number of recipients with the intent of selling something.

PRIVACY PROTECTOR

One way to deal with spam is simply to delete it without reading it. As you become familiar with using e-mail, you'll be able to recognize subject lines you probably don't want to bother with. They might read, "Make a million dollars!" or "Money! Money! Money!" These are dead giveaways for junk.

Some messages actually say something along the lines of: "If you don't want to receive any future messages please return this message with the word REMOVE in the subject line." Unfortunately, this is often a clever way of determining if your e-mail address is active. So you might think twice before you do it.

If you want to avoid seeing the spam altogether, you can try using a **filtering system**. Both Netscape Messenger and Microsoft Explorer's Internet Mail provide mechanisms for filtering mail. Basically you tell your mail-reader to look for subject headers with certain words in them (*money, cash, big bucks*), or to look for a specific sender address. After filtering out these messages, your mail-reader will put them wherever you tell it to—into a folder labeled *Junk*, or into the trash.

VOLUNTARY DISCLOSURE

One program working toward making the Net more privacy-conscious is TRUSTe (**www.truste.org**), which awards a branded logo or seal to websites. You can look for a displayed trustmark to signify that the website is adhering to TRUSTe's monitoring, oversight, and consumer complaint resolution process. The site also provides useful tips on privacy and security issues.

reviewed by
TRUSTe
site privacy statement

Phone privacy

Can other people listen to your cordless and cellular phone conversations? The answer is yes. In most cases, conversations are probably heard only briefly and by accident. But there are people who make it a hobby to listen to cordless and cellular phone calls by using radio scanners.

Cordless phones work like mini radio stations. They send out radio signals from the base unit to the handset and back again, and the signals carrying your conversation can usually be transmitted and overheard up to a quarter mile away. These signals can be picked up by a number of devices—including radio scanners, baby monitors, radios and other cordless phones.

Since others may be listening to your conversations, avoid discussing financial or other sensitive personal information. For example, if you buy something over the phone and give out your credit card information, your cordless or cellular call could be monitored, and you might end up the victim of credit card fraud.

You can also look into PGPfone at **http://web.mit.edu/network/pgpfone**. PGPfone (Pretty Good Privacy Phone) is a software package that turns your desktop or notebook computer into a secure telephone. It uses speech compression and strong cryptography protocols to let you have a real-time secure telephone conversation via a modem-to-modem connection. It also works across the Internet.

PRIVACY PROTECTOR

Check with your cellular phone company to see what kind of antifraud features they have. Always use the lock feature (this feature renders your phone keys unresponsive and requires a password to "unlock" them) on your phone when you aren't using it. Check your cellular phone bills carefully each month. Report a stolen or lost phone immediately to your carrier.

Blocking and Filtering Information

You can determine what gets through to you—and what shouldn't.

From a philosophical and legal point of view, the ready access provided by the Internet is a double-edged sword. While you can find virtually any type of information on the Net, there may also be things you don't want, or don't want your children to be exposed to.

The same is true of cable and satellite TV. While programming is varied to suit many tastes, not all of it may be to your liking, especially where children are concerned.

Fortunately, there are ways you can **block**, or **filter**, material you don't want on your home screen.

METADATA is data that describes other data

Blocking systems create an electronic wall that allows you to screen out specific sites you find objectionable.

A filter oversees the e-mail coming into your mail-reader. It uses a set of agreed-upon standards to determine what kinds of information should be restricted and which should pass through. Neither blocking nor filtering software actually controls the content but lets you, as the end user or viewer, control access to it.

ONLINE BUT OFF LIMITS
Most major online services let you restrict access to certain chat rooms, newsgroups and e-mail based on a list of preset topics. There are also software programs that locate unacceptable subject matter and automatically put it off limits.

A filtering program called Net Nanny (**www.netnanny.com**), for example, supplies a list of sites that are to be blocked. You can add to it, and you can download updates containing sites you may want to block. And it can be run invisibly so kids don't know what is being blocked. Other programs include Surf Watch, NetShepherd and Snag. To find these and other programs, use a search engine and type in the word *blocking*.

CyberPatrol uses a standard search engine to identify sites that contain words like *sex*, *drugs* or *satanic* in their description. Reviewers look at the sites and at the potentially offending words in context. If they find the use objectionable, they can block access, listing it under the category CyberNOT. If it meets their standards, it is categorized as CyberYES.

By using people to assess the sites and determine what's objectionable, programs like CyberPatrol avoid wholesale blocking of sites that may contain valuable information. Likewise, they can ferret out sites with veiled but offensive material.

HOT LABELS
The Massachusetts Institute of Technology's World Wide Web Consortium has developed a set of technical standards called **PICS**, short for **Platform for Internet Content Selection**, as a way to make electronic, computer-readable labels about content and other site characteristics easily available.

The labels can be included in the site or document itself, sent automatically when a site is accessed, or stored separately and provided in response to a particular query.

Since PICS provides a shared understanding of what the ratings mean, organizations can use PICS to publish their cyber-ratings and to evaluate the ratings of their own sites and materials as they develop them.

You can use the labels to specify the kinds of materials you want blocked. For example, using the Recreational Software Advisory Council (RSACi) (**www.rsac.org/homepage.asp**) system for rating nudity, sex, violence and obscenity, you could ask Net Nanny or CyberPatrol to block sites with any violence, or only those with gratuitous violence. You can visit PICS at **www.w3.org/PICS** to learn more about what the labels or ratings mean.

THE POSITIVE APPROACH

Labeling is often the most effective when the labels are created by people whose views you share, and when *you* make the ultimate decision about what information to access and what to make off limits. Several organizations, including Net Nanny and Net Shepherd, evaluate websites using specific criteria. You can set up your Web browser to check the ratings published by these groups and then highlight or exclude specific sites. Net Shepherd, for example, has a database, or label server, of more than 300,000 descriptive rating labels that you can use to check the content of a website. If you trust the labels, you can reasonably rely on the system to screen out what you find offensive.

PRIVACY AND THE COURTS

Attempts to limit Internet access or to label material as unacceptable are always controversial. One key issue is whether you want to make the final decisions yourself about what you see, read or hear, or whether you want a regulatory agency to do it for you. A related matter is whether or not you or your children should have to be exposed to things you find unacceptable. Any really workable system has to take both those positions into account and be easy to use yet sophisticated enough to provide a meaningful basis for making judgments.

TELEPHONE BLOCKING

You can block access to or from specific telephone numbers, and you can block calls to certain categories of numbers. For example, you can block all outgoing paid calls, or those described as entertainment numbers (900 numbers), which may offer pornography, psychic readings and fortune-telling services.

You can also block incoming anonymous calls using caller ID and a service called **anonymous call rejection**. If an identifying phone number doesn't appear on your caller ID display screen, the caller gets a message that you don't accept private anonymous calls. If the caller chooses to reveal his or her name, the call can go through. You can call your phone carrier to learn more about these services.

BLOCKING THE TUBE

Although television broadcasters and cable operators participate in a voluntary, age-based rating system similar to the one used by the movie industry, television sets are being built with **V-chips**. These chips detect program ratings and then block adversely rated programs from view.

For example, you can set a V-chip to block access to individual shows, to movies with specific ratings, or to particular channels, programs or time periods.

The first televisions containing the V-chip were unveiled in December 1997, along with a line of set-top boxes that allow you to modify your existing television.

KID POWER

America Links Up: A Kids Online Teach-In is a public awareness and education campaign sponsored by a broad-based coalition of nonprofits, education groups and corporations concerned with providing children with a safe and rewarding experience online. You can find it at **www.americalinksup.org**.